Hollywood's Second Sex

Hollywood's Second Sex

The Treatment of Women in the Film Industry, 1900–1999

AUBREY MALONE

McFarland & Company, Inc., Publishers
Jefferson, North Carolina

Library of Congress Cataloguing-in-Publication Data

Dillon-Malone, A. (Aubrey)
Hollywood's second sex : the treatment of women
in the film industry, 1900–1999 / Aubrey Malone.
p.   cm.
Includes bibliographical references and index.

ISBN 978-0-7864-7978-8 (softcover : acid free paper) ∞
ISBN 978-1-4766-1951-4 (ebook)

1. Women in the motion picture industry—United States—
History—20th century.   2. Sex discrimination in employment—
United States.   3. Sexual harassment of women—United States.
4. Women in motion pictures.   5. Motion pictures—
United States—History—20th century.   I. Title.

PN1995.9.W6D54 2015   791.43082'0973—dc23   2015011373

British Library cataloguing data are available

On the cover: Marilyn Monroe, 1954 (Photofest); Clara Bow,
Katharine Hepburn, Demi Moore (author's collection)

Printed in the United States of America

*McFarland & Company, Inc., Publishers
Box 611, Jefferson, North Carolina 28640
www.mcfarlandpub.com*

Table of Contents

Table of Contents

Preface

A book of this brevity can hardly hold pretensions of comprehensiveness. All it can do is give selective (and, one hopes, representative) examples of a mindset extant in the front offices of the studios featured, and the often cruel and dismissive men within.

I've combined an examination of the lives of a range of famous (and un-famous) actresses with an analysis of many of the films in which they appeared. The themes of these films often echo the tragedy and victimization of some of their lives. They are a sober reminder of a business that plucked people from obscurity and later cavalierly thrust them back into obscurity (or toward an even worse fate) when their time was up.

Introduction

"Hollywood," said Mamie Van Doren, "is a haunted town, full of ghosts and memories. A lot of blond bombshells and platinum goddesses didn't make it. They died long before the wrinkles and lines they lived in fear of had a chance to appear in their beautiful faces." There were also those who made it and then lost it, for any number of reasons—the cruelty of the moguls, the streamlining of their careers, personal involvements with men who didn't have their best interests at heart, or an industry that wasn't quite ready for them.

In our progressive era, we might think that Hollywood's war on women is over. But this is far from the case. Women in the Hollywood film industry might endure less sexual harassment than in years past, but has much really changed about who holds the reins of power or what kinds of films are being made? Pauline Kael once speculated that the history of American movies could be encapsulated in a marquee poster she once saw with the words *Kiss Kiss, Bang Bang.*[1] This book explores that theory.

We begin with silent screen vamp Theda Bara, a woman seen as evil by the pioneers of cinema because she peddled sex. The Bara Syndrome, if we may call it that, continued with *noir* movies, which generally portrayed women as rotten to the core. In contrast, so-called "women's pictures" placed them on pedestals. But, as Betty Grable liked to joke, a man only puts a woman on a pedestal to get a better look at her legs. Or did men put them there simply to get them out of the way?

To succeed as an actress, Ethel Barrymore observed, a woman had to have "the face of Venus, the brain of Minerva, the memory of Macaulay, the figure of Juno and the hide of a rhinoceros."[2] Otto Preminger saw it differently. In his view female stars in Hollywood generally fell into two categories: those who were exploited by men, and those who survived by *acting* like men. "Female movie stars," wrote Sean French, "were symbols of transcendent glamour who turned into equally symbolic victims of a culture that fetishizes young female beauty. Most actresses began their career intoxicated by the first until they ran up against the second."[3]

After Bara I investigate the flapper era and the promises it afforded women before being blunted by the sad plight of stars like Clara Bow and Louise Brooks, whose careers ended far too soon. After this came the foreign influx of androgynous stars like Greta

3

Garbo and Marlene Dietrich. Garbo fought against the domination of MGM boss Louis B. Mayer before becoming disenchanted by Hollywood's value system, while Dietrich struggled to assert herself under the controlling influence of her Svengali, Josef von Sternberg. When Mae West arrived, she shook the paternalistic ethos of the film industry to its foundations with her lewd humor but she too fell under the sway of the male hierarchies in time, and under the *diktats* of a censorship system that eventually broke her, even if she joked that she made a fortune from it.

Bette Davis was a different kind of phenomenon. Like West, she came in like a lion, leaving no doubt that she was there for the long haul. She had to fight constantly against typecasting and also against mediocre roles, studio domination, and men who were intimidated by her personality. She challenged Jack Warner's "ownership" of her in 1936 in a seminal court case challenging contractual binding. She lost it. But the very fact that she put her head over the parapet paved the way for stars like Olivia de Havilland, who challenged the system with more success in later years.

This book is also concerned with those who failed to make their mark on movies for one reason or another. Chief among these, perhaps, was Frances Farmer, who paid the ultimate price for her headstrong personality when she was sent to a psychiatric institution. Not long after, Judy Garland began showing the strain of being a child star catapulted into the public consciousness by producers who seemed to care little for her mental health. In time Garland would become addicted to diet pills, sleeping pills and other concoctions that resulted in her premature demise.

Other victimized actresses under scrutiny in the book include Rita Hayworth, a bashful star who was both used and abused by the men in her life and also her bosses, in particular Harry Cohn, for whom she represented little but a dollar sign. Hayworth was exploited for her sexuality as well, like many of her contemporaries, including Jane Russell, an actress only slightly more famous than her breasts after *The Outlaw* (which exhibited these assets with some aplomb) went on release in 1943.

When America entered World War II after the attack on Pearl Harbor, women benefited briefly from the absence of male stars from the screen, enjoying the kind of prominence they'd sampled during the flapper era. But when Johnny came marching home again, hurrah, hurrah, the ladies were shunted back to the shadows once again and slotted into subsidiary roles as the token eye candy. Gone suddenly were performances like that of Greer Garson in *Mrs. Miniver* and Joan Crawford in *Mildred Pierce*. Instead we saw a multiplicity of jingoistic excesses that once again relegated women to the sidelines as "moral support" to the male.

The forties ended with the suicide of Carole Landis (after she was jettisoned by Rex Harrison) and the pillorying of Ingrid Bergman, who did nothing worse than fall in love with a man who wasn't her husband (Roberto Rossellini) and have his child. It would be seven years before she was forgiven and brought back into the Hollywood fold.

In the fifties we saw Rita Hayworth elbowed aside when she was no longer considered beautiful enough to captivate the masses. In place of this love goddess, one was invited to sample the charms of Marilyn Monroe. The fifties was also the decade of Hugh Hefner and *Playboy* magazine. Monroe was its first centerfold and she became as much a victim of this culture as Jayne Mansfield and Diana Dors—her alleged clones—as well as a multitude of other women Hollywood waved in audience's faces for their delectation, most of them with breasts even more alluring than those of Jane Russell.

In the later years of the decade we had more foreign "imports," most notably Brigitte Bardot, with others like Gina Lollobrigida bringing up the rear. We also saw a brief example of "black power" when Dorothy Dandridge landed the lead role in *Carmen Jones*. Dandridge, like Monroe, would eventually be cast aside by Hollywood and die by her own hand. So would Jean Seberg, an actress who, like Dandridge, was brutalized by Otto Preminger.

Kim Novak was a more manufactured sex symbol than either of these and had a tough time trying to crawl out from under the shadow of Monroe. Harry Cohn tried to dominate her and when she began a romance with Sammy Davis, Jr., he told her it would destroy her career if she pursued it. Davis received death threats and backed off, retreating to Frank Sinatra's Rat Pack where things seemed much safer. Sinatra had divorced his wife by now and was involved in a tempestuous relationship with Ava Gardner. She suffered his explosive moods and even forgave him for faking a suicide attempt to soften her attitude toward him. Sinatra also treated Lauren Bacall badly after Humphrey Bogart died, becoming engaged to her and then breaking it off when she leaked the news to the press. He was even supposed to be intending to marry Marilyn Monroe for a time but in the end he seemed only to give her bad habits.

Monroe died in 1962, giving rise to a debate that's still going on today as to whether she brought most of her problems on herself or had them imposed on her by an industry intolerant of her demons. Gail Russell died a year earlier, having succumbed to alcohol addiction, an affliction shared by Veronica Lake, yet another siren cast into the Hollywood wilderness when her looks faded.

This could also have been the fate of Bette Davis but she turned Hollywood's penchant for beauty on its head by playing the town at its own game. In 1962 she embraced a makeup department that did its darnedest to "uglify" her in *What Ever Happened to Baby Jane?* and in so doing prolonged her career by a few more decades. Joan Crawford didn't quite enjoy the experience as much as she did, having bought into the idea that one had to be glamorous to be a "real" star—a myth the industry liked to perpetuate.

Doris Day was an actress of whom Oscar Levant once said, "I knew her before she was a virgin." Day was physically abused by her first husband Al Jorden and almost bankrupted by her second, Marty Melcher, but somehow she survived. So also did Susan Hayward, another siren unfortunate enough to marry someone less successful than she was, Jess Barker. Barker, like a lot of Hollywood men, couldn't adjust to the fact that his wife was more successful than he was. He tried to clean her out financially after they divorced but failed.

In 1963 Alfred Hitchcock directed *The Birds*, in the process subjecting its star Tippi Hedren to some of the most horrendous ordeals ever visited on an actress. He oversaw her being attacked viciously by the birds in question, at one point making her fear for her life. His cruelty towards her also continued off-set, which made it all the more amazing that she returned to the scene of the crime the following year when she signed with him again for *Marnie*. One was reminded of Jean Seberg agreeing to be directed by Otto Preminger in *Bonjour Tristesse* the year after being humiliated by him repeatedly on the set of *Saint Joan*. The need to find work sometimes exhibited itself as masochism in this poisoned goldfish bowl.

In the same year that *Marnie* was made, George C. Scott was busy beating Ava Gardner up for reasons best known to himself. In another country, Alain Delon deserted Romy Schneider after having lived with her for five years. And in Mexico Pina Pellicer (Marlon Brando's petite co-star in *One-Eyed Jacks*) killed herself when she realized she couldn't reach the stellar heights of that film again, or indulge the fascination she had for Brando. Rachel Roberts also attempted suicide that year when her marriage to Rex Harrison started to spring leaks. Soon afterwards both Inger Stevens and Pier Angeli killed themselves, each of them apparent embodiments of the fact that when a beautiful woman starts to age in the film world, she starts to develop a fear that her career (and/or love life) is over. Julie Birchill summed up the situation chillingly: "Suicide is much more acceptable in Hollywood than growing old gracefully."

Jane Fonda made it her life's ambition to put the lie to that tenet, being made of stronger stuff than the tragic figures who preceded her. Once she emerged from the shadow of Roger Vadim she gave a new voice to women both on and off the screen. She became a political figure as well as a campaigner against sexism and male pomposity. She even spearheaded a keep-fit regime with her workout videos. Some people laughed at her for her about-turns but half a century on she still remains a force to be reckoned with by those who made it a practice to steamroll "the fair" sex when the opportunity presented itself.

In the seventies, things started to go wrong for women again, with films like *Last Tango in Paris* blurring the distinctions between pornography and mainstream sexuality and *Deep Throat* taking things a step further. The stars of these films, Maria Schneider and Linda Lovelace respectively, never recovered from them nor forgave their makers. Elsewhere people like Michelle Triola and Sondra Locke were campaigning for different types of justice as they pitted themselves against two iconic figures of male machismo, Lee Marvin and Clint Eastwood. Both of them claimed victory in landmark court cases though the men in question denied this, as they would.

The final chapters of the book look at what we might call a "post-feminist" attitude to the plight of Hollywood women, taking in stars like Jessica Lange, Michelle Pfeiffer, Glenn Close, Barbra Streisand, Demi Moore and Sharon Stone. In many ways these women have learned how to play the system while also trying to reform it from within. Have they been successful? Only mutedly, one has to say, and sometimes they've had to hide their intelligence to do so. Close, Moore and Stone have been forced to play demonic women opposite one actor alone—Michael Douglas (in *Fatal Attraction*, *Disclosure* and *Basic Instinct*). As Marie McDonald said after being asked if she was embarrassed by being continually referred to as "The Body": "Not at all. I found out long ago that in Hollywood a girl doesn't get very far by being known as 'The Brain.'"

As an addendum to the above themes, and often running concurrently with them, I've examined the achievements of women who stepped behind the camera to make their voices heard. This list includes directors Lois Weber, Dorothy Arzner, Leni Riefenstahl, Susan Seidelman and Donna Dietch, director-screenwriter Frances Marion, director-actress Ida Lupino and producers Sherry Lansing and Dawn Steel.

The conclusion I've drawn is that the battles the beautiful women of the early years of the last century started to fight continued to the end of it and are still going on today. The salaries of female stars may have approached parity with men, at least for the Meryl Streeps and Julia Robertses of this world, and men seem more politically correct in their pronouncements about women. But is this genuine or merely cosmetic? If we scratch a New Man, are we in danger of seeing an "old" one underneath?

One fears this is true. For every *Silkwood* Hollywood turns out, there's a corresponding *National Lampoon's Animal House*. For every *Erin Brockovich* there's a *Shallow Hal*. For every *Indecent Proposal* there's a *Pretty Woman* and for every *Thelma & Louise* there's a *Lethal Weapon*. There are still quality parts being written for women today but not as many as for men and that will probably never change. Neither will we ever see as many elderly women in films as we see elderly men, or as many action heroines. The Sigourney Weavers and Uma Thurmans may be more feisty than, say, Maureen O'Hara, who tended to underline male values instead of undermining them (even as a pirate queen) but at least we're aware of that disconnect today, which is hopefully the first step in doing something about it.

The disquieting reality is that women will probably continue to be "Hollywood's second sex" for as long as movies are made. They'll continue to play demeaning roles like the "best friend" or the "glamorous granny" when they reach a certain age and continue to be aware that in the Hollywood jungle they will have to do everything twice as well as men to survive.

But as one of them wryly observed, "Fortunately this isn't difficult."

Birth Pangs of a New Medium

Hollywood's anti-female bias dates at least as far back as 1906. That was the year the French-born Alice Guy Blaché directed *La Vie du Christ*, which in most filmographies was credited to Victorin Jasset, her assistant. Blaché was virtually ignored by historians despite having made a staggering number of films between 1896 and 1920.

Another one of Hollywood's earliest female directors was Cleo Madison, who had over seventy features to her credit. She started out as an actress, reaching stardom with the serial *The Trey O'Hearts* (1914) in which she played a double role. When she hit upon the idea of directing, she met with resistance everywhere she went. She then decided that what she couldn't get by request, she'd get by force. She hatched a plan to be as difficult an actress as she could so that directors would be glad to be rid of her in this role. It worked and before long she was making films at Universal Studios. Asked if she was nervous on her first day, she replied, "Why should I be? I had seen men with less brains than I have getting away with it." She made an enormous number of features between 1914 and 1924 but today she is little more than a footnote in film history. "One of these days," she pronounced, "men are going to get over the fool idea that women have no brains and quit getting insulted at the thought that a skirt-wearer can do their work quite as well as they can. I don't believe that day is very far off."[1] Unfortunately it was.

Lillian Gish also directed (or helped direct) many films from 1912 onward. She proved adept at it but ultimately found that "directing is no career for a lady." Gish cited her film career as the reason she never married: "What kind of wife would I have made? A good wife is a seven day a week, 24 hour a day job. [But] I was devoted to the studio. I loved many beautiful men but I never ruined their lives."[2] One would have to ransack many archives to find a similar sentiment expressed by a male director—or indeed a male star.

Perhaps the most famous female director of this time was Lois Weber. She directed *Hypocrites* in 1914 but landed herself in hot water with the censors because of a scene featuring a nude statue of a young woman. The film caused riots and so would Weber's next feature *Where Are My Children?*, which broached the issue of abortion. The fact that she managed to carve out a career—and a lucrative one at that—as a controversial female director was nothing short of a miracle. Her thought-provoking dramas dealt with everything from prostitution to capital punishment. If some of the conclusions were pat, this was a small price to pay.

The key to Weber's success at a time when women behind the camera were an anomaly was the manner in which she talked down her position. As one writer put it, "The message from the culture was loud and clear. If you want to play in this business, you play like a man or you're out. And if you happen to be a woman, better not mention it to anybody."[3] The downside of this was that she never received her just deserts from Hollywood. When her career faded, she was quickly forgotten, despite having worked in 400 films as actress, writer, producer and/or director.

The preeminent male figure behind a camera at this time was D.W. Griffith. In 1915 he directed his masterpiece *The Birth of a Nation*, but the film had problems. Apart from its heroic depiction of the Ku Klux Klan, it portrayed women in a subservient Victorian light—or darkness. According to the film's star Lillian Gish, Griffith was terrified of women in real life. Maybe that was why he tended to feature them on screen as "delicate, ghostly images" that were "the very essence of virginity." Gish herself had once harbored ambitions to be a nun and on set was chaperoned by her mother. Between scenes Griffith forbade his women players from entertaining men in their dressing rooms. They also faced dismissal if they developed blemishes on their skin, such imperfections being, in his mind, indicative of "a debauched character." He subjected them to endless sermons on the necessity of avoiding promiscuity "or you will end up with some disease." He even forbade women from kissing on screen, merely allowing them to embrace their lovers instead.[4]

The most famous female star of the day was Mary Pickford, who was known as "The Girl with the Curls" when she first hit the screen rather than by her own name. This was deliberate policy on the part of the Motion Picture Patent Company. It was felt that if she was named directly, she'd demand more money.[5]

Personifying all the virtues and values of Hollywood as its especial "sweetheart," the homespun rural values of stars like Lillian Gish (above) became eminently dispensable once heroines, or rather antiheroines, became more savvy and sophisticated.

"Little Mary," as she was called, was earning $500 a week in 1913 but two years later that figure rose to $2,000. In 1916 she formed her own production company, the Pickford Film Corporation, thereby becoming Hollywood's first female mogul. In this capacity she earned over $1 million a year and went on to make a successful transition from silent movies to the talkies. But her private life was anything but smooth.

At the beginning of her career she was married to alcoholic Owen Moore. She divorced him for the swashbuckling hero Douglas Fairbanks. In 1919 she set up United Artists with Fairbanks, Charlie Chaplin and D.W. Griffith, prompting Richard Rowland to utter his famous line, "The inmates have taken over the asylum." Her "sweetheart" image slipped somewhat when she married the also-divorced Fairbanks. She was maligned in the press for a time but this stopped when it was revealed that Moore had been abusing her. It was a symptom of the "new" Hollywood that her liaison with Fairbanks didn't spell the end of her career, or indeed his. In contrast they became Hollywood's first example of an almost royal couple. Their lush Beverly Hills mansion, Pickfair, was the closest the film colony could approximate to a palatial residence.

Gloria Swanson, like Pickford, made a successful transition from silent movies to the talkies. She had a controversial private life as well. She appeared in Cecil B. DeMille's *Don't Change Your Husband* in 1919 but hardly carried that philosophy off screen, going on to divorce no less than five spouses. Her first one was Wallace Beery. Beery raped her on their wedding night in 1916 and went on to trick her into swallowing medication that caused her to abort their baby.

The fact that Swanson openly professed her disenchantment with marriage—hardly surprising after her experiences with Beery—caused Paramount, her studio, to insist she settle her second divorce, from Herbert Somborn, out of court. (This came about after Somborn charged her with adultery.) She agreed, and thereby saved the studio's blushes. Far from causing her popularity to slip, by now she was receiving up to 10,000 fan letters a week.

One of the other leading actresses at this time was Theda Bara. It's a salutary reminder of Hollywood's wildly divergent attitude to men and women that its prime male sex symbol of the early 1900s was the dashing Rudolph

The career of Theda Bara, pictured above in *Cleopatra* (1917), crumbled when the "Vamp" era ended. She was discarded by Hollywood to make way for the Roaring Twenties, and a more user-friendly type of sex symbol than her convulsive, cannibalistic one.

Valentino and its prime female one the malevolent Bara, a woman whose name could be converted into the oddly applicable anagram Arab Death. She was marketed as an unconscionable man-eater in films like *The Serpent* and *The She-Devil* but in real life she was a happily married woman from Cincinnati. But of course that was far too dull to feed the gossip presses of the time.

When Bara arrived on the scene, her publicity machine went into high gear, creating a backstory for her that was as demonic as it was weird. She'd been suckled by crocodiles; her lovers died of poisoning from mysterious amulets; she was raised on the Nile. In reality she was Theodosia Goodman, a tailor's daughter. Bara had to be made into a foreigner to protect the honor of American women. Nobody so venal could possibly have been born on native shores, could they?

To audiences she was like a human version of a praying mantis, a woman who delighted in destroying her victims and afterwards posing beside them like some bejeweled big game hunter bagging her latest kill.

Bara's contract forbade her to marry within three years. It demanded she be "heavily veiled" while in public. She wasn't allowed to appear in the theater, take Turkish baths, pose for photographs or go out in the daytime. And if she was driving at night, she had to close the curtains on the windows of her limousine.[6]

A new word entered the language with her: As a result of her she-devil antics, "vamping" became the latest sensation: "All over America women writhed and wriggled, snaked and snarled, batted their lashes, nibbled their pearls and trampled on the groveling bodies of worshipping men, if only in the wishful shadows of a movie matinee."[7] So terrifying was the image she projected on screen that women who saw her on the street were reputed to hold their children (and of course their husbands) extra tightly for fear they'd fall under her spell.

She did her best to break out of her contract's stranglehold by appearing in *Romeo and Juliet* in 1916 but it was a forlorn hope, the film more resembling *Romeo and Bara* than anything else. The dejected star capitulated to studio demands afterwards with roles in *The Vixen* and *Cleopatra*. These projects better suited the career direction it had planned for her.

As Bara's star fell, her black-lidded look gave way to the more muted creations of Helena Rubinstein and Elizabeth Arden. Platinum blonds like Jean Harlow and ebullient damsels like Clara Bow and Colleen Moore were now the new role models. As the waltz became replaced by the Charleston, so did the general pace of living speed up. A hedonistic credo was embraced by Bow, Pola Negri and Alla Nazimova.

Bara made all of her 39 films in less than five years. By 1919 she was finished, postwar audiences looking for something more sophisticated in their heroines (or anti-heroines). She tried to send herself up in a Mack Sennett comedy but the joke was on her. She even attempted a stage comeback but it did no good. Her persona, and all that went with it, had already passed into lore, the gothic excesses of the melodramatic angel of death so many burnt offerings on Hollywood's altar of consumerism. She was sent packing from Tinseltown's gilded glory with the same reckless abandon she herself used to dispense with unwanted suitors in her films. A new age was dawning and if people wanted ponderous love scenes in tents, it was to Valentino they now looked.

Bara's era effectively ended when that of Cecil B. DeMille began. DeMille is primarily known for his religious epics but he also made a string of films like *Old Wives for New* (1918), *Don't Change Your Husband* (1919), *Male and Female* (1919) and *The Affairs of Anatol* (1921). His films often had the theme of wives having to work harder at their marriages to save their husbands from straying into the arms of vamps like Bara. The idea that the husbands might be to blame for the straying doesn't seem to have entered the equation, the onus being on the wife to compete with possible mistresses by making herself more sexual. Bara wouldn't have stood a chance in a DeMille film but there was no need for her anyway, seeing as his emphasis was always on the sanctity of marriage. As was the case with his Biblical work, DeMille seemed to enjoy showing sin as much as the moral *cost* of sin but he was never castigated for this—nor indeed for his extra-marital affairs offscreen.

Fritz Lang was another director whose private life was "protected" by his status in the film industry. In the winter of 1920 his wife Lisa Rosenthal is alleged to have discovered him in *flagrante delicto* with his scenarist Thea von Harbou. As a result, the story goes, she shot herself. But rumors of her being murdered by Lang flew about the place. It was, after all, his gun she used, a gun he'd waved at her some months before during an altercation. Whatever happened, it was hushed up by the media and Rosenthal was removed from all publicity to do with Lang in future years. Did the director, who subsequently married von Harbou, kill Rosenthal or was he in some way responsible for her death? In his biography of Lang, Patrick McGilligan suggests there are enough reasons to suspect he might have been, one of which was the fact that Rosenthal had planned to go on a shopping trip at the time of her death. As McGilligan put it, "What sort of woman plans a shopping trip before committing suicide?"[8]

One wonders what would have transpired if a *female* director had been embroiled in a scandal like this. It would probably have ended her career. On the credit side, things were changing for the "gentle" sex in the political sphere at this time. In 1918 women over the age of thirty were given the vote. The flapper era had also started, though the denial of a flapper vote delayed full female suffrage.

Flapper girls claimed their right to do what men had been doing since time immemorial: behave badly. In real life this didn't always have consequences but in films it did. Liberated or not, the Jazz Babies of the early twenties still had to pay the price for their sins, reverting back to dull reality in the last scene with their wings clipped, their brief Rabelaisian spree at an end.

Sometimes it did have consequences in real life. Barbara La Marr had a child out of wedlock in 1922 and put him in an orphanage for fear of the scandal the birth would cause. She later "adopted" him. Other stars dealt with their extra-marital pregnancies by having abortions, most notably Gloria Swanson. The thinking was that a child could wait whereas a career couldn't. As one star put it, "Abortions were our birth control."[9]

Theoretically the twenties was a groundbreaking decade for women. They were driving cars, raising their hemlines, asserting themselves more with their menfolk and attending films without chaperones. This would have been unthinkable a decade earlier. As well as wearing their skirts shorter, many of them chose to go without their corsets—those items they wore to "improve" their figures for men (and potentially destroy their own pulmonary systems).

Women rebelled against the mores of their parents but conformed with one another, the classic antinomy beloved of the youth of every era. It was the beginning of the "Anything Goes" culture, or subculture. In olden days the glimpse of a stocking may have been looked on as something shocking, but now young women were being encouraged to shed their inhibitions, an imprecation buffeted by the writings of people like Sigmund Freud, who brought terms like "libido" into the public realm.

The Roaring Twenties meant women could party until dawn and indulge their sexual desires without fear of pregnancy. Margaret Sanger had introduced diaphragms in 1916, and three years later condoms made their first appearance. In 1921 Sanger organized the first American Birth Control Conference. Women could now have sex before or outside marriage without having to fear the encumbrance (or scandal) of a child. Inside marriage they could plan their families and perhaps even contemplate combining the twin roles of wife and career woman. Having said that, contraceptive devices were mainly sold under the counter at this time, at least unless they were prescribed by doctors under the coy euphemism "feminine hygiene."

The arrival of Prohibition, ironically, gave women a different kind of power, lending glamour to the activity of alcohol, which was previously only the preserve of fallen women. They could now kick up their heels in speakeasies, the "forbidden fruit" syndrome adding an extra dose of allure to an already daring practice.

Smoking also became fashionable for women, the cigarette manufacturers cleverly proposing it as a gesture of emancipation when their primary goal was monetary rather than anything more egalitarian. It was promoted as a slimming aid as well, a thin figure being part of the package for members of the Jazz Age.

Impressionable young women looked up to stars like Lillian Gish. Gish swam every morning to keep herself fit and also watched her diet carefully, all too well aware that much of her appeal came from her petite figure.

If birth control freed women to have fewer children, or none at all, the increasing prominence of labor-saving devices in the workplace gave them more time to devote to self-development as opposed to the drudgery of incessant domesticity, the legacy of their forbears.

Something else gave them an unexpected power: The outbreak of World War I meant that many of them supplanted men in the workplace. After it ended, their appetite for a life outside the home grew, as did their desire for careers and free love. Selwyn Ford wrote, "The decimation of a whole generation of young men made girls more competitive than their mothers would have dared to dream of. [They] had no time for the leisurely courting and betrothal rituals of the prewar era."[10]

No longer was it necessary to be born in the shadow of the pyramids like Bara—at least if her promotion was to be believed—to want pre-marital sex. Girl-next-door types were also "doing" it.[11]

The movies of the day reflected this climate change. Norma Shearer became a sort of poster girl for the louche generation, despite Florenz Ziegfeld telling her she wasn't pretty enough, or D.W. Griffith insisting her eyes were too close together to register properly in close-ups.[12]

Shearer was one of the first actresses in Hollywood to play liberated women, but she did so in such a nuanced manner that it didn't appear like it. She didn't have the exoticism of a Garbo or the mystique of stars like Marlene Dietrich but she played a diverse range of roles that could be classified as pre-feminist in a lengthy career. She did this with an authenticity that gave the lie to those who ascribed her success to the fact that she was, as Joan Crawford once put it, "sleeping with the boss" (Irving Thalberg, her husband).

Shearer appeared in *Main Street* in 1923. The film gave her the oft-quoted lines, "Solitary dishing isn't enough to satisfy me or many other women. We're going to chuck it and come and play with you in the offices and clubs and politics you've cleverly kept for yourselves." It was a cheeky taunt at men but one that was honored more in the breach than the observance in the following years.

Pola Negri arrived in Hollywood shortly after *Main Street* was released. She announced her intention of making her mark in movies as soon as possible, citing Gloria Swanson as her main adversary. Gossip columnists wildly exaggerated their rivalry to sell their movies. In her autobiography Negri wrote: "Every unkind thing that was said about me was attributed to Gloria Swanson so the Paramount publicists could keep interest high in our imaginary fight."[13]

Films suddenly seemed awash with exotic, adventurous women but there were other types too. Colleen Moore, Hollywood's most famous flapper, gave off a "safe" version of wildness in films like *Flaming Youth* (1923), *The Perfect Flapper* (1924) and *Flirting with Love* (1925). The title of her 1927 film *Naughty but Nice* seemed to sum her up. Concealing a wholesome persona behind her effervescent exterior, she was the acceptable face of modernity in an industry trying to come to terms with early feminism. She was the kind of heroine directors like Cecil B. DeMille liked because she posed no serious threat to domestic harmony. She was the "bit on the side" whom heroes were prone to fall for temporarily before running home to the hearth with their tail firmly placed between their legs.

In real life Moore was happily married to a producer for First National, John McCormick. Her claims that she spent most of her time baking cakes for him was no more than media spin as she spent up to 18 hours a day on set and ate most of her meals in a bungalow just off it. Hollywood pedaled her as a party animal who went home when the parties were over, someone who both worked and played hard but basically knew what side her bread was buttered on, even if she didn't butter it herself.

For some, though, such "parties" had dire consequences. In 1926 Barbara La Marr died in a sanatorium of a drug overdose. She was just 29 but was already burned out from cocaine and alcohol. Another cause of death was alleged to be excessive dieting. She was hounded by the press on the basis of having "loose moral standards," the latter charge being based mainly on the fact that she married six times in her short life. La Marr was a *bon viveur* who fell prey to most of Hollywood's excesses. As with so many other victims of its blandishments, there was nobody on hand to guide her through the film world with anything approaching common sense.

A more prominent scandal of the time was that involving a possible charge of statutory rape against Charlie Chaplin as a result of his relationship with the 15-year-old Lita Grey. Chaplin cast Grey as his love interest in *The Gold Rush* in 1924 but before it began shooting he had impregnated her, which caused her to be replaced. He wanted her to have an abortion but her age ruled this out.

Reluctant to marry her, he instead offered her a dowry of $20,000 as well as "assistance" in finding a suitable husband for herself. He thought this would solve things for him but her parents pressured him into protecting the girl's honor. He went ahead with a "quickie" wedding in Mexico in November 1924, spending the wedding night on a train bound for Los Angeles where he was believed to have remarked to his friends, "Well, boys, this is better than the penitentiary. But it won't last." He's reported to have thought up a more chilling resolution to the marriage when he said to Grey as the train hurtled onwards, "You know, it would be easy if you'd just jump. We could end this whole situation."[14]

Chaplin's marriage to Grey was stormy. He was unfaithful to her and she was subjected to much emotional cruelty from him, as well as many sexual demands that bordered on the perverse, some of them involving a third party.

She filed for divorce from him in 1927 and was about to cite five prominent actresses with whom he'd been "intimately involved" during their marriage when he agreed to a cash settlement of $625,000 instead.[15] Revelations of infidelity and oral sex flew in the face of the image of the innocent Tramp that Chaplin spent so many years finessing on screen. For a time such revelations threatened to spell the end of his career. Outraged women called for his films to be withdrawn from circulation and/or banned. He survived, but his reputation with women was tarnished forever.

Chaplin, in the view of Otto Friedrich, wasn't really interested in women as people, only "toys" to be taken to bed "and then put aside when he had serious work to do." He once said, "I must find a woman who understands that creative art absorbs every bit of a man." Was he suggesting that even after his "creative art" was finished, he would still be unavailable to such a creature? "When I am working," he admitted, "I withdraw absolutely from those I love."[16]

Another former hero whose reputation was tarnished was Rudolph Valentino. When he died in 1927 there was almost national mourning on the part of women, but as time passed he became not so much the Lothario of legend as a "powder puff" figure who married two lesbians, the first one (Jean Acker) locking him out of the boudoir on his wedding night.

Valentino subsequently married the actress Natascha Rambova but because he hadn't waited the required time for his divorce from Acker to become final, he was declared bigamous and threatened with a lengthy prison sentence. He avoided this by claiming he hadn't slept with Rambova during their honeymoon, a proposition that caused him some humiliation. Was it possible that the Great Lover of celluloid had two unconsummated marriages in such a short time span?

Stories also emerged of his poor opinion of women in general. Rambova said during their marriage that she was fed up with a husband who "goes on the lot at five a.m., gets home at midnight and receives mail from girls in Oshkosh and Kalamazoo." Valentino famously expostulated, "I don't like women who know too much."[17] And "One can always be kind to a woman one cares nothing about, but only cruel to a woman one loves or has loved." It augured ill for women's future chances that the pioneer of dusky love in Arabian tents was quite possibly an impotent misogynist to boot. Was he also a closet homosexual? It's unlikely, but he was an effeminate sex symbol, as female in his ways as Bara was male. And therein lay the irony. In Hollywood's first two icons, somebody seems to have got their genders mixed up.

Part of Valentino's appeal, despite his effeminate overtones, was his aggressive sexuality, particularly as portrayed in his signature movie *The Sheik*, "riding off into the desert on a white steed, carrying a woman against her will to red-hot romance under the moon." In such films Hollywood seemed to be conspiring in a kind of "attractive rape" against the female of the species. And society at large followed suit: "Arab designs flooded the day's fashions and interior design and sales of hair pomade skyrocketed. So did the sales of a new brand of condoms that took the name 'Sheiks.' Jazz babies and flappers took to calling their fellows sheiks as well, and soon it was a household word."[18]

Valentino's death caused a style shift in the kind of films audiences wanted, Pola Negri being the main casualty. She left Hollywood soon afterwards, her brooding histrionics no longer attractive to a film public about to immerse itself in the more subdued fervor of Greta Garbo. She continued to work hard in Europe but when the 1935 film *Mazurka*, a favorite of Hitler's, led to rumors of a romance with the Fuhrer,

Louise Brooks was immortalized as the hedonistic Lulu in *Pandora's Box* (1929) but she always felt used and abused by Hollywood's coercive star system and railed against it, to her detriment.

17

she returned to the U.S., having sued the French magazine *Pour Nous* for printing the rumor.

Louise Brooks had arrived in Hollywood by now and, like Valentino, changed not only the way women were portrayed on screen but also the fashions of the time. She opted for sleek suits and furred gowns in contrast to the lumpy sweaters that had been in vogue up until then.

Hollywood, unfortunately, didn't appreciate her talent properly. After an apprenticeship as a Ziegfeld showgirl and a few forgettable features like *Another Blond* (1926) and *A Girl in Every Port* (1928), she set sail for Berlin where the German director G.W. Pabst cast her as Lulu in *Pandora's Box,* the film that made her name. With her dizzy charm and a fringe that reminded one of a jet bead curtain, Brooks epitomized the hedonistic excesses of the Jazz Age. In *Pandora's Box* she played a dancer who becomes the protégée of a newspaper editor. It was the ideal showcase for her cheeky eroticism.

She claimed that she was treated by Pabst "with a kind of decency and respect unknown to me in Hollywood."[19] She played a prostitute in *Diary of a Lost Girl* the following year but offers thinned out after that. When she refused the role eventually played by Jean Harlow in *The Public Enemy* in 1931, she sent out a rebellious message to the powers-that-be which sealed her fate in the U.S.

Maybe her mistake was immersing herself so much in Lulu's character that she expected the dancer's dominance over men to be replicated in the real world. This was never going to be the case in 1920s Hollywood, even for a flapper. Over the next decade she fought many wars with the studio bosses and usually came out second best. She retired young, her fall from grace almost as sudden as that of the characters she played so endearingly on screen. She became a film critic in her later years, using her pen as a kind of scalpel to eviscerate the industry that spat her out when it felt it had no need any more for her bobbed hair or her skittish sense of fun.

There were many in line to take her place, either as dancers or chorus girls, the latter job description often serving as a euphemism for prostitution. These functions offered films the easy opportunity of disposing of such *femmes fatales* in the finale. They spent much of their time

> falling off the stage or down a flight of stairs, getting run over by a trolley or being sold into white slavery. If they chose to deny temptation and suppress ambition they were rewarded by a handsome hero who would remove them from that sordid world altogether. The sound of babies, not applause, would fill their ears and satisfy their egos. With this idiom, Hollywood not only baked its cake but ate it too.[20]

The message was clear: Hollywood used its women as long as they were viable and then disposed of them just as clinically.

Mabel Normand was another major figure of cinema's early years who disappeared suddenly and is now a mere footnote in movie history. Normand fell for Mack Sennett (the man behind the Keystone Cops films) in 1908 and they spent seven years together. One day in 1915 she came home unexpectedly and found him in the arms of a naked actress, Mae Busch, who was supposedly Normand's best friend. Two weeks later Normand attempted suicide by jumping off a Los Angeles pier. She was rescued but was never the same afterwards.

It's not generally known that Normand was a director as well as an actress, having helmed many of the Keystone productions in which she appeared. After William Desmond Taylor was shot in 1922, her career suffered severe damage and when her chauffeur was implicated in a subsequent murder (while using a gun that belonged to her) the damage was irreparable. Sennett refused to put her back in films. She made a partial return in 1926 but her heart wasn't in it. She died of tuberculosis in 1927 at age 35.

That was also the year Valentino died. What twist would the film world take now? A gloomy Swede by the name of Greta Garbo provided the answer to that question in a series of films that elevated romance almost to a sacred status.

Entrances and Exits

When Garbo made *Flesh and the Devil* with John Gilbert in 1927, she was earning $600 a week, as opposed to his $5,000. When she demanded parity with him, Louis B. Mayer threatened to have her deported to Sweden for her "high-powered temperament." Garbo shrugged her shoulders at this, which shook him. He wasn't used to dealing with women who cared so little for his power, or their own future.

When *Flesh and the Devil* was a runaway success, MGM decided to build on this by rushing Garbo into a similar "vamp" vehicle, *Women Love Diamonds*, for the same fee. This time, however, the lady wasn't for turning. Instead she demanded $5,000 a week from Mayer. He almost choked at her arrogance, offering her the sop of a modest increase in salary if she reported for work immediately on *Women Love Diamonds*. To this offer Garbo uttered her by now famous, "No more bad weemen. I theenk I go back to Sweden." Mayer thought she was bluffing but she wasn't. He placed her on suspension and made the movie with Pauline Starke instead. But Starke was no Garbo and the returns reflected that. Mayer caved in and begged her to come back at her asking price. The rest is history—or her story. The fact that she stood up to Mayer made her a role model for her peers. In the words of Louise Brooks, her stubbornness "rocked all of Hollywood."[1]

Women were making significant strides behind the camera as well as in front of it by now. Dorothy Arzner directed her first feature, *Get Your Man*, in 1927. It starred Clara Bow, who was none too pleased with the director at first. But Arzner asserted herself with the "It" girl, letting her know in no uncertain terms that she would have no nonsense on the set.[2] As shooting progressed, the relationship between them improved, Arzner learning a lot from Bow's instinctiveness before the camera. She also used her the following year in *The Wild Party,* Paramount's first talkie. This was the first Hollywood film to show female bonding almost to a lesbian degree. Here and afterwards, Arzner sought to undo the stereotypes of women as "scheming witches and light-hearted husband-chasers."[3] She was fortunate in the fact that most of her films were made before the introduction of the Hays Code, so themes like this, and indeed drugs and prostitution, weren't yet taboo.

Mae West was also making her presence felt by now. In 1927 she wrote a play called *Sex* which dealt with homosexuality in a sensitive manner. It played to packed houses in

New Jersey but was subsequently closed down and West ended up serving ten days in jail for "public obscenity."

She always denied that her play was "dirty": "There wasn't any nudity and the language had less profanity than some other Broadway shows. What they objected to was that it told the truth. Prostitutes aren't the only ones who are in the sex business. A lot of very respectable dames sell it too, and for a high price, like [when they marry] a man for his money."[4]

A new age was dawning. Even Mary Pickford cut her golden curls in 1928, the first sign of the former conformist breaking away from studio dominance. Pickford and Douglas Fairbanks co-starred for the only time in their careers in 1929 in *The Taming of the Shrew*, a limp adaptation of Shakespeare's play directed by Sam Taylor. (It carried the laughable credit, "By William Shakespeare, with additional dialogue by Sam Taylor.") Pickford found her husband an ordeal to work with. Perhaps he took the part too seriously, playing it off screen as well as on. His biographer wrote, "He would dawdle and delay shooting sched-

"What, when drunk, one sees in other women," said Kenneth Tynan, "one sees in Garbo sober." She used her Nordic gloom to beguiling effect in a raft of romantic dramas but offscreen she fought tougher battles for equality against the likes of Louis B. Mayer.

ules, costing a lot of money. He failed to learn his lines. He demeaned [Mary]." Her confidence was shattered as a result. She was never at ease again before a camera.[5]

The pair were having personal problems as well by now, the glitter having worn off Hollywood's first "golden couple." Fairbanks made her feel isolated and she took to drink as a result—a family failing. After the marriage broke down, screenwriter Frances Marion (a friend of Pickford's) tried to console her by saying, "Remember, Mary, you're America's sweetheart." Pickford replied, "I only want to be one man's sweetheart and I'm not going to let him go."[6] But eventually she had to.

Clara Bow's luck also ran out at the end of the decade when her affair with a married man caused her to be sued by his wife. Paramount punished her for her breach of its morality clause by seizing her escrow account. Things got worse for her in 1931 when Daisy De Voe, her former secretary, was convicted of stealing large amounts of her money and jewelry. De Voe subsequently published a kiss-and-tell book outlining Bow's sexual adventures and this resulted in her being fired from Paramount. Bow's future years were characterized by various nervous breakdowns. Her mother had died in a psychiatric institution and she feared she would too. A solid marriage to Rex Bell gave her some stability in her life but she struggled with depression constantly and she failed to make a screen comeback, much as she tried.

Lillian Gish was another high-profile casualty. By the end of the 1920s her appeal, and era, had gone. (Louise Brooks felt she was "stigmatized at the age of 31 as a grasping, silly, sexless antique.") Hollywood afterwards did to her what it did to all its treasures once they lost their luster: It turned her into a character actress. She continued to give great performances in old age but the sweetness that was her trademark became superseded by the more frivolous ambience ushered in by the new decade.

In many ways this decade belonged to Marlene Dietrich. Dietrich exploded onto the screen in Josef von Sternberg's German film *The Blue Angel* (1930), playing a cabaret performer Lola who destroys the professor who's besotted with her, played by Emil Jannings.

She opened movies up to a new way of viewing romance. Her "Live now, pay later" credo carried Clara Bow's party antics into a more sophisticated domain. Her sexuality was also more diverse than Bow's, if not more prolific. "It doesn't matter if you're a man or a woman," she declared, "I'll make love with anyone I find attractive."[7] If Hollywood had its eyes opened by Garbo shortly before, Dietrich turned them in a more provocative direction, replacing Garbo's legendary search for love with a more reckless abandonment to the moment.

Clara Bow's reign as Hollywood's self-styled "It" Girl was brief but glorious. It ended when her ebullient behavior became too hot for the industry to handle. A messy divorce followed by the tawdry revelations of a secretary precipitated her early retirement from movies, and an ongoing problem with mental illness.

Von Sternberg was a huge figure in her emergence but he exaggerated this out of all proportion to the media. "In my films Marlene is not herself," he blustered, "Marlene is not Marlene. I am Marlene." Sam Jaffe explained: "Von Sternberg wanted to impose himself on everyone to a point where anyone with any individuality could no longer tolerate it. [He] tried to absorb you."[8] Elsewhere von Sternberg proclaimed, "I gave her nothing that she did not already have," which seems to contradict the other claim.[9]

Her subservience to him was in stark contrast to the domineering influence she exerted over men in her movies. One viewer wrote: "That she can be had, but not possessed, is a test for the male ego. Her attitudes deprive men of the excitement of the chase as well as the triumph of conquest. The male sexual target may be led to feel that he's attacking but all too soon the real nature of the situation becomes clear: Marlene has selected him. How humiliating to have performed a love dance for such a cool spectator!"[10]

Her most notable trait was expanding women's appeal to both sexes without special pleading to either. Kenneth Tynan observed, "She has sex, but no gender."[11]

Dietrich also made *Morocco* for von Sternberg in 1930. In the film's most talked-about scene she kisses a woman when dressed in top hat and tails and then hands a flower to Gary Cooper. In a few brief moments here she manages to usurp both male courting rituals and apparel. Was this a covert lesbian move or is she merely being mischievous and/or playing hard to get? Whichever, it sent out a clarion call to men that a new breed of woman had made her appearance. Can we draw a line from Dietrich's cross-dressing to a suggestion of bisexu-

Marlene Dietrich ushered in the era of the androgynous woman on the American screen, dressing like a man in films like *Morocco* (1930), above. She threatened the old order by her sartorial and behavioral arrogance and defiant (metro) sexuality.

ality on her part? Not in Danny Peary's view. Peary wrote: "Marlene chooses to wear men's clothing just as she chooses to approach sexual satisfaction with a freedom ordinarily considered a masculine prerogative."[12]

There were rumblings of discontent among moralists about all this ribaldry. "Women," *Variety* proclaimed in a front-page story in 1931, "are responsible for the ever-increasing public taste in sensationalism and sexy stuff." They made up the bulk of cinema audiences, it contended, and were also the main readers of "the tabloids, scandal sheets, flashy magazines and erotic books."

"Women love dirt," it went on. "Nothing shocks 'em." The mind of the average man, in contrast, was "most wholesome."[13]

Society's double standards were already becoming apparent. Any effrontery on the part of women was seen as licentious whereas for men it would be merely forward, or fun. One is accustomed to view pre–Code films as liberal but they still had blind spots, not only in the manner in which misbehaving women had to kowtow to their men but also in the naive depiction of ladies of the night who tended to fall into the "Hookers are always looking for love" stereotype in films like *Girls About Town* (1931).

People have often wondered why Depression-era films featured so many women as prostitutes. Writer Barry Norman posited the theory that it was because many Depression era women *were* prostitutes: "At the tail end of the Jazz Age, films showed prostitution as a means whereby girls could get their share of the good life, a shortcut to the American Dream. But by the early thirties, taking to the streets had become a last, desperate way to earn a living. In 1930, 20 percent of America's ten million women were unemployed but in one in six urban families the only wage-earners were women, and they were paid 60 percent less than the men."[14] Films like *Blonde Venus* and *Faithless* showed women resorting to prostitution as a necessity. By now the "fallen woman" had become almost a stereotype.

There were of course, different opinions of what constituted "fallen." Many films made in 1931 depicted free-spirited women without judging them. In *The Common Law,* Constance Bennett played a nude model who moves in with her artist lover. In *Tonight or Never* Gloria Swanson was a singer whose voice improves when she takes a lover. *Illicit* had Barbara Stanwyck as a dynamic young woman who doesn't want to marry the man she's living with for fear it will destroy the bohemian life they have, her fears becoming realized when they do marry and find themselves drifting apart. The resolution is old-fashioned and contrived but Stanwyck conveyed the idea of a very well-defined "modern" woman: sweet, kind, faithful but still craving adventure. What a shame the so-called Hollywood "purge" removed gems like this from circulation when the Hays *fatwa* rode roughshod over anything smacking even vaguely of liberalism.

Lenore Coffee scripted *Possessed* for Irving Thalberg that year. Like most of her films it was a success but Thalberg never appreciated her. He only paid her half of what she got from Louis B. Mayer and dumped her in a dingy office to pen her scripts.

Bette Davis was just starting out now. One of her first auditions called for her to don a revealing dress and lie on a couch. She had to act as "a test girl for thirty or forty men, give or take a few. These try-out actors would plop themselves on my bosom, flattening it and me." For Davis the whole process was like "feudal serfdom": "If we didn't behave ourselves we got tongue-lashed. And if we slaves revolted we could have our contracts cancelled."[15]

One of the most controversial films of the year was William Wellman's *The Public Enemy.* This launched James Cagney onto the screen as a hoodlum, his energy papering over the melodramatic cracks of the kind of film that would come to define him. In one memorable scene he squashed a grapefruit in the face of Mae Clarke. Doris Day remarked, "When he did that, he was epitomizing one of the great mysteries of all time: Why do women prefer bastards?"

Clarke, regrettably, was remembered for this indignity more than anything else she did in her career. It was as if it was indeed what gangsters' molls were for, to act as background scenery for male aggression.

Later that year she gave a towering performance as an ill-fated prostitute in James Whale's *Waterloo Bridge* but the film was banned when the Production Code was introduced in 1934. MGM bought the rights to it in 1939 and a year later released the Mervyn LeRoy adaptation starring Robert Taylor and Vivien Leigh. After being stored in a vault for 35 years, the 1931 Mae Clarke version was re-discovered but a joint agreement between MGM and Universal meant it wasn't seen publicly for two more decades. She never received the recognition she deserved for it, going to her grave as a forgotten star. In some ways the character she played in *Waterloo Bridge* was like a metaphor for her life. Before she died she gave an interview to *Premiere* magazine in which she purported to be sick to death of people ranting on incessantly about the grapefruit scene, which eclipsed everything she did afterwards. Her career was also blighted by a car accident she had in the thirties, and some medical and psychological problems she developed as a result of it.

Most people saw *The Public Enemy* as Cagney's coming-of-age film but they should also have noted Jean Harlow's part in it. In one scene she asks him for his phone number, an unprecedented gesture for a woman of the time. But then, that was Harlow. She wasn't going to stand on ceremony when she wanted something.

She appeared in *Red-Headed Woman* the following year, playing a character who sleeps her way to the top without remorse and gets away with it. It was a new kind of woman and a new kind of movie. Puritans were enraged and liberals gratified. Those in the middle wondered if the "victory" was pyrrhic, if the enslavement to men that was woman's heritage heretofore was in danger of being replaced by a potentially more fearful sell-out to consumerism.

A bigger danger according to the woman herself was being typecast in such roles. Such typecasting continued immediately with her playing Clark Gable's floozie in *Red Dust*. When shooting of this was over, she asked her agent, "What kind of whore do you want me to play next?"[16] She meant it only half in jest, all too aware of the rules of Hollywood's game. More worrisome by far was Louis B. Mayer's view of her as "the freak whore."[17]

Harlow was free with her body. She was one of the first screen heroines to transmit the fact that sex could be fun, that it wasn't a guilty pleasure. Her brash demeanor and smoke-soaked voice promised men every soldier's dream. The way she carried herself— even in a bath towel—took that promise to

When Jean Harlow hit the screen, everything was up for grabs—literally. She flouted convention and gave the men as good as she got in films where her brash sexuality redefined woman's role both in the real world and the reel one.

the next level. Either inside or outside marriage she was available to hot-blooded males for fun and "maybe something extra." Her sassiness also had a knock-on effect on other films that were being made at the time, films like *The Animal Kingdom* (1932) where Ann Harding describes herself as "a foolish virgin," adding "Well, foolish anyway."

Harlow's career was threatened when her husband Paul Bern killed himself and there was a question mark over whether she'd been a factor in his suicide. (He wrote a note which pointed to some sexual shame on his part on their wedding night.) But the situation changed when a previous relationship of his came to light: Bern had had a common law marriage with a young actress called Dorothy Millette but it broke down. Afterwards Millette became unhinged and had to be placed in a mental hospital. When she was released and heard about Bern's marriage to Harlow, she visited him and an argument broke out. Millette may have threatened to charge Bern with bigamy. She then drowned herself, or was drowned. Rumors that she could have been murdered persisted.[18]

In the same year the British actress Peg Entwistle jumped to her death from the 50-foot electric HOLLYWOODLAND sign, frustrated over a failed marriage and a career that didn't seem to be going anywhere. She'd appeared opposite Irene Dunne in the film *Thirteen Women* and chose the thirteenth letter of the sign from which to jump, perhaps as a result of this. Entwistle had been a successful actress in London but once she reached Hollywood she fell prey to the "casting couch" syndrome and was advised to make a "sensational stag reel" movie to "make your hair curl" and possibly impress the likes of Darryl F. Zanuck. That was the way things were done, she was informed. Men called the shots and women, if they were lucky, brought up the rear.

Clark Gable was about to become "king" of Hollywood now. He was the alpha male of his generation, bedding women as they presented themselves to him, which happened with some frequency—though not as often as legend would have it. ("Hell," he liked to tell reporters, "if I'd jumped on all the dames they say, I'd never have had time to go fishin'.")

Carole Lombard appeared with him in *No Man of Her Own in* 1932. Sparks flew between them both on- and off-screen but each of them were married to other people at the time. It was years before they started living together. They didn't marry until 1939 because Gable's wife refused to give him a divorce. Many people thought the relationship wouldn't work because of Gable's overt machismo but he was secure enough in himself to enjoy "ballsy chicks" like Lombard. She fought hard for women's equality in the film world and had the vocabulary of a trucker to drive her points home when men seemed more interested in her vital statistics than her causes.

Trailing clouds of notoriety from Broadway, Mae West had arrived in Hollywood by now and hit the ground running. She appeared with George Raft in *Night After Night* and, according to Raft, "stole everything but the cameras."[19] The film gave viewers their first exposure to her classic wit. When a girl looks at her jewelry in one scene and gushes, "Goodness, what beautiful diamonds!" West replies, "Goodness had nothing to do with it, dearie."

Paramount was in receivership when West arrived on the scene. She was 39, an age that would have ruled most actresses out from even having a career, never mind bringing an age of prudery tumbling down. But that's what she did, allowing a whole generation of women to laugh about sex by dint of her naughty one-liners. The fact that they were delivered in her nasal drone only made them more enticing.

West was a lot more savvy about men than she pretended. "When a man was courting me," she said in one of her rare serious moods, "he'd want to put a diamond on my finger. As soon as he thought he had me, he wanted to put an apron around my waist. I lived in the world of show business, which was a man's world as far as where the power was concentrated." Her mother told her she'd do better with men if she concealed her intelligence, advice she took to heart: "Men don't like a woman to be smarter than they are. Brains are an asset as long as you hide them."[20] West made a lot of money for Paramount with *She Done Him Wrong*, a film version of her play *Diamond Lil* in which she gets to say the legendary line "Why don't you come up sometime and see me?" to Cary Grant. The following year she made another film with Grant, *I'm No Angel*. This contained another immortal West one-liner: "It's not the men in my life, it's the life in my men." It would have been more raunchy throughout but was toned down by the Production Code Administration—so much so that at one point West burst into tears.[21]

W.C. Fields referred to her as "a plumber's idea of Cleopatra." Other people saw her as a caricature of sex, a female impersonator of females. Her *double entendres* were really *single entendres*: There could only be one meaning. She was ribald in a jaunty manner. Her scripts intimated not so much a hint of sex as a delight in their own ingenuity. Hollywood allowed her to prosper not because she was threatening but for precisely the opposite reason: She was lightweight. Her attitude to sex was really a male one. She

More than any other actress of the time, Mae West spearheaded the idea that a woman could, and should, take the initiative in relationships with men, but her outrageous oneliners got her into hot water time and again with the repressive ideologies of the 1930s, eventually resulting in her muzzling by the powers-that-be.

saw it as lewd and naughty. Her wicked barbs were really the stuff of men's postcards, construction workers' wolf-whistles. When she said things like "When I'm good I'm very good but when I'm bad I'm even better," this was like a male line fed through a woman's lips. She may have invited men to come up and see her sometime but the invitation seemed to have as much interest for her as the visit. In this sense, the foreplay was the sex; she was always more verbal than physical.

Despite her later problems with censors, West was much more innocuous than another siren about to be launched upon the American public: Hedy Lamarr. In 1933 Lamarr made headlines when she appeared nude in the Czech-Austrian film *Ecstasy*. Later in the year she married munitions manufacturer Fritz Handl. Handl tried to buy up all prints of the film to stop people outside Europe from seeing it. (He was unsuccessful in this gambit.)

Lamarr acquired the tag of "the most beautiful girl in the world" after she reached Hollywood but she remained unimpressed by the adulation. "American men are only interested in two things," she pronounced, "women and breasts." And elsewhere, "The ladder of success in Hollywood is usually: press agent, actor, director, producer, leading man. You're a star if you sleep with each of them in that order."

"Any girl can be glamorous," Lamarr sniffed, "all you have to do is stand still and look stupid." She had the same arrogance as Garbo, an added attraction to men. Also, as with Garbo, it seemed to come with a sultry pout. The golden curls of Mary Pickford suddenly seemed a long way away. It looked as if Hollywood was going to have trouble with one so unawed by its value system even if she was content to play into its myopic undertow for the immediate career kickbacks.

Katharine Hepburn, who'd also burst upon the scene, was a different type of threat to the old order, serving notice that she wasn't going to curry favor with the studio bosses or suffer fools gladly on film sets. "I didn't realize until quite late," she stated, "that women were supposed to be the infe-

"It's easy to be glamorous," said Hedy Lamarr. "All you have to do is stand still and look stupid." She was anything but that, though she had a hard time convincing the studio bosses of her intelligence, particularly since her career began with a nude appearance in *Ecstasy*. Afterwards it was stymied all too often by substandard vehicles.

rior sex."[22] From the start the Bryn Mawr bluestocking demanded roles that suited her "Katharine of Arrogance" mien and she got them more often than not. The fact that she wasn't hugely popular at the box-office hinted more at the fact that the world wasn't yet ready for a woman who looked as if she'd be more at home in a library than on a film set. (In her leisure time she read "serious" literature rather than the penny dreadfuls of the day.) She dressed in trousers and stern collars, leading to rumors that she was part of the notorious "sewing circle" of bisexual stars.

Hepburn appeared in Dorothy Arzner's *Christopher Strong* in 1933, playing a woman who has to choose between her career as an aviatrix and her love for a married man (Colin Clive). Even before the enforcement of the Code, this was a situation Hollywood could only resolve in one way: i.e., Hepburn's kamikaze-style suicide. The question audiences were left facing was: which was Hepburn's greater "sin," having a career or an illicit love?

Arzner was none too pleased at the compromises she had to agree to in order to get the film made but half a loaf was better than no bread. She was all too well aware that it was men who were running the industry and she had to keep her head down about the "messages" in her films, concentrating instead on the fuzzy plotlines. She said in an interview, "There should be more [women] directing. Try as any man may, he will never be able to get the woman's viewpoint in directing certain stories. A great percentage of our audience is women. That too is something to think about."[23]

She had some Hepburn-like qualities herself, dressing in men's clothes and keeping her hair tightly cropped. She wasn't an aggressive person—she couldn't have survived as a woman at such a time if she was—but she was sufficiently confident of herself to walk off a movie if she wasn't given what she wanted. "Get yourself another boy" was her favorite parting shot under such circumstances.[24] But this never happened. It helped that her films made money.

Arzner kept her private life private. Was she a lesbian? The common

Katharine Hepburn made it clear that she would never be intimidated by the top brass from her very early days when she became branded as "Katharine of Arrogance," a pose she continued right through her career. She brought a flinty hauteur to an industry that had previously viewed women as "Adam's Rib" creations, to use the title of one of her films.

consensus today is that she probably was, but this was something else she kept under wraps. Her androgynous dress sense, as was the case with Hepburn and Dietrich, was indicative of a sea-change not only in Hollywood's sartorial priorities but also its view of the upcoming crop of screen goddesses and their orientations. As far as the public was concerned, they could be lesbian and/or bisexual. New parameters were being opened to male-female concourse in an impish manner that hinted at erotic adventures rather than nailing down any new manifestos. These stars opened the door for others to follow "suit," like Sandra Shaw in *Blood Money* (1933) where she dons a tuxedo and monocle. There were no overtly revolutionary statements in their films and they usually ended by affirming, or confirming, a heterosexual credo—but along the way some variations were considered, perhaps for future elaboration.

Miriam Hopkins pushed the envelope for women in a different direction by playing a woman who seems to enjoy living with the man who rapes her (Jack La Rue) in *The Story of Temple Drake* (1933). "There is no beauty," *The Hollywood Reporter* ranted, "in seeing a lovely girl stripped of all charm on the screen, standing before her audience [as] a base and vile representative of all that is disenchanting in sex."[25] What this "review" overlooked was that it was La Rue who was base and disenchanting. It was also he who instigated the sex. The fact that Hopkins appeared to collude in it, and afterwards endorse it, was too much for audiences of the time to comprehend. If Hopkins' character was male, she might have had the cult following of a Cagney or Bogart, but being female she became an object of revulsion.

Cagney himself appeared in *Picture Snatcher* that year, playing a photographer this time, but with familiar bile. In one scene he knocks a moll out by tossing her into the back seat of a car—routine treatment by his standards even when he wasn't playing a gangster. One writer observed, "On their own turf the sassy women of the 'bad girl' cycle took no guff but in the masculine environs of the gangster film the dames, molls and dishes are pushed around and cast aside."[26] The "good girls" of the time were also pushed around, but in more subtle ways. This was apparent in two other 1933 releases, *Female* and *Employees Entrance*.

Female appeared to be a feminist film but the manner in which it ended made it even more threatening to women than anything more overtly sexist. Instead of the traditional "maiden in distress" figure, this presented us with a career woman (Ruth Chatterton) flouting the old verities of men and marriage as she rises to the top of the corporate ladder. So far so good but after an hour it plunges us back into that twee comfort zone beloved of controlling men as she realizes the error of her ways and decides to leave the boardroom behind and instead marry and have no less than nine children. The white picket fence and Mom's apple pie aren't mentioned but one imagines they'll be part of the package too as our erstwhile society lady settles into the joys of suburbia.

In *Employees Entrance* Loretta Young sleeps with her boss as a result of being annoyed with her husband, a steamy theme for the time, but she's made to attempt suicide afterwards in remorse for her *amour fou*. There always seemed to be an ethical seesaw at play in "issue" films of this kind. Casual cruelties were meted out to women who tilted at traditional windmills, however tentatively.

Sometimes the cruelty was directed at actresses as well as th...
Cukor had the image of being a woman-friendly director. His repu...
supreme performances from them was well established but he could also be...
when he wished, and use mischievous psychology to either flatter or coerc...
doing things they didn't want to do. Neither was he slow to tell his female stars w...
displeased him. He actually struck Katharine Hepburn on the set of *Little Women* w...
she spoiled a dress that was being used in one of the scenes, something most other director...
would have balked at with this lady.[27]

of the Code

Female was pulled from circulation in 1934 as Will Hays rode over his metaphorical hill with the Production Code, cutting down screen Jezebels with the self-righteous indignation of a fire-and-brimstone Bible-thumper. So was *The Story of Temple Drake* and numerous other fine films, including Alfred Green's *Baby Face* and Rouben Mamoulian's *Queen Christina*.

After the enforcement of the Code, sexual themes had to be dealt with *in* code, either through the kind of innuendo preferred by Mae West or by trivialization in screwball comedies, where stars like Irene Dunne and Carole Lombard were free to misbehave in a zany manner and let audiences draw their own conclusions. If sex was turned into a joke as far as the censors were concerned, it lost its edge of danger. The Marx Brothers were also allowed free rein from this point of view. Blatant sexual sins were dealt with more severely after 1934. In a squeaky-clean cosmos, wandering wives and girlfriends were forced to embrace traditional morality with undiluted commitment before the end credits rolled.

Not too many actresses raised their heads above the parapet at this time, not even Bette Davis. She appeared in *Fashions* (1934), a film where she caved in to studio demands regarding her image for one of the very few times in her career. "They made me up to look like Miss Garbo," she griped, "which of course is utterly impossible. They gave me the lovely long bob and the nice beautiful wide mouth and the long long lashes. It was sickening because it wasn't my type and thank God I had the brains enough to know that." It was the first and last time she became a "product." After that it was, "Either fire me or let me be what I personally am."

Her talent allowed her to prosper in later years but others weren't so fortunate; many actresses allowed themselves to be manhandled and even physically altered as plastic surgery "corrected" bad teeth, skin, noses, whatever: "Those who had any individuality never made it because they looked phoney."[1]

Davis was unfairly denied an Oscar for her performance in RKO's *Of Human Bondage* in 1934. She played Mildred, the tragic female lead character of Somerset Maugham's acclaimed novel. Her name appeared in small print under that of her co-star Leslie Howard when the film was first released, but when it performed well at the box-office, the print size increased.[2] With men it seemed to work the opposite way: A star's name in big letters "persuaded" audiences to think an actor deserved such prominence.

Another bone of contention for Davis was the manner of her death in the film, which had to be changed from syphilis (as it had been in Maugham's novel) to pneumonia to placate the censors. All in all it was an unhappy experience for her, as were many of the films she made for Warner Brothers around this time. She tried to expand her horizons in them but directors either didn't understand her intentions or didn't want to know, anxious only to develop in her a stock type, something she fought resolutely against. Her frustration reached boiling point in Michael Curtiz's *Cabin in the Cotton*. She did her best to give a performance of quality but all Curtiz could say was, "Who'd want to go to bed with her?" as if that was all that mattered.[3]

The German director Leni Riefenstahl suffered from a different type of problem: a political one. When Riefenstahl made *Triumph of the Will*, a documentary on Hitler's Nuremberg rallies, it was castigated as being one of the most galling propaganda films of all time even though this wasn't her intention at all. She went on to be accused of being an apologist for almost every Nazi excess that followed in the years ahead, thereby becoming one of the most wronged directors in history. In an attempt to defend *Triumph of the Will* she said, "In 1934, Hitler had acquired a certain credit in the world and he fascinated a certain number of people, among them Winston Churchill."[4] It was understandable that she would also have found herself a victim of his mass hypnosis. But posterity chose to see her differently. One writer concluded, "She was an ambitious artist born in the wrong time and place and of the wrong sex."[5]

Back in Hollywood, more prosaic concerns perpetuated themselves. Myrna Loy starred with William Powell in *The Thin Man* in 1934, the first of six films in which the husband-wife detective team hit the screen. They were highly successful but Loy never really commanded the salary she deserved at MGM. Whenever she looked for a raise, executives threatened her with being replaced by their rising star Rosalind Russell. The following year the perennially-popular Fred Astaire and Ginger Rogers were paired for the fourth time in *Top Hat*. It became one of their best-loved films but Rogers, like Loy with Powell, always lagged behind Astaire in the salary department. She made an issue of it during *Top Hat*, halting production for a time as she clamored for a raise, but what she got was minimal. This despite the fact that, as Rogers herself declared, "I did everything Fred did—except backwards, and in high heels."[6]

Marlene Dietrich's collaboration with Josef von Sternberg ended with *The Devil Is a Woman* in 1935. The decision was his rather than hers. He wasn't able to accept the fact that she was now a star and could soar without him. Like many Svengalis, he needed his control over her career to be extended indefinitely. When he saw that she was now having an independent one, his devotion to "the creature whose image was reflected on film" dissipated.

The up-and-coming Frances Farmer travelled to Russia that year and in doing so managed to enrage those who'd already heard her anti–God pronouncements. To this they could now add "anti–America." She returned with only good things to say about it and while her remarks didn't have any immediate effect, they were on public record and gave those of a reactionary bent a further reason to do her down when erratic behavior patterns began to emerge at the beginning of the next decade.

Loretta Young became pregnant by Clark Gable after they starred together in *Call of the Wild*. As was the case with Barbara La Marr in 1922, Young had the child quietly and told her she was adopted. It was only when she reached adulthood that she learned the truth of her heritage. (One was reminded of the old joke: "In Hollywood an aristocrat is someone who can trace their heritage all the way back to their parents.")

Also in 1935 the silent star Thelma Todd was found dead in her car in the family garage. The cause of death was asphyxiation, leading to rumors that she'd been murdered. A more likely cause is that the man she was living with at the time, Roland West, locked her in to the garage to "punish" her for being drunk and she passed out at the wheel without him being aware of this. West never admitted to having had any part in her death so he didn't face a charge of manslaughter but his involvement was corroborated by his friend Chester Morris, who claimed he confessed as much to him on his deathbed in 1951.[7]

Later in the year, Judy Garland signed up with Metro-Goldwyn-Mayer, beginning a career that would be more of a lifestyle than a job. She summarized it like this: "I was born at the age of twelve on the MGM lot." Almost as soon as she stepped in front of a camera, Louis B. Mayer started to worry about the fact that she could have a tendency towards pudginess. "From the time I was thirteen," she groaned, "there was a constant struggle between MGM and me: whether to eat, how much to eat, what to eat. I was on prisoner's rations. The only salt I got was that of my tears as I gazed on an empty plate."

The kinds of films Garland was making at this time fed into the post–Code preference for domestic harmony, something that was also prevalent in most of the offerings with adult stars. In *Alice Adams*, for instance, we saw social climber Katharine Hepburn settling for marriage with the dull Fred MacMurray, something one severely doubted would have happened in real life.

In *The Bride Walks Out* (1936) we had the familiar sight of a Hollywood groom (Gene Raymond) denying his wife (Barbara Stanwyck) the right to work even though they were having a tough time making ends meet on his salary. Despite her wish to bump up the family budget by going back to her pre-marriage job, he prefers her learning the finer points of cooking. Stanwyck wants to leave this to the maid, Hattie McDaniel. McDaniel could almost have put "movie maid" on her screen Actors Guild card as her career, so many times did she essay such a role.

Marlene Dietrich had lost her edge by now, playing a mere shadow of her former self in *The Garden of Allah*, a film which gives her lines like, "Nobody but God and I know what is in my heart." Having Dietrich as a devout Catholic seemed about as credible as casting Theda Bara as a virgin or Carole Lombard as a nun. Dietrich was also "cleaned up" at the end of Frank Borzage's *Desire*, playing a jewel thief who falls into the arms of Gary Cooper at the end in a manner that would hardly have been countenanced before the enforcement of the Code. As if that wasn't bad enough, in *The Moon's Our Home* Henry

Fonda subdues the bubbly Margaret Sullavan who at first refuses to give up her career for him but in the end seems glad to do so. Sullavan is much more believable before her sacrifice. (Neither did it help the credibility of the piece to know that Fonda and Sullavan were divorced in real life when it was being made.)

Jean Harlow starred with William Powell in *Libeled Lady* in 1936. The pair fell in love but Powell stopped short of marrying her because of her sex symbol status, a decision that seemed to place a question mark over just how deep his love went. "In my declining years," he huffed, "I don't want to be married to a girl men kill themselves over."[8] He didn't have to worry about such an eventuality, Harlow dying soon afterwards of uremic poisoning brought on by kidney failure, a problem misdiagnosed by her physician at the time.

Frances Farmer got her first big break in 1936's *Rhythm on the Range*, a film she made with Bing Crosby. Even this early, the temperament that would get her into such trouble with moguls down the road was starting to make itself manifest. She refused studio chief Adolph Zukor's injunction to dress more formally off-camera, preferring sweaters and slacks to evening wear, and also refused to change her name or style her hair in the way she was asked. She drove a wreck of a car, lived with her husband in what she herself described as "little more than a shack" and denounced the plight of women in a male-dominated industry to all and sundry.

Because she was "hot property" she was allowed such indulgences by Zukor, who dismissed her insolence as "eccentricity," but there was bigger trouble brewing when she made *Come and Get It* the following year for William Wyler. Wyler dismissed her with the comment "The nicest thing I can say about Frances Farmer is that she's unbearable."[9] Farmer countered by remarking that acting in a film directed by Wyler was the nearest thing she could think of to slavery.

Notwithstanding all this, the movie (in which she played a double role) turned out to be a huge hit. She refused to follow it up with another one, however, electing to go instead to Broadway where she appeared in Clifford Odets' *Golden Boy*. It wasn't a wise choice, the abuse she suffered under Wyler being nothing compared to that dished out by Odets, a man to whom she was at first sexually attracted. They had an affair and then he deserted her, having branded her as "cheap" for succumbing to his advances.

Farmer's next film was *The Toast of New York,* which she made with Cary Grant. She wasn't impressed by the actor, berating him for wanting to be "Cary Grant" rather than his character. This led to a mechanical performance on his part in her view, and a poorer film. When the Spanish Civil War broke out shortly afterwards, she aligned herself wholeheartedly to the Loyalist cause and began campaigning for it. This set many tongues wagging about the pro-communist actress so recently returned from "red" Russia.

Mae West was also getting into hot water. William Randolph Hearst described her as "a menace to the sacred institution of the family" and the censorship police continued to get on her case, scrutinizing her scripts for offensive material. This wasn't too difficult to find and it wasn't long before she became the special "cause" of Joseph Breen, the director of the Production Code Association. Brought before magistrates, she refused to bend the knee. Asked once, "Are you showing contempt for the court?" she replied, "No, I'm doing my best to *hide* it." She always put a brave face on her plight, claiming that she liked censorship because she "made a fortune out of it." But when Paramount cancelled her contract, caving in to the pressure exerted by Breen and his henchmen, she started to become concerned about where her career might go.

A guard appeared on the set of *Belle of the Nineties*, watching her every move. Charles Laughton used to say they couldn't censor the gleam in his eye but with this lady they seemed to want to do even that. After so many years of playing havoc with enemies of spontaneous expression, by the mid-thirties she seemed to have become a shadow of her former self, her role in *Klondike Annie* (1936) as a Salvation Army nurse on the run from the law a total abnegation of everything she'd stood for up to this point.

By the end of her career she was almost totally defanged by Breen, who made it his business to go through her scripts with a fine-tooth comb. When movies failed her she slipped sideways into radio but a 1937 broadcast with her as the Biblical Eve drew such negative reactions she was banned from the airwaves indefinitely. Feeling rejected by both media, she went back to her first love, the theater, and revived *Diamond Lil* there.

Bette Davis was another star beginning to feel the studio heat. She realized she was tough but this was misinterpreted: "When a man gives his opinion he's a man but when a woman gives her opinion she's a bitch."[10] Some directors quivered at the prospect of working with her but she wasn't temperamental: "I got into trouble because I was a perfectionist."[11]

In March 1936 when Warner Bros refused to loan her out to RKO for *Mary of Scotland*, she became so angry she delayed returning to the studio for post-production work on *The Golden Arrow*, a film she'd just finished shooting, unless her contract was changed. She wanted her salary increased from $100,000 to $200,000 a year, her contract to run for four years instead of seven, and to be called on to make no more than four films in any given year. She also wanted a clause granting her the freedom to do one film a year for another studio, and to have a three-month holiday included in it as well as a choice of cameramen.[12] Jack Warner flatly refused all these demands, offering her a role in the bland *God's Country and The Woman* instead. When she said she wasn't going to do this, she was suspended without pay. She sailed for England because "not one film company in Hollywood would touch me with a ten-foot pole" as a result of her taking Warner on.

Warner sued Davis for breach of contract, claiming that any film she made in England would "hurt" Warner productions. Davis countersued Warner Bros., referring to her contract as a form of slavery. "This slavery has a silver lining," the Warner Bros lawyer pointed out, "because the slave was well remunerated."[13]

Davis hadn't a leg to stand on in court and lost her case. It had a positive impact, though, because it let Warner know she wasn't afraid of him. He ended up paying her legal fees and pleading with her to come back to Hollywood. When she did, it was to make *Marked Woman* (1937), a film much superior to the fare she'd been getting before her walk-out. In it she played a woman testifying against an underworld figure, Eduardo Ciannelli. After she does so, her face is cut with a knife. To cover the scar, Davis was given a gauze contraption that seemed to her to resemble an Easter bonnet. She refused to wear this, going instead to a hospital for a more authentic covering. Though beaten in court, she hadn't lost her fighting qualities—and Warner knew it.

Many people thought she deserved an Oscar nomination for her performance but she didn't receive one. Luise Rainer won that year for *The Good Earth*. Rainer had also won the previous year for *The Great Ziegfeld*. Everybody was perplexed at her back-to-back wins. Rainer herself felt she peaked too soon in her career. As was often the case with Oscar winners, a lot of dross followed, Louis B. Mayer presenting her with substandard material in the years ahead. Her frustration at this state of affairs finally boiled over the day she told Mayer she wouldn't do any more poor scripts. Mayer roared back at her, "You'll do what I tell you. We made you and we can break you." Rainer replied, "God made me," and left his office. And Hollywood.

Not everyone was as forthright as Rainer or Davis when it came to looking for their rights. Most actresses just took what they were given, for better or worse. Life wasn't much fun on suspension with bills to pay. Often the thinking was that if you took the bad parts, the good ones would come along in their own sweet time. But often they didn't. Actresses who settled for less also appeared to put a small price on their heads. This dissuaded "quality" directors from considering them for the juicier roles. It was a delicate balancing act.

Even when one did get a part with a highly-regarded director, it wasn't always plain sailing. Sylvia Sidney made *Sabotage* for Alfred Hitchcock in 1937 but found the experience daunting. Sidney's husband dies in the film and Hitchcock wanted to shoot Sidney's reaction to his death before the death scene itself, which discombobulated her. "How do we do the end of the scene before we've even rehearsed [it]?" she asked, understandably. But Hitchcock argued that if they did that, she'd probably be too tired to work up the emotional range for her close-up. It was hardly a Method approach but she gave in: "You begin to say to yourself, 'My wishes are not that important. Give him what he needs.' I could not have worked with [him] if my attitude had been any different."[14] Later in the year she made *Dead End* for William Wyler and found him to be "probably one of the most sadistic directors in motion pictures."[15] Frances Farmer felt the same about Wyler but many actresses got on fine with him. Sometimes it was simply a question of a temperamental clash.

That also seemed to be the case with George Cukor. Cukor had a reputation of being kind to actresses, but as we've seen he could be manipulative with them too. Cukor was also tough on female screenwriters like June Mathis, Jeanie Macpherson and Frances Marion.

Marion wrote the screenplay for *Camille*, which was directed by Cukor in 1937. The film was a hit, as was another film Marion scripted for him, *Dinner at Eight,* in 1933. Marion was one of the most gifted female screenwriters Hollywood ever produced, with a string of other successful films to her credit like *Stella Maris, Anne of Green Gables, Humoresque, East Is West, Abraham Lincoln, The Scarlet Letter, Anna Christie* and *Stella Dallas,* but Cukor was negative about her talent. Was he jealous of her? It's possible. She was also the only woman on the first board of directors of the Screenwriters Guild. One of the main reasons she was allowed such power as a woman was because few people took moviemaking seriously.[16]

Marion, like most writers of her time, had to deal with the prudes at the Hays Office in crafting her screenplays. Exhorted to "make your scenario sound awfully sweet, and don't describe your heroine as sexy," she ran the risk of going to the other extreme and making her scripts seem "imbecilic and fit only for ten-year-old consumption."[17]

When she first applied to Twentieth Century–Fox for a screenwriting job, William Fox asked her derisively, "Why does a pretty girl like you want to be a writer?" Her reply was crisp and to the point: "Because I like to write." He then asked, "Why ain't you in a dress from a stylish store? Why don't I see no jewelry? A girl like you should have rings on her fingers." Marion countered, "And bells on her toes?" The "interview" ended with Fox telling her, "Nobody cares about female writers. Actresses, yes, they got glamour. But writers ... the poor *schlemiels*.[18]

Marion wrote for her third husband, the actor Fred Thomson, under various *noms de plume* because she didn't want to steal his thunder, her career being more famous than his. One of her favorite themes for scripts was, "The woman who earns more than her husband loses her love." She was content to hide her light under a bushel—if not to massage his ego unduly.

Her best years were spent under Irving Thalberg but after he died she was virtually ignored by the powers-that-be. Her contract was drawn up on a week-to-week basis and no longer could she be guaranteed screen credits for her scripts (or her name even used for publicity). Her work she likened to "writing on the sand with the wind blowing. They chew up and disgorge your stories until they're so far removed from your original idea that all you recognize is your name, and often that isn't even spelled correctly."[19] Maybe the bonus was that it was there at all. Men, on the contrary, were assured of a credit even if their contribution to a final script was minimal.

Rita Hayworth started to gain fame almost at the same time as Marion started to lose it. In 1937 she got a part in a film called *Hit the Saddle* mainly due to the efforts of her first husband Edward Judson, a 40-year-old car salesman who offered a Columbia executive a discount on a vehicle in return for the favor. Judson went on to secure a seven-year contract for her at Columbia after they were married. As the deal was clinched, he asked Harry Cohn, "What bride ever received a better wedding gift than a movie contract?" Cohn replied tartly, "It looks to me as if an old man has just found himself a seven-year meal ticket with free room and broad."[20] The pun was good; the sentiments not too idealistic.

Cohn was desperate to get Hayworth into his bed and pursued her relentlessly. He had spies everywhere, reporting back to him on her every move. He even hid microphones in her dressing room to eavesdrop on her conversations. She rebuffed his advances and he became demeaning to her. When she was in his office, sometimes he'd go to the toilet and leave the door open purposely, "as if he wanted to show her that no matter how successful she might be on screen, as far as he was concerned she was still nothing."[21] Cohn, in the words of Jack Cole, "just hated actors. You didn't have to be Glenn Ford or Rita. He thought they were all a tub of shit and he could replace any of them in a minute."[22]

Judson encouraged Hayworth to have affairs with other men to "improve" her profile.

"It seemed to me," said an acquaintance, "that Eddie would have sold his wife to the highest bidder if it would have enhanced her career."[23] He was more of a pimp to her than a husband.

His pushiness meant she was now subjugated to him as well as to Harry Cohn. She had her name changed (she was born Margarita Carmen Cansino), her hair dyed and her hairline raised by electrolysis. Such transmogrifications became the pattern of her life both on and off the screen as she submitted herself to the tender (and sometimes not so tender) mercies of men who thought they knew what was best for her and expected her to blindly agree. Alas, all too often she did.

Judy Garland was another vulnerable soul who submitted herself to Hollywood's Dream Factory aspirations with incurable optimism, not yet realizing that its only religion was the almighty dollar at the box office. She appeared with Mickey Rooney in the racetrack musical *Thoroughbreds Don't Cry* in 1937. She was still trying to curb her appetite as Louis B. Mayer's spies followed her to ice cream parlors to make sure she didn't partake of any sundaes to wind down from the day's filming.

The diet pills her doctor prescribed were giving her insomnia. Seconal was added to the mix to help her sleep. This made her woozy in the mornings so she took uppers to increase her energy levels for her singing and dancing exertions on the set. By nighttime she was unusually adrenalized so her body clock was upside down. She now needed more Seconal or Nembutal to bring on sleep, and was then roused at cock-crow for the next day's shoot. It was an insane spiral and would take its toll sooner than later.

Rita Hayworth was the love goddess to end all love goddesses, but she was manipulated by most of the men in her life, even those who loved her, like Orson Welles. Welles revamped her image for the ill-fated *The Lady from Shanghai* (above), a film he promised would revive her career. In effect it almost destroyed it—not least due to "that" peroxide hairstyle.

All Mayer allowed her to eat was chicken soup. She said with grim humor, "I swear there must have been a vat full of chicken soup at the MGM commissary with my name engraved on it."[24] As well as the soup, she lived on black coffee and eighty cigarettes a day, a combination guaranteed to play havoc with anyone's health even without the pills.

In defense of "Uncle" Louis, with whom Garland always remained friendly, he knew she had a sweet tooth and, if left entirely to herself, could have poured on the pounds. But even if she did, she wouldn't have been overweight, only overweight by Hollywood standards. Mayer couldn't have this because of her unique money-earning capacity. The film world thus became a kind of prison to her, a slimming club.

Even more stringent than Mayer was her mother Ethel, the classic "stage mom" who monitored her career—and bank account—with a zeal approaching the obsessive. When Garland wrote her name in the wet cement outside Grauman's Theater, Ethel took it upon herself to hover over her daughter's shoulder and straighten one of the letters in her signature. The superstar wasn't even allowed this one moment of individual expression.

Babes in Arms, another Garland-Rooney package, came out in 1939. Twelve hours after it wrapped, they were at work on *Andy Hardy Meets Debutante*. When that was finished, they were thrust into Busby Berkeley's *Strike Up the Band*. The grueling schedule meant even more pep pills to keep them singing and dancing and then a trip to the studio hospital to knock them out cold with sleeping pills. Then after a few hours sleep they were woken for further gymnastics. "Half of the time we were hanging from the ceiling," a bemused Garland recalled.[25] Any semblance of a social life was a strict no-no. She went on occasional dates but only for promotional purposes: "Judy Garland Is Dating Mr. X" became an attention-grabbing headline in any movie magazine even if they only shared a sundae. Or, as was more likely, some chicken soup.

Even when a film was in the can, there were more responsibilities. After spending two or three hours in makeup and then fourteen hours a day in front of a camera for a month, or two months, or even three, and finally breathing a sigh of relief when a director shouted "Cut" for the last time, she was often called upon to criss-cross the country advertising her films in countless theaters, and sometimes singing songs from them in such theaters, if not executing dance moves, or both. There were also radio interviews to be done. It was a workload designated to kill a horse, never mind a delicate sixteen-year-old *ingenue*. All the studio cared about was that she was present and correct when the director shouted "Action!" She was their prize product and they worked her into the ground.

Other stars of the time had different kinds of problems. Claudette Colbert starred in *Tovarich* (1937), which caused Kay Francis to sue Warner Bros as she'd been promised the role. She dropped the suit eventually but hung on at Warners for her juicy salary of $5,250 per week, appearing in much drivel for them in the years following and also taking a lot of abuse from Jack Warner in the process. "I didn't give a damn," she confessed, "I wanted the money." In a sense it was her way of rebelling against Warner because she knew he would have been happier to be rid of her. But she played the bad parts and he had to honor her contract.[26]

Hedy Lamarr now divorced Fritz Handl and moved to London. There she met Louis

B. Mayer. He was reluctant to offer her a movie contract because *Ecstasy* had been released in the U.S. with her nude scene. He eventually gave her one but cast her in a number of films that did little more than display her female charms.

She wasn't the only one being put into movies that downgraded women. Miriam Hopkins played an architect who sacrifices her career for marriage with Joel McCrea in the giddily-titled *Woman Chases Man*, a film that failed to establish any logic behind her decision. Paramount put Frances Farmer into the grossly substandard *Escape from Yesterday* to lure her back from Broadway, where she was still enjoying a break from dull contract movies, and also to punish her for any anti–Hollywood sentiments she espoused during her theatrical sabbatical. She hated doing the film but she couldn't afford to turn it down: A refusal would have meant indefinite suspension.

In 1938 Leni Riefenstahl released *Olympia,* her two-part record of the 1936 Berlin Olympics. It's difficult to evaluate this as a cinematic achievement considering it came out on the cusp of World War II. Fair-minded people realize today that she cared more for art than propaganda but in her lifetime she was almost perma-

Judy Garland should have won an Oscar for *A Star Is Born* (above). The fact that she didn't was yet another example of the "death by a thousand cuts" that Hollywood inflicted on her from the days when she was worked to the bone as a child star and put on slimming tablets that led to a later addiction to pills and other substances, resulting in her early death.

nently under the cloud of an imagined alliance with Hitler's regime. This is a pity because it blinds us to the wonderful cinematography she employed here. Later editions of the film have mercifully excised all footage of Hitler himself. Today we can evaluate it on its own merits even if we don't go as far as Jim Card, who suggested that it might well be "the best film ever made in history."[27]

Riefenstahl's only crime was the fact that Hitler admired her. Those who claimed such feelings were mutual over-argued the case. The rest of the world had the benefit of hindsight. Those caught in the eye of the Nazi storm weren't quite as observant, but to view her films as subversive Nazi tracts is unfair. Instead we should see them as documentaries in their own right, so many triumphs of film grammar.

The effects she achieved in *Olympia* were stunning. She didn't have the benefits of technology, instead going underwater and into trenches with her viewfinder. In a 1973 interview she put her feelings in perspective when she said, "I was fascinated by Hitler but took no political position. I have always been a romantic and loved beauty. People have been stoning me for years to destroy me. There is a Mafia-like conspiracy against me."[28] Only by expunging the mindset of the time, wrote B. Ruby Rich, and coming to terms with the attacks on her as "Hitler's girlfriend" do we stand a chance of seeing her as "Goebbels' victim, a defenseless parrot under a patriarchal pantheon."[29]

Lois Weber died in 1939 at the age of just 56, her passing greeted by a flimsy obituary in *Variety*. She was so hard up for money she couldn't even afford to pay for her own funeral, Frances Marion instead picking up the tab.[30] Weber was abandoned by Hollywood when her films started losing money from the mid–1920s onwards. One imagined it would be the censors who would cut her career short rather than lack of commercial appeal but she found it difficult to make her films entertaining enough for the skittish party set of the Jazz Age. In the last years of her life, this gifted lady was reduced to testing young stars for Universal Studios, a heartbreaking downturn for a woman who'd once earned up to $50,000 per picture. Her marriage also broke down as her star faded, which led to other kinds of problems.

Joan Crawford fought her way up the Hollywood ladder, beginning by playing shopgirl roles and advancing to those of more moment. She ended her days a prisoner of her legend.

By now the marriage of Joan Crawford and Franchot Tone had started to crumble as well. Tone spent many nights out drinking and sometimes when she quizzed him about what he did on such nights, he struck her. She thought the only way to regain some stability in their relationship was to have children but after two miscarriages she was informed she could never reproduce. Tone was also unfaithful to her, as she discovered one night when she walked into his dressing room unannounced and found him canoodling a starlet. "I suppose this has been a regular occurrence," she remarked coolly. "Of course," he replied. The next day she received a call from a reporter who wanted to do a story about the different backgrounds of the pair of them. "I've got a better story for you," Crawford told the reporter blithely, "I'm divorcing him."[31] And she did.

Crawford's career was in a slump at this point. She had a brief fillip as a homewrecker in George Cukor's *The Women* but one was entitled to expect a less misogynistic offering from Cukor here, or indeed from Clare Boothe Luce, who wrote the play upon which it was based. Most of the characters resembled one another in their unbridled bitchiness, courtesy of a screenplay co-written by Anita Loos and Jane Murfin. The women in the audience who'd waited so many years for a film that would showcase their gender were left scratching their heads at such a wasted opportunity. Allied to the inveterate sniping was a "Marriage beats career" message tacked on at the end, an extra slap in the face to anyone of an even vaguely feminist stripe.

Cukor wouldn't have been able to make *The Women* if he hadn't been fired from the most expensive film made that year—indeed, that decade—*Gone with the Wind*. This was the one everyone was talking about. The search for an actress to play Scarlett O'Hara, its fiery heroine, had begun as far back as 1937 and was almost as dramatic as the movie itself. A brace of traveling salesmen claiming to be studio scouts inveigled aspiring actresses into their beds in every town west of Manhattan. Very few of these were caught, though in Flagstaff, Arizona, two of them were arrested on charges of statutory rape. Five more were arrested in Alabama but the cases were dropped when the girls in question failed to testify.

David O. Selznick was producing the movie and hundreds of hopefuls arrived at his office every day clutching pieces of paper given to them by these traveling salesmen, announcing them as the person most suited to play Scarlett. (Their tawdry testaments to grandeur were usually printed on hotel notepaper.) Many of these already had their pictures in the newspapers of the small towns they came from. Often they were too humiliated to return after the trickery was exposed. Some stayed on and had a future but most fell by the wayside. One enthusiastic starlet had herself parceled up and delivered to Selznick's home on Christmas morning. When he opened the packing case, he was somewhat startled to see a naked girl jump out of it and trill "Happy Christmas!" to him and his family.[32] Another aspirant presented herself at his house wrapped inside a giant replica of the Margaret Mitchell novel on which it was based.[33]

Norma Shearer didn't know what all the fuss was about. "Scarlett O'Hara is going to be a thankless and difficult role," she contended. "The part I'd like to play is Rhett Butler!"[34] An actress by the name of Susan Hayward also tested for Scarlett but was found wanting. Selznick advised her to consider another career besides acting but her reply to him was prophetic of the tough-skinned actress Hollywood would come to know (if not always love) in years to come: "I like oranges. I think I'll stay."[35] Katharine Hepburn even auditioned for the role, her enthusiasm crushed when Selznick taunted, "I can't imagine Rhett Butler chasing *you* for ten years."[36]

When the film began shooting, Vivien Leigh was bothered by Gable's bad breath, particularly in their kissing scenes. Of more concern to her was the fact that he refused to put on a Southern accent for the role. Gable felt Cukor was "throwing" the picture to Leigh and favoring her too much in the closeups. He also thought Cukor was too effeminate to handle a film of this epic nature. "I can't go on with this picture!" he exploded at one point, "I won't be directed by a fairy. I have to work with a real man!"[37]

Cukor ended up being sacked and replaced by Gable's friend Victor Fleming. Fleming's style of direction was much less nuanced than Cukor's. "Ham it up," he advised Leigh (whom he nicknamed "Fiddle-dee-dee" to make her feel small) one day when she asked him how she should play a scene. Another day he told Walter Plunkett, the costume designer, "For God's sake, let's get a good look at the girl's boobs." Plunkett was then forced to have Leigh's breasts taped and thrust upward to give her a bodice-ripper look. Leigh was furious but could do nothing. On the quiet, though, both she and Olivia de Havilland continued to visit Cukor on weekends for acting tips. He told them he felt more famous for *not* directing *Gone with the Wind* than he did for anything he'd actually completed.[38]

Leigh won an Oscar for her performance but a furious Gable got nothing, which made Cukor feel a lot better. If he'd helmed the film, no doubt Gable would have blamed him for this turn of events, but because it was directed by his friend Fleming he had nothing to complain about. Hattie McDaniel beat Olivia de Havilland to the Best Supporting Actress award but there was an element of tokenism about this. As mentioned, McDaniel played the same part for most of her career. The value of the win was negated by the fact that when the film premiered in Atlanta, neither McDaniel nor Butterfly McQueen (another black member of the cast) was invited. In fact, their photographs were even removed from the programs distributed at the premiere.[39] It would be another ten years before another black actress would be Oscar-nominated: That was Ethel Waters for *Pinky* (1949). Such a fact was reassuring but it couldn't

Vivien Leigh was irritated by Clark Gable's grandstanding in *Gone with the Wind* (1939), pictured above, especially after George Cukor was removed from the director's chair and replaced by Gable's buddy Victor Fleming, who had a sexist attitude towards Leigh and the film.

disguise the fact that the main role had a white actress, Jeanne Crain, playing a black role.[40]

The fact that a "Brit" had snared such a huge role from under the noses of a bevy of American stars gave Leigh a huge degree of confidence, even if the universe Scarlett O'Hara occupied was run by the opposite sex. As Judith Crist remarked, her story taught women that making it in a man's world left one "bereft of child and Clark Gable, with only a hope of a better tomorrow."

Outside the Trenches

The advent of World War II changed the fate of Hollywood actresses significantly. Because women would now comprise the lion's (or lionesses') share of audiences, that meant films would largely be tailored towards their wants. Secondly, the absence of male stars meant there would be more women on screen. There were also more writing opportunities for women during these years. Men made up 85 percent of Hollywood's writers at this time but most of these were now conscripted. That led to more work for the remaining 15 percent, if not other women being employed to do the work of the absentees.

All of this meant serious re-empowerment for women. The status they'd enjoyed before the enforcement of the Code in 1934 returned to them as they joined the workforce vacated by their menfolk. They had disposable income now, and an unexpected release from the home. The films that were made around this time embodied that seismic shift in two ways: first with the phenomenon of the "woman's picture" and second with that of the *film noir* and its dusky centerpiece, the *femme fatale*.

The former genre, or mini-genre, had gritty heroines like the Joan Crawford of *Mildred Pierce*, while the latter one fed more into the lowbrow mode of the gangster's moll. Somewhere in the middle of these two iconic templates we had a third type of military maiden: the Locker-Room Pin-Up.

Men who enlisted may have had sentimental feelings for the women they left behind but in public it was a more blowsy female image they publicized. Photographs of semi-clad sexbombs were pinned onto the noses of their B17s and cheesecake damsels on their barrack room walls. Pneumatic firebrands pouted at them from the inside of tanks and planes while in their lockers Betty Grable stood perched in a yellow swimsuit and pink high heels, hand on hip and wearing a smile that said, "Hello, soldier, fancy a good time?"

Many people were confused about what exactly a "woman's picture" was, but of course women's pictures were as old as pictures themselves; they just weren't *called* that. When the term arrived, it gave such films a self-conscious patina that served them ill. It was as if women were some kind of third sex that had to be over-praised and perhaps pandered to. They were placed on pedestals as doughty individuals suffering all for love or glory. They negotiated bad marriages and performed Herculean tasks of survival in a manner that didn't so much individualize them as subsume them under an umbrella one could loosely describe as Noble Sufferers.

In the other films made at this time, things went on much as before. Esther Ralston's musical escapades ended with *Tin Pan Alley*. She could have had a thriving career at MGM but it ended when she rejected a pass made at her one night in a restaurant by Louis B. Mayer. The following morning he called her into his office and snarled, "You think you're pretty smart, don't you? Well, I'll blackball you. You'll never get another picture in any studio in town." That didn't quite happen but her spurning of Mayer's advances led to her departure from MGM for Universal.

Mae West appeared with W.C. Fields in *My Little Chickadee* (1940), but the combination, while amusing, didn't light as many sparks as it should have. Fields was credited with co-writing the screenplay but West claimed he only wrote "about three minutes of it where he talks to a fly on the bar." She said he insisted on the credit as revenge for her having him thrown off the set one day for drinking too much.[1] Fields preferred drink to movies. And indeed to women. "The great earthquake of 1906 destroyed my marriage certificate," he joked once, "which proves that earthquakes aren't all bad."[2]

A sarong-clad Dorothy Lamour joined Bob Hope and Bing Crosby in *Road to Singapore*, though she'd later say that the sarong felt more like a straitjacket. In subsequent years she was similarly attired for *Road to Zanzibar* (1941), *Road to Morocco* (1942), *Road to Utopia* (1945), *Road to Rio* (1947) and *Road to Bali* (1952). All lucrative work, no doubt, but did it amount to a career? The problem wasn't so much the movies themselves, which were popular, but what they cut her off from. What director would think she could do anything else, sandwiched as she was between two inane jokesters as the lubricious background scenery? Because she made money for Paramount the studio was loath to part with her, or stretch her. Today she's virtually synonymous with the Road series, anything else she did (like gangster films and musicals) raising nary a murmur.

Frances Farmer made *Flowing Gold* (1940) after her return from Broadway but it wasn't a pleasant experience for her. One scene called for her to fall face down in mud and the director, Alfred E. Green, insisted it be shot 14 times. Farmer felt it was Hollywood's "get-even" gesture towards her, its way of putting manners on her for her perceived snooty attitude to the establishment.

Laraine Day appeared with Joel McCrea in Alfred Hitchcock's *Foreign Correspondent* but she too found the experience dispiriting: "Your performance was Hitchcock's performance. You read the lines the way Hitchcock read the lines. You added nothing and you took away nothing. You did exactly as he told you. He had drawn it out on paper. You'd see the scene like a comic strip and that's the way you played it. You'd bring nothing but [your] body to the set."[3]

The rising Irish star Maureen O'Hara made *Jamaica Inn* for Hitchcock, having been taken under the wing of Charles Laughton, but shortly after shooting the film she found herself trapped in a marriage with George Brown, a production assistant she hardly knew before she tied the knot with him. She was about to go to the U.S. with Laughton but Brown insisted on meeting her before she left. When she agreed, the venue turned out to be a house where he'd recruited a man to marry them. She then felt a ring being slipped around her finger and panicked. She said "Yes" merely as a quick means of escaping him, only half-aware of what was happening. She then ran off into a cab, hyperventilating. "The horror of what I'd done was choking me," she recalled.[4] The marriage was later annulled but no sooner was she out of the frying pan with Brown than she found herself being pestered by John Farrow, who directed her in her next movie, *A Bill of Divorcement*.

Farrow, who was married to Maureen O'Sullivan, invited himself to her house, bringing dinners (and even waiters) with him. If she came home and saw his car outside her door, she drove around the block instead of going in. Eventually he got the message that she wasn't interested in him and took to badmouthing her on the set with taunts like, "She must be a lesbian." In his office, he kept a photograph of her and threw darts at it. One day doing a scene with Adolphe Menjou, she had to strike him; Farrow thought she was hitting him too gently. He barked: "Hit him hard." O'Hara snapped, striking Farrow instead with the line, "You mean like this?"[5] After that he stayed away from her.

Arguably more a victim of Hollywood's casual cruelties than any other star of her time, or any time, Frances Farmer (pictured) was pilloried and then cast into the horrific world of psychiatric institutions for the better part of a decade, for no better reason than the fact that she had a volatile temperament and refused to play the star game by Hollywood's rules.

Farrow was up to his tricks the following year again with Anna Lee when he directed her in *Commandos Strike at Dawn*. "Lock your door, Anna," O'Hara advised her. Lee took the advice but Farrow still barged into her room one night. When she told him she wasn't interested in a relationship with him, he roared back at her, "You pious little Puritan. You're probably no good in bed anyway but I'm not going to waste my time tonight finding out. Just remember, if I want something badly I always get my way, no matter how long it takes."[6]

Lee was a fine actress but she never got the exposure she deserved. She was a star in England but in the U.S. all too often she was slotted into character roles. "It was the beginning of the end when I came to Hollywood," she groaned.[7]

O'Hara's next film was *Dance, Girl, Dance,* directed by Dorothy Arzner. Today it's mostly remembered for a scene towards the end where O'Hara, playing a dancer, berates an audience of men gazing lustily at the scantily clad ladies in her troupe. "I know you want me to take my clothes off," she taunts, "so you can look your fifty cents worth. Fifty cents for the privilege of staring at a girl your wives won't let you.... We'd laugh right back at the lot of you only we're paid to let you sit there and roll your eyes and make your screamingly clever remarks. What's it for? So that you can go home when the show's over and strut before your wives and sweethearts and play at being the stronger sex for a minute? I'm sure they see through you like we do." Judith Mayne believed this speech signaled a seminal moment in feminist film history, foregrounding as it did the sexual hierarchy of "The Look" men give to objectify women.[8]

O'Hara had her marriage to George Brown annulled in 1941 but almost immediately plunged into another disastrous marriage with the producer Will Price, a hopeless alcoholic who almost bankrupted her in the ensuing years as well as being both verbally and physically abusive. Her next film was *Ten Gentlemen from West Point*, a military offering co-starring George Montgomery. One day during a romantic scene, Montgomery gave her an open-mouthed kiss that "damn near" choked her to death. "I know today they practically lick each other's faces clean," she said afterwards, "but back then it just wasn't done."[9] She walked off the set in disgust. Montgomery was later cautioned but she knew if she wasn't such a big star, nothing would probably have been done.

O'Hara had two ovarian cysts removed that year. She was recovering in hospital when Darryl F. Zanuck, who wanted her to appear in *Son of Fury* with Tyrone Power, suspected that she was extending her stay in the hospital to get out of making the film. When he accused her of this, she became livid and told him her surgery had been really serious. An unconvinced Zanuck even went as far as bringing in a top doctor from Fox to verify her condition. When he looked at her charts he sneered, "It's probably just a fragment left over from an abortion." If a comment like this was made to an actress today, it would no doubt land a man in court but these were different times. O'Hara was too shocked to say anything.[10]

Zanuck never molested O'Hara sexually but he had a huge libido. He was small in stature and may have become over-intent on proving his virility to counteract that. In the view of his biographer Leonard Moseley, copulation for him was "just another form of pugilism or arm-wrestling, and part of the crusade to prove he was as big as any six-foot hulk on the team and more successful with the girls."[11] The downside was that he viewed them as "tramps," with the exception of his wife Virginia—though not enough to stay faithful to her.[12] He treated the younger actresses on the Fox lot as so many disposable playthings, contemptuously slapping them on their rear ends when he felt like it, and curtly silencing them if they objected.[13]

Zanuck was instrumental in the rise to fame of Carole Landis, whose career took off dramatically with hits like *Moon Over Miami, I Wake Up Screaming, Dance Hall* and *Cadet Girl*. There was a price to be paid for such success, however, as Zanuck used her, like many other actresses on his roster, for sexual favors.

One of the most notorious exponents of the "casting couch" syndrome, Zanuck "entertained" starlets almost on a daily basis. One day when he was urinating on a flower bed, his assistant stood in front of him in case some actress that was passing by might see him. A chortling Zanuck waved his penis at the aide with the words, "If you know a young lady on the lot that hasn't already seen *this*, I want her in my office by five tonight."[14] There was a rumor that Landis was Zanuck's mistress but then tired of her. Afterwards her career trailed off, Zanuck even refusing to take her phone calls when his ardor cooled.[15]

There were a number of significant marriages in 1941. Not only did Maureen O'Hara go to the altar, so also did Gene Tierney, Doris Day and Judy Garland—all four of them in decidedly different circumstances. Tierney eloped with the designer Oleg Cassini, in the process angering studio executives so much by her choice of husband (he was out of favor in Hollywood) that they ostracized the couple from social events for months afterwards.

Doris Day married the trombonist Al Jorden, primarily because she was pregnant by him. The day after the wedding she gave a fellow musician a peck on the cheek to thank him for a wedding gift and Jorden, beset with jealousy, beat her senseless. Shortly afterwards she was passing a newsstand with him when she saw a photograph of herself wearing a swimsuit on the cover of a magazine. When she drew his attention to this, he again grew enraged and slapped her repeatedly across the face in front of shocked fans. In subsequent months he beat her to a frazzle for little or nothing, often collapsing in tears afterwards. (This had the odd effect of making her feel she was the guilty party.) He also accused her of infidelity, calling her a "dirty whore" when it was he who was unfaithful in the marriage.[16]

When she told him she was pregnant, he denied the child was his and again beat her, this time so badly she almost miscarried. He ordered her to

Doris Day may have appeared feisty in films like *Calamity Jane* and *Love Me or Leave Me* (above) but in her private life the Professional Virgin (as she was called) was a victim of much male cruelty and exploitation, both of her career and her finances.

abort the baby and she was so much under his spell she almost acceded to this request. In typically dramatic fashion, Jorden then decided he wanted her to engage in a suicide pact with him. He even bought a gun with this in mind, thrusting it into her stomach one day. She was meant to shoot herself and then he intended to blow his own brains out. She managed to talk him out of the mad plan but he continued to beat her until she summoned up the courage to divorce him for emotional cruelty.

As the divorce proceedings progressed, Day locked him out of the house. She also put a restraining order on him, at which point he started stalking her, often following her into restaurants and sitting at tables near her to spook her. He begged her to take him back but she refused, even after he broke down in his familiar tears. In 1967, carrying through on his original suicide threat, he put a bullet through his head when a subsequent marriage went sour.

Judy Garland married the bandleader David Rose at 1 a.m. on July 28, 1941, in Las Vegas but within 24 hours she was ordered back to the studio for work on her latest movie *Babes on Broadway*; her "honeymoon" had lasted less than a day. When she became pregnant by Rose, he was less than happy at the prospect of becoming a father so soon. Garland's mother Ethel felt a baby would impede her career as she'd already been lined up for her next movie, *For Me and My Gal*. It was decided above Judy's head by Ethel and some studio executives that the best course of action would be to have the baby aborted even though abortion was illegal at that time in California. Garland agreed to the decision grudgingly but became wracked by guilt in the ensuing months. She was back at MGM doing overdubs for *Babes on Broadway* 48 hours after the termination. Paul Donnelley wrote: "There was no way anything as minor as an abortion was going to stop the studio from making Judy work."[17]

Garland had a hit with *Ziegfeld Girl* later that year but wasn't happy about her career. She felt she was in that awkward stage between child actress and budding adult. She described herself as an "in between" girl who was "too old for toys but too young for boys." The star once claimed to have stopped believing in Santa Claus the day she sat on his lap in a department store and he asked her for her autograph. Her view of MGM was scathing: "They wanted you either five years old or eighteen, with nothing in between."[18]

Greta Garbo made her final film, *Two-Faced Woman*, in 1941. It was such a poorly conceived work, one is hardly surprised it was her last hurrah. A limp attempt to Americanize her, the war having led to the decline of her audiences in Europe, it totally backfired in its ambition, robbing her of most of her mystique and all of her dignity. The storyline was also absurd, casting her as a woman who tries to expose her husband's infidelity by posing as her promiscuous twin sister. The Legion of Decency had a problem with this so insisted a scene be added in which her husband (Melvyn Douglas) becomes aware of her subterfuge early on, thereby making her vicarious seduction of him farcical. The film's joke was now on Garbo rather than Douglas, a familiar piece of sexist Hollywood's game-playing. The added scene also killed the film as drama. It bombed at the box office as a result.

Louis B. Mayer now informed Garbo he was going to "rest" her until the war ended—

"rest" being a thespian euphemism for "drop." Garbo got the message, tipped her figurative hat to him and bade her farewell to the studio that made her. She would be a hard act to follow but Mayer decided he'd try to fill her shoes with his latest acquisition, Hedy Lamarr. Katharine Hepburn and Greer Garson had been his substitutes for Myrna Loy and Norma Shearer and now he had a third juggling act to perform. If Lamarr didn't work out, there was always Lana Turner. He moved his stars around like ninepins, working the percentages as he tried to second-guess the public. But for now there was no more Garbo. She slid into the sunset almost imperceptibly, becoming as famous for her early retirement as she was for her incandescent rise to grandeur. If she wanted to be alone, as people surmised from her most misquoted line, now was her chance. Asked by David Niven why she was leaving films, she drawled somberly, "I have made enough faces."[19]

Another interesting star on the rise was Susan Hayward, though she wasn't too popular in Hollywood at this time because of her fiery personality. "I was pushed around in those years," she complained, "so I spoke up. The studio kept referring to me as a promising young actress. What I wanted to know was just how long could a girl be promising? I got the reputation of being, to put it politely, a wavemaker." The reasons for her abrasive personality were complex: "All my life I've been terribly frightened of people.... The only way I knew how to protect myself was to try and scare [them] before they scared me. Other girls were going to the top while I got the parts no one else wanted. I was getting a good salary by then but, being basically an honest person, I felt like a fraud for accepting it."[20] She was a sheep in wolf's clothing, developing a shell of aggressiveness to conceal that fact. "Susan was painfully shy," one of her early colleagues recalled, "a trait which took the form of brutal frankness. She was almost sullen with people she didn't know well. Even with her close friends—and they were few—she was undemonstrative. But when she was affectionate, you knew she meant it."[21]

Susan Hayward burst upon the film scene in *Adam Had Four Sons* (1941), playing a role that laid the foundation for her "spitfire" persona. Her private life was dogged by the physical and financial abuse of men, and the traumas she underwent as a result led to depression and, ultimately, a suicide attempt.

The Best Actress Oscar of 1942 went to Greer Garson. She did one of those "Heroine Suffers All for Her Family" roles beloved by Hollywood in *Mrs. Miniver*, the role she was always most remembered for. Garson's son in the film was played by Richard Ney. He was older than she would have liked, which made her feel that she would also be seen as old by audiences, and typecast in that vein afterwards. She ended up falling in love with Ney and then becoming engaged to him. Louis B. Mayer was aghast at this and told her he didn't want her to marry him until after the film's release. She agreed to this but it was still one in the eye for Mayer and for his ageist attitude towards women.

Mayer showed a different type of prejudice towards Lena Horne, Hollywood's first glamorous African-American star, offering her the role of a maid in *Cairo* as if this was still the post–Hattie McDaniel status for women. Horne's father advised her to refuse the role, telling Mayer, "I can *hire* a maid for her. Why should she act as one?"[22] She went on to star in a number of all-black musicals like *Cabin in the Sky* and *Stormy Weather* (both 1943) but found it difficult to break out of this genre. Some people viewed her success as

a step in the right direction for black actresses while others thought it was mere tokenism, a stage act with the cameras turned on. Horne, like Dorothy Dandridge, was "the acceptable face of black beauty," with tanned skin and Caucasian features. Horne saw this happening and spoke out about it. "I'm *in* Hollywood but not of Hollywood," she declaimed. "I'd like to do [a] good serious role in a mixed-race movie instead of being confined to café singing parts."[23]

This was unlikely to happen. She campaigned for the role of the mulatto Julie in *Show Boat* (1951) but didn't get it. Audiences from the Deep South, it was thought, wouldn't have it. Ava Gardner was chosen instead, darkening her features with a makeup known as Light Egyptian. Horne departed Hollywood and resumed her stage career. In a sense, she'd never left it.

When Gardner first arrived in Hollywood she did a screen test for Mayer. His reaction was fairly typical of moguls' attitudes to starlets of the time: "She can't act, she can't

A feisty Texas lass who partied like a man and refused to behave like a lady even though she was one, Ava Gardner fell foul of male chauvinism in all three of her husbands, Mickey Rooney, Artie Shaw and Frank Sinatra. She also had to deal with a disastrous relationship with George C. Scott, who beat her violently on more than one occasion.

talk, she's terrific!" But Gardner let it be known from the get-go that she wasn't going to be a studio product, eating in the cafeteria with the truck drivers and grips for starters, which was regarded as "abominable" behavior by the studio heads.[24] She also resisted the studio's makeover process, refusing to thin her eyebrows or have a dimple removed by plastic surgery.[25]

She married Mickey Rooney in 1942. She was fascinated by his energy but it wasn't long into the marriage before she came to realize that golf and carousing were closer to his heart than keeping the home fires burning. They parted after little more than a year. According to Gardner, Rooney looked on marriage as "a small dictatorship, with you-know-who as the one in charge." He put her second to boozing, broads and bookmakers—and that was only the Bs. They were scarcely married two months when he started entertaining other women in the marital bed, something she couldn't countenance: "I don't cheat and I don't want anybody cheating on me. Maybe I'm stupid because I know every man in the world is going to do it." She realized the marriage was over the night Rooney got drunk and, upon the instigation of his cronies, pulled a notebook out of his pocket with a list of his female conquests and began reading it out in front of her.[26]

Another actor who liked to boast about his conquests was Errol Flynn. "My main problem," he joked, "is trying to balance my gross habits with my net income." But the smile went from his face in 1942, the year he played the boxer Jim Corbett in *Gentleman Jim*. His offscreen behavior didn't appear to be too "gentlemanly" when he was charged with two counts of statutory rape. There were murmurings that his career could be over but the charges were quashed. In fact, the publicity generated by the case actually increased box office receipts for the movie. A few years later Ingrid Bergman would have a seven-year time-out placed upon her career because of a sex scandal. With men, it seemed, different standards—or lack of standards—applied.

Bergman's situation became worldwide news while other people's predicaments were hushed up. It was an open secret in Hollywood, for instance, that Katharine Hepburn and Spencer Tracy became lovers after they appeared in 1942's *Woman of the Year*—the first of their nine films together—despite the fact that Tracy was married. His Catholic wife wouldn't give him a divorce so he lived with Hepburn without marital decree and the public seemed content to accept this, as did Hepburn.

She wasn't a great advocate of marriage anyway. "Sometimes I wonder if men and women really suit each other," she said once. "Perhaps they should live next door and just visit now and then."[27] And elsewhere, more trenchantly, "If you want to sacrifice the admiration of many men for the criticism of one, get married."[28]

Rita Hayworth experienced the truth of this dictum at first hand, her marriage with Ed Judson falling apart when she realized she meant little to him but a dollar sign. He once threatened to disfigure her if she ever left him but she now found the courage to do that. At their divorce hearing he asked for $30,000 from her for furthering her career—a fact she never denied—and she gladly gave it to him. What pained her more was the emotional neglect of their time together. "I was never permitted to make any decisions," she told the divorce judge. "He robbed everything of excitement."[29]

"I married him for love," she added, "but he married me for an investment."[30]

Other stellar marriages started to crumble at this time too. Judy Garland separated from her husband David Rose in 1943 and began a slow mental collapse. She started seeing a psychiatrist and he put her on even more pills than she was already taking. Having been ordered to take diet pills almost from the moment she started acting, she was now on uppers and downers to try and regulate her moods. But they only made them more erratic.

Gene Tierney also divorced Oleg Cassini. Their problems had increased dramatically from the stress of having a severely handicapped daughter, Daria, whom Tierney had to put into care when she found herself unable to cope with her debilities. Daria's handicaps had been caused by the fact that Tierney had developed German measles when she was pregnant with her, contracting them as a result of being hugged one night in a canteen by an infected fan. Tierney beat herself up in the following years even though it wasn't her fault. She suffered a mental collapse which prematurely ended her career.

Jane Russell got her best-known role in *The Outlaw* in 1943, though mostly for the wrong reasons. Her cleavage became the main selling point of the rather flat Western, a fact attested to by the posters advertising it, which showed her chest bursting out of her blouse. Producer Howard Hughes referred to her as "the two and only Jane Russell." He filmed her at angles that flattered her physique rather than moving the plot forward. This was most noteworthy in a scene where she was dressed in a low-necked nightgown shot bending down over a set of milk pails. She said of the photographers: "They were not looking at the pails."[31]

Russell is raped in the film and afterwards bound in ropes and gagged. This was a kind of coded bondage scenario that increased her sexual charge. The poster for the movie professed that there were "two good reasons" for seeing it, again drumming home the importance of Russell's mammaries. The shot of her bending over the milk pails was hung on many an adolescent's bedroom wall as well as adorning locker rooms and garages across the nation. In many ways it was a precursor of Marilyn Monroe's famous "air vent" shot from *The Seven Year Itch* a decade or so on. Hughes specified that all Russell's dresses be low-necked, "and by that I mean as low as the law allows, so that the customers can get a look at the part of Russell which they pay to see."[32]

She grudgingly accepted the excessive attention that was given to her breasts during the shooting of the movie and such attention continued right up to its premiere. Here she heard a member of the audience call out to his friends during the first scene, in which she leaned forward to exhibit her "assets": "Bombs away!"[33] Some sex symbols outgrow their early movies but there was no way Hughes was going to let her forget this one, even donning his aviator's hat to advertise it. One writer prophesied: "From the moment that a San Francisco skywriting plane drew two circles in the sky with dots in the middle, Russell must have known she would be haunted by the publicity campaign for *The Outlaw* for the rest of her life."[34]

Another actress who struggled against pigeonholing, Olivia de Havilland, finalized her seven-year Warners contract by making *Government Girl* (on loanout to RKO) in 1943. She looked forward to spreading her wings when it was in the can but no sooner was shooting completed than Jack Warner informed her he was adding six further months to her contract to punish her for her repeated suspensions over the years. He offered her a new film called *The Animal Kingdom* but she turned up her nose at it.

Warner's extension, according to advice de Havilland received, violated an old California law against peonage. The reason all Hollywood contracts were for seven years was because anything else, according to this law, constituted slavery. It was an obscure legal point upon which to take on the studio but de Havilland went for it. What had she to lose now?

A lot, as it happened, because Warner blacklisted her. He also warned all the other studios not to employ her or he'd take them to court. The upshot was that she remained idle for two years, her legal bills mounting. Warner refused to pay them and also started to play dirty with her, having his lawyers put out a rumor that the reason she refused *The Animal Kingdom* was because she was having an affair.

Jane Russell became as famous for her breasts as her talent, largely on the basis of her breakthrough role in *The Outlaw* (1943), a routine Western where her generous cleavage was exploited relentlessly by Howard Hughes and his voyeuristic camera crew.

Joan Fontaine knew what a pickle her sister was in. A suspended star, she warned, couldn't even take a job behind a counter in a department store. The system was rigged so that the studio held all the aces, foisting a fusillade of bad scripts on its stars with the "hangman's noose" of suspension forever hanging over their heads. "If the studio didn't have a script ready for you," according to Fontaine, "they would send you one they knew you would turn down. They could send you the dictionary or the telephone book and you would have to turn it down and you would be suspended. That meant they didn't have to pay you until they submitted something else to you. Meanwhile, the children had to go to school and the bills had to be paid."[35]

At Paramount, Veronica Lake was starting to show signs of mental fatigue. Her career had started off on a high with hits like *This Gun for Hire* and *The*

Glass Key but as the decade went on she started to enjoy film making less, and also the all-too-prevalent pairings with Alan Ladd, whom she didn't get on with as well as was generally perceived. The so-called "Peekaboo Girl" started to have doubts about her ability as the mediocre movies built up. "You could put all my talent into your left eyelid," she quipped, "and still not suffer from impaired vision."

Her private life was troubled as well. She married a man called John Detlie who always had trouble with her fame, and the fact that she was earning more than he was. When their only baby died shortly after being born in 1943, it was the last straw in a fraught relationship and they divorced. The following year Lake married the Hungarian-born actor and director André De Toth. She had two children by him but he was physically and emotionally abusive to her and basically lived off her earnings.

All the promises of the war years, it seemed, were evaporating for women as it neared its end. The kind of films being made seemed to reflect that as well. *In Together Again* (1944) Irene Dunne played a widowed mayor who's advised by her former father-in-law to re-marry because he doesn't consider it normal to be "a big shot in your office and a non-entity in your own home." The following year Rosalind Russell played a psychiatrist in *She Wouldn't Say Yes*. At first she refuses to marry because too many of her patients are attending her clinic as a result of marital problems but the film cops out to traditional values at the end when she agrees to marry Lee Bowman.

In real life the treks to the divorce courts continued. Judy Garland ended yet another marriage in 1944. The trauma drove her to a psychiatrist to look for some peace but Louis B. Mayer stepped in and cancelled her appointments, feeling they distracted her from concentrating on her forthcoming movie *Meet Me in St. Louis*. It was like hitting someone over the head to "cure" a headache. Herman J. Mankiewicz gave this estimation of Mayer: "He has the memory of an elephant and the hide of an elephant. The only difference is that elephants are vegetarians and Mayer's diet is his fellow man."[36]

Mary Astor played Garland's mother in the movie. She was typecast in such

Peekaboo Girl Veronica Lake enraptured audiences with her radiant insouciance but when her star faded she was dispensed with and forced to forage for a buck. The men in her life also let her down. She took to drink to drown her sorrows and died in obscurity like so many divas of yore.

roles by now. "Metro's mothers," she griped, "never did anything but mothering. They never had a thought in their heads except their children. They sacrificed everything; they were [either] domineering or else the 'Eat up all your spinach' type. Clucking like hens. Eventually every actor on the Metro lot called me Mom. I was in my late thirties and it played hell with my image of myself."[37]

Towards the end of the year, Olivia de Havilland got pneumonia when she was on a trip to the Fiji Islands to entertain the troops. She started to cough blood. Her weight shrank to ninety pounds and her temperature reached 104 degrees. As she slowly started to recover, the news came through that she'd won her case against Jack Warner. The California Supreme Court ruled in her favor, stipulating that suspension time against stars couldn't be added on to contracts after they expired. It was a landmark decision that changed the goalposts for every actress. One hoped that this would mean better parts for women across the board, especially those written for them by other women. Bette Davis took credit for paving the way for de Havilland after the stand she took against Warners some years before.[38]

The writer-producer Joan Harrison outlined the basic differences between male and female producers, the most significant one being that men didn't have to worry about their appearance: "They can spend Saturday afternoon playing golf instead of wasting endless hours at the hairdresser's. They can report to the office looking like the shadow of a roaring evening without giving it a second's thought, or others tossing them a second glance. The absence of a long-needed shave gives them a certain carefree dash, hollows under the eyes suggest they've been working hard, and rumpled clothes stamp them as intellectual, rugged individualists." Men, on the other hand, lost out because they "don't know the delights of buying three hats at one time" and neither could they try a new hairdo if they got tired of the old one. More importantly, "They're not allowed the woman's privilege of changing her mind."[39] Some of Harrison's attitudes may appear quaint today but they were reflective of the thinking of the time. She showed a harder edge when she remarked, "I don't think women can be directors. To be a director you have to be an s.o.b."[40]

Much of her work was done for Alfred Hitchcock. She found him very frustrating. "You see before you a thwarted writer," she told a journalist in 1944. "Everything I wrote was either shelved or turned out so badly I asked to have my name taken off it."[41] Her post–Hitchcock career was as much producer as writer, which gave her more control over the process. (Virginia Van Upp also became a producer for the same reason.)

One of Hitchcock's favorite films that year was *Double Indemnity*, a film he would have been proud to have made himself. Barbara Stanwyck had the best role of her career as the scheming murderess. She was brave to take it on, many other actresses having turned it down for fear they'd damage their reputation. "My only problem," she sighed, "was finding a way to play my fortieth fallen woman in a different way from my 39th."[42] She needn't have worried, however: Phyllis Dietrichson became the woman audiences loved to hate.

Susan Hayward had auditioned for the role but failed to get it. The rejection, she confessed, was her greatest disappointment since being passed over for Scarlett O'Hara five years earlier. Hayward was also promised the lead role in *Dark Waters* that year but studio chief Buddy DeSylva changed his mind at the last minute and Merle Oberon got the part. "You've been rude, snippy and uncooperative with stars and directors," he accused, "Maybe this will teach you." Hayward disputed this. "I never held up production in my life. I've fought for what I thought was right. I don't call that temperament. I call that being honest and fair."[43] Hayward reacted to the slight by leaving Paramount altogether. DeSylva realized he'd gone too far and begged her to come back. He even offered her a new contract on a raised salary but she told him what he could do with it.[44]

Hayward married the small-time actor Jess Barker in July 1944 after becoming pregnant by him. Her mother thought he was a gold-digger and persuaded her to have him sign a pre-nuptial agreement so he wouldn't get her money in the event of a divorce. He signed it grudgingly but it got the marriage off to a poor start. It would be characterized by many arguments in the years to come, both verbal and physical, before they finally called it quits a decade later.

Shortly after Hayward married Barker, her career skyrocketed and his nosedived. "Call it coincidence or bad timing," wrote Hayward's biographer Beverly Linet. Whatever it was, Barker couldn't handle it, becoming sulky and resentful as a result of his inactivity. A wardrobe assistant to Hayward asked her, "Don't you get a little upset when you come home and find Jess has been sitting around all day?" She rose to his defense, telling her he worked very hard, but the bottom line was that he was an unemployed actor and the marriage was already looking creaky.[45]

This seemed to be the pattern with most of Hollywood's love goddesses, their off-screen romances as tempestuous as their screen ones. It was also the case with Rita Hayworth. After escaping the clutches of Ed Judson, she fell into the arms of Orson Welles, imagining him to be the man who'd rescue her from her twin dominations by Judson at home and Harry Cohn at work. He did, but as time went on she realized that a life with him was merely a substitution of one form of domination for another. Welles decided to marry Hayworth even before he met her, having been entranced by a photograph of her in *Life* magazine.[46]

He told her he loved her and she believed him. Maybe he did, but to be loved by a man of this stature was to be consumed by him. And *with* him. Dorothy Parker said of a rendezvous with him, "It's like meeting God without dying." Marlene Dietrich added: "You should cross yourself when you say his name."[47] These women weren't intimidated by him, merely awed. His self-belief was such, he almost *expected* such awe. He and Hayworth were both victims, he believed. She was used by men and he by the film business. But now they were going to launch an assault on the world on both fronts.

He wanted to take her away from cheesecake, to put her into films of more substance. He was, after all, the world's greatest filmmaker, wasn't he? Hayworth believed he was, becoming infatuated both with his presence and his promises. At last she'd found a man who could sweep her up in his arms and carry her off to Valhalla, or Xanadu.

Welles made *Jane Eyre* during his marriage to Hayworth, exhibiting the same arrogance with the cast here as he did with his wife. On the first day of shooting, Joan Fontaine (who played Jane) recalled, "He strode in, followed by his agent, his valet and a whole entourage. Approaching us, he proclaimed, 'All right, everybody, turn to page 8.' And we did, even though he wasn't the director."[48]

Welles had a blinkered attitude to women. "We made civilization," he said once, "to impress our girlfriends." And elsewhere, "It's improbable that [women] will ever be as numerous as men in the arts [but] if there had never been women there would never have *been* art."[49] Hayworth was too blinded by her love to see this arrogance before she committed herself to him, Welles having hypnotized her with his charisma.

He liked performing magic tricks and celebrated their engagement by sawing her in half during one of his acts. Hayworth went along with it but some people viewed the action as symbolic of how he might treat her in the marriage itself. They were like forerunners of Marilyn Monroe and Arthur Miller, the Body and the Brain. "I'm not Mrs. Orson Welles," Hayworth sighed, "I'm Rita Hayworth."[50] But how could she assert herself under his genius?

He treated her well in the early days of their marriage but there was no way this man could ever commit himself to any one woman, even if that woman was the fantasy wife of most red-blooded filmgoers at this time. Before long his attention drifted from her to other film projects. And to other women.

Judy Garland was a surprising conquest of his. One night he returned home from a rendezvous with her and Hayworth spotted a bouquet of flowers in the back of his car. She thought they were for her, understandably enough. Welles' secretary Shifra Haram managed to get to them before Hayworth and remove a note to Garland that he'd pinned onto them.[51]

Welles conducted other affairs behind Hayworth's back as well but as Glenn Ford's son Peter observed, "Orson was mostly in love with Orson," perhaps an even greater problem for her.[52] There were also rumors that he was consorting with prostitutes. Hayworth came to inhabit the role of so many famous actresses: adored by her fans and neglected by her spouse.

Something similar happened to Bette Davis. She married for the third time in 1945 but this betrothal was hardly any better than the other two: Her husband William Sherry actually threw her out of a car on their honeymoon. Asked why she took this kind of treatment from the men in her life, she revealed that the image of toughness she projected on screen didn't always extend to her private life: "I'm an Aries, and we under the Aries sign are always patsies about our own problems. We take a lot. Of course I shouldn't have taken it. And that's why I had to go." (She divorced him in 1950.)

There were two other marriages of some significance that year: Betty Hutton and Ava Gardner. Hutton married the Chicago businessman Theodore Briskin. He wanted her to give up her career but she refused. They had two children together but divorced in 1951. Gardner married Artie Shaw, who'd been married before and would go up the aisle many times again after this. Asked why she married him, she replied, "Everyone married Artie Shaw!"[53]

Howard Hughes pursued Gardner both before and after her marriage to Shaw, imploring her to hook up with him no matter how many times she said no. One night after she had dinner with Mickey Rooney—they still met occasionally after their divorce—she found Hughes in her bedroom and he proceeded to hit her for reasons she could never decipher. He beat her black and blue and in retaliation she hurled a bronze bell at him, hitting him on the temple with it. Hughes ended up in an ambulance as a result.

Gardner's marriage to Shaw went the way of all his other ones. The honeymoon was hardly over before he started complaining about her lack of intelligence. He humiliated her in company and took on a paternalistic role with her, making it his business to "improve" her mind. At one stage he forced her to put down *Forever Amber*, a novel she was enjoying, and take up Thomas Mann's *The Magic Mountain* instead. Gardner hated *The Magic Mountain*. "I thought I'd never finish that damn book," she groaned, doing his bidding for the sake of peace.[54] "I wasn't Artie's wife in any real sense of the world," she reflected, "only one of his possessions. I was charming as a girlfriend but as a wife I was a hindrance." If she was quiet when they were entertaining friends, he would say, "Don't you have anything to add to the conversation?" but if she tried to make a point he'd say, "Shut up." He thought it would do her good to learn to play chess so he taught her. Then one day she beat him and he never played with her again, peeved beyond words at the indignity of being bested by a "mere" woman.[55]

Shaw married Lana Turner after Gardner. Turner almost had as many husbands as Shaw had wives. "I started off wanting one husband and seven children," she joked, "but it ended up the other way round." Louis B. Mayer had started to show a professional interest in Turner and was grooming her to take over from Hedy Lamarr at MGM as their star attraction. Lamarr ended her tenure at the studio with the limp romance *Her Highness and the Bellboy* (1945). Afterwards she formed her own production company and went on to make more fulfilling films, thereby going some way towards sidetracking Hollywood's "revolving door" system of hiring and firing stars.

Her situation was an example of how so many actresses had to fight to get what they wanted. They usually had a choice between kowtowing to the system, accepting the bad movies and becoming reasonably secure, or rebelling like Davis and de Havilland and risking a premature end to their careers. It was a tough choice to make and it usually boiled down to how confident or ambitious they were. Most actresses felt constrained to take what was dished out to them. In the war years, with some notable exceptions, this was either jingoistic tosh, screwball service comedies or the kind of escapist harem movies made by stars like Maureen O'Hara, Maria Montez and Yvonne de Carlo. There were some interesting storylines for women during these years but most of them either sugarcoated the horrors of war or dressed them up in love stories like O'Hara's *The Immortal Sergeant* where she played a typically loyal lover waiting for her man to come home from the trenches and make her life meaningful again.

Frances Farmer's career had declined by now and so had her mental health. She was reeling from a botched love affair with Clifford Odets and an equally disastrous marriage to Leif Erickson. The success of *Come and Get It* wasn't reprised by her later movies and Paramount had started to lose interest in her, as studios always did when the grosses dipped.

Farmer was now being seen as a "difficult" performer so the studio heads kept a watchful eye on her. Her mind seemed to be elsewhere during the shooting of *Son of Fury* with Tyrone Power, the film that would be her last for sixteen years as she sank into a haze of alienation and psychological turmoil.

On October 19, 1942, on the way to a party at Deanna Durbin's house, she decided to have a few drinks to give herself courage to meet the other revelers. After leaving a Santa Monica bar she pulled her car over to the side of the road and burst into tears, the turmoil of the past few years finally catching up with her. She forgot to turn off her head-lights and because it was a dim-out zone a policeman confronted her and upbraided her for her misdemeanor. Never one to take correction lying down, she told him he bored her, which instigated a train of events that would have lasting repercussions for her. He booked her on a charge of drunk driving and she was taken into custody and booked. In a court-room the following day, she was sentenced to 180 days in jail.

While this was a suspended sentence it was still grossly unjust for a first offender. One had to conclude that other factors were at work. Farmer had what is now referred to as an "attitude problem" with authority figures and this applied as much to figures of law and order as it did to the moguls in the film colony. People were waiting in the wings to "get" her and by losing her temper with the police officer she gave them the opportunity.

The immediate impact of the sentence was to see her excluded from Hollywood's A-list for social engagements. Studios also had problems getting insurance for her now. In 1943 she had a chance of a career revival with a film called *No Escape* but the title proved ironic when she lost her temper with a hairdresser shortly into shooting. Farmer struck her and as a result was kicked off the picture. Shortly afterwards she was arrested for failing to report to her probation officer regarding her 180-day sentence, a gaggle of police-men breaking into her hotel room. She fought with them and was afterwards taken into custody. Photographs of the scuffle were seen all around the world. At her court hearing she threw an inkpot at the judge and fought with policemen again, resulting in her being placed in a straitjacket, the first of many during the next five years.

Afterwards she was sent to a sanitarium and here she was subjected to repeated electric shock treatments. Her predicament was sensationalized by the media and her mother also fed the gossip mills, informing reporters that she was mentally ill. (Her "evidence" for this allegation seemed to be the number of left wing causes Frances had embraced in the past.) Everything seemed to be pointing to a kind of conspiracy to destroy the "insolent upstart."

The conditions in the institution were horrendous: In her autobiography, Farmer wrote about having to eat her own feces on one occasion. At other times the inmates had to make themselves sexually available to visiting soldiers. Orderlies raped them on a regular basis. Rats also patrolled the wards.

After she was released from the sanitarium she went back to her native Seattle to live with her mother, who'd been appointed as her legal guardian. This was the worst thing she could have done: The mother was more unbalanced than Frances. The pair of them argued constantly, her mother behaving almost like another jailer to her, making her feel as if she was under house arrest. The threat of sending her back to captivity was also held over her head, exacerbating the tensions that were already there.

On the morning of March 21, 1944, Frances came down to breakfast and heard her mother saying excitedly, "Hurry and finish your juice, the boys are here." A moment later three employees from the mental institution where she'd previously been detained wrestled her to the ground, put a straitjacket on her and dragged her back to the psychiatric ward of Seattle's Harborview Hospital. Her mother felt her mind was still corroded by communist infiltration and that this was the only place she could be cured.

In his biography of Farmer, William Arnold speculated that there may have been a conspiracy between Seattle politicians and some psychiatrists to put Farmer out of commission because of her frequently-aired left wing views. If this is so, she was the earliest casualty of the "red-baiting" that would inform much of the latter half of this decade when Senator Joseph McCarthy issued a virtual *fatwa* on any form of freethinking at the HUAC investigations. Maybe Farmer would have been better off to be hauled in front of some tribunal like this. At least then she would have "merely" been regarded as a subversive rather than a full-scale schizophrenic.

Whatever misdemeanors she was responsible for in her youth, she paid for by the hundredfold in the succeeding years, the terrors and indignities she experienced in captivity from 1945 to 1950 far in excess of what she deserved. Psychological problems weren't as understood then as they are now so she was basically left to rot in hospital. There was no rehabilitation, no counselling, and not much Christian care either. Patients were left to sink or swim, at the mercy of whatever demons assailed them as they lived in what can only be described as medieval conditions. There were also frequent beatings, and threats of permanent confinement. Maybe the miracle is that she came through it at all.

She captured the horror of these years in detail in her autobiography, a book so graphically written it seems to belie the logic of her being in such a place at all. If one of the symptoms of mental illness is being unable to look outside oneself, Farmer was far from this, her ability to capture a scene and document it faithfully being indicative of a highly vigilant sensibility.

Being famous enabled her to highlight the conditions that had been extant in such institutions for years. "My story is not unique," she believed.[56] The fact that her tenure of confinement exceeded a year meant she was considered incurable, which meant she wasn't given any treatment after a certain point. As a recidivist, her mental state wasn't re-evaluated upon her return. Instead she was just led to a barracks and caged like an animal.[57]

Farmer's career was over by now, her decline dressed in the emperor's clothes of self-destruction to gloss over the fact that the business she graced, and which disgraced her, spent most of its time fearing her and then, when she lost her composure, felt the way was open to have done with her.

Her story is that of a woman who refused to be a cog in the Hollywood machine, which meant the machine saw fit to brutalize her. She tried to buck a system that proved unbuckable and in the process destroyed herself. She never claimed to be perfect but she was sorely let down by her family, her industry and her country. Could anyone have foreseen the fact that a beautiful young woman like this could have her life stolen from her because of a series of uncanny events consequent upon her failing to dim her lights one night on the way to a party on the Pacific Coast Highway?

If it was a film, people probably wouldn't have believed it.

Postwar Transitions

The war years didn't live up to their early promise for Hollywood women, but they were given a fair degree of exposure, though much of it was of the wrong kind (as Jane Russell discovered). After the war ended, however, they moved back into the subservient positions they'd occupied before it. In the view of one commentator, the reason was three-fold: "Relief that the war was over, happiness that their men were back, [and] desire for stability. The postwar period was not a time for sexual revolution."[1]

Bette Davis put it in a nutshell: "During the war, women had done men's jobs. After [it], Hollywood must have thought the best way to get [them] back in their traditional place was by going back a few decades on the screen. Careers were out, home was in."[2] The postwar baby boom caused a dramatic decline in women attending movies and also led to a noticeable change in the kinds of movies studios put out. The babysitting era hadn't yet arrived so there didn't seem to be much to be gained in gearing films towards women.

Harry Cohn certainly didn't think so. After the last bullets were fired, he engaged in one of the most objectionable actions of his life by putting Rita Hayworth's picture on the first atom bomb that was tested by the U.S. She wasn't consulted about the tasteless stunt and didn't appreciate it. "I was under contract and they threatened to put me on sus-pension if I put up a fuss. Harry was the Gestapo at Columbia."[3]

Hayworth made *Gilda* in 1946 and soon became synonymous with her character in the public imagination. "Men went to bed with Gilda and woke up with me," she famously intoned. She uttered these words almost as an apology but Hayworth was much more endearing than Gilda even if men were too blind to see that. "I never really thought of myself as a sex goddess," she said with typical self-effacement, "I felt I was more a comedian who could dance."[4]

By now her marriage to Orson Welles was on the rocks but she still appeared in a film with him called *The Lady from Shanghai*. Not only that, she even agreed to have her beautiful waterfall of hair cropped and bleached blond for the role, an action some saw as making her resemble "a photographic negative of herself." She was transformed into a white goddess: "unfeeling, implacable, spectral [rather than] carnal."[5] She became like a female Samson shorn of her locks. And, by extension, her power. No longer would the former Salomé perform her dance of death.

"Orson sometimes gave me cause to think he married me so he could direct me," she said after they divorced, "If the film we did had been more successful with the public, our marriage might have lasted longer."[6] (She could have added, "He went to bed with *The Lady from Shanghai* but woke up with me.")

In the view of one writer, it was shot by Welles with "a fascinated loathing" for Hayworth.[7] As well as destroying her hair, he had her looking older and more severe. It was as if he was seeking revenge on her for being so enticing in *Gilda*, the film she had the audacity to make when they were apart from one another. It had made her name, he knew, but did that mean it was it any good? At the end of the day, was it not just another *noir* staple with hammy acting? He told her *The Lady from Shanghai* would be more cerebral, more ambitious. And she believed him. As she always believed him, as she always believed all men no matter what they told her, even when they were selling her down the river. *The Lady from Shanghai* flopped miserably at the box-office—the unfortunate fate of so many of Welles' films.

Neither did it benefit from Harry Cohn's skepticism about Hayworth's image overhaul. "Orson was trying something new with me," said Hayworth, "but Harry Cohn wanted The Image—the image he was going to make me [keep] till I was ninety."[8] Maybe he was right in this instance, however. "The six people who saw what Orson Welles did to Rita in *The Lady from Shanghai* wanted to kill him," he snarled, "but they had to get behind me in line."[9]

The film's most famous scene involved a hall of mirrors. It was difficult to pick out the "real" Hayworth and audiences didn't like this sort of confusion. They wanted the Hayworth they knew and loved: accessible, predictable—and with red hair.

So they stayed away in droves. For Welles it was "as you were" time. Once again he was broke. He'd borrowed money repeatedly from Hayworth when they were married but that wasn't an option for him since their parting. Maybe this affected him more than the parting itself.

"Mr. Welles [*sic*] showed no interest in establishing a home," Hayworth testified at their divorce hearing. "Mr. Welles told me he should never have married in the first place as it interfered with his freedom in his way of life."[10] Welles gave a more ominous reason why the marriage hadn't succeeded: "Women are stupid. I've known some who are less stupid than others, but they're all stupid."[11] Whatever accusation could be leveled at his ex-wife, this shouldn't have been one of them. If his definition of intelligence was somebody who could wade through a dense tome about the history of an ancient civilization with eagerness, then he was the one displaying tunnel vision. (Artie Shaw had also suffered from this.) Hayworth provided a third reason why the marriage failed: "I can't take his genius any more."[12] In a more jocular mood, she gave their liaison this coda: "All's Welles that ends Welles."

After The Lady from Shanghai bombed, Hayworth was tarnished goods as far as Cohn was concerned. She'd just turned thirty, a dangerous age for a love goddess. He began to think about who might take her place when the time came. One likely candidate seemed to be Lauren Bacall. Bacall became an overnight sensation when she appeared opposite Humphrey Bogart in *To Have and Have Not* in 1944. The pair of them fell in love and co-starred again in Howard Hawks' *The Big Sleep.*

Hawks surprised many people when he employed Leigh Brackett, a female screen-writer, for this film as he was generally regarded as a "macho" man of the old school when it came to things like this. In actual fact, Hawks originally thought Brackett was male because of her Christian name but he kept her on after he realized his mistake, a gesture she appreciated.[13] He found it difficult to believe a woman could write as she did, especially when she looked like someone who played tennis rather than one who drove a truck. "I grew up as a tomboy," she explained. She read Edgar Rice Burroughs and "every book on Indians I could get my hands on."[14] When she started writing, her aunt exhorted her to tailor her style for *The Ladies Home Journal*, advice Brackett ignored. "A lady never did anything for herself," she contended, "somebody always did it for her."[15]

William Faulkner was co-writing the script with her and he too was surprised at her "ballsy" style. Bogart found some of the dialogue too genteel and complained to Brackett, only to discover that it was Faulkner who'd penned the genteel lines, the "tough guy" ones coming from Brackett. Suitably chastened, he took to calling her "Butch" afterwards.[16]

There were also "tough *gal*" ones. Ironically, Hawks liked these more than Brackett did, things eventually getting to the stage where she felt her female characters were getting too pushy. She asked Hawks if she could tone them down but he refused. More than once, she joked, she asked him if it would be possible for her to let "the poor boob of a hero" make just one decision by himself, but she was always overruled.[17] Matters had come to such a pass that a reconstructed New Man was conferring reluctant benison on an unlikely Old Woman.

Hawks was unusual in that he liked strong women. Most other directors were like Elia Kazan. Katharine Hepburn and Spencer Tracy starred in Kazan's turgid farm drama *The Sea of Grass* in 1947. Marguerite Roberts, the film's screenwriter, wanted to strengthen Hepburn's character by having her threaten to leave Tracy because he was so obsessed with his work. When she put this to Kazan, he wouldn't allow it. "Kazan's politics were very liberal at the time," Roberts maintained, "but he was a chauvinist." She was left in little doubt that at MGM there were only two types of women: angels and whores. She tried to get around the problem by writing about men instead. "You could do anything with a man," she enthused.[18] Roberts, sadly, was hauled before the House UnAmerican Activities Committee during the McCarthy witch-hunt and blacklisted in 1951 when she refused to name names. Her Metro contract was terminated as a result and her name even wiped from the credits of *Ivanhoe*, the film she was working on at the time.

Elsewhere women were punished heavily for minor infractions, or even a mild show of temper. Jayne Meadows walked off the set of *Song of the Thin Man* (1947) in a huff one day and was promptly informed she'd better return pronto if she wanted to have a career. She heard the alarm bells ringing and "walked back, and fast" to resume normal service.[19] A few years later Viveca Lindfors refused to appear in *Backfire* (1950) because she objected to its violence but changed her mind when placed on suspension. "I sold out," she admitted.[20] Those who stuck to their guns, she knew, might never be heard of again.

It was one thing for major stars like Bette Davis and Olivia de Havilland to threaten the established order but Meadows and Lindfors were eminently expendable.

So was Celeste Holm, at least in the eyes of Darryl F. Zanuck. Holm won a Best Supporting Actress Oscar for *Gentleman's Agreement* and used the accolade to campaign for a raise in salary. When Zanuck refused, she threatened to leave Fox. Zanuck reacted by calling the head of every other studio to tell them he fired her because she was too difficult to work with. Fortunately Joseph Mankiewicz didn't believe him and put her in *All About Eve* for three times the salary she'd been getting. Zanuck was furious and arranged for her dressing room to be put in an alley outside the sound stage to get his revenge.[21]

Elsewhere, more subtle humiliations took place on a daily basis. Audrey Totter starred as a psychiatrist in *High Wall* but she wasn't given makeup to wear in the film because the studio felt that career women of this nature should look plain. Clearly, women's liberation was a long way away. What happened to the kind of roles Katharine Hepburn had been playing a decade before? It was as if Hollywood was still suffering from the "Adam's rib" syndrome. How dare a woman be both pretty *and* professional!

Ann Sheridan played a dusky nightclub singer in *Nora Prentiss*, her 1947 signature movie, but her career failed to take off as it might have if she played it more compliant with the powers-that-be. She found Hollywood a cold place inhabited mostly by untrustworthy people, which meant she kept herself at arm's length from many of its blandishments. Warner Bros. tried to soup up her image by inserting a clause in her contract stipulating that she spend at least three nights a week in nightclubs but this kind of manufactured partying only had the effect of alienating her further from the cocktail set. Her career rumbled on for another decade but never reached the heights it might have if she was a "type." She rejected the sex symbol status pined for by the more shallow and blatantly ambitious.

Some stars only managed to break out of a mold due to the tender mercies of those who had their best interests at heart. Anne Baxter wanted to play the racy Sophie in *The Razor's Edge* but Darryl F. Zanuck thought she was unsuitable for it because, as he put it, she was "a cold potato." Baxter's friend Gregory Ratoff said to Zanuck, "Darryl, I've had it [*sic*] and it's marvelous," meaning he'd been to bed with her. It was a lie but it worked. Baxter got the part and as a result her career took an upswing. The story confirmed Baxter's belief in the narrow-mindedness of producers who divided stars into either "librarians" or "broads." Before *The Razor's Edge*, Baxter had been a "librarian." After it, as far as Zanuck was concerned, she was a "broad."[22] What being a "broad" meant was explained by Baxter: "They had a can of stuff they called 'Sex.' It was Vaseline and you rubbed it on your shoulders to make them gleam. You felt ridiculous but what were you going to do? It was, 'Wet your lips, honey, and suck in your tummy and look sultry.'"[23]

The Best Years of Our Lives continued the sexist strain. This was a highly regarded film but it had an anti-women subtext. The soldiers were home from the war now, it seemed to say, so it was time to put women back where they belonged. In William Wyler's intense chronicle we're presented with three men trying to come to terms with life on Civvy Street in markedly different ways. Harold Russell has to face his fiancée after having had his arms blown off. Dana Andrews is confronted by an unfaithful wife. Fredric March finds it difficult to adjust to civilian life. March's daughter (Teresa Wright) says to him at one point, "Don't worry about us." He doesn't, actually, and the film doesn't seem to either, Wyler dealing with all three situations primarily from the men's point of view.

Virginia Mayo played one of her few strong dramatic roles in the film and received good notices, but it didn't lead to better things and afterwards she was dispatched back to light comedies. She was still "the pretty girl in Danny Kaye movies" as far as audiences were concerned. It was a question of putting up with that or walking the gangplank: "We were made to toe the line. Jack Warner kept a record of the first take in the morning and at what hour it was in the can. And he kept a record of each individual. If you made a mistake and it had to be done over, that went on your record. If you goofed, that was a black mark." If you accumulated too many black marks, your option wouldn't be picked up after your contract ran out.[24]

Maureen O'Hara was another star who took the "stinkeroos" that were given to her over a career that spanned many decades, arguably for that reason. She made noises about being under-used now and again but didn't really do anything about it, receiving high salaries for her various escapades as "The Queen of Technicolor," the pirate queen or the queen of the desert, Maureen Sahara. In 1947 she had a fairly typical role in Bruce Humberstone's *The Homestretch* opposite Cornel Wilde. She plays a refined Boston girl, Leslie Hale, who's engaged to a dull diplomat called Bill. When she meets the big-spender racehorse owner Jock (Wilde), he sweeps her off her feet. Another woman from his past, Kitty, is also on the scene but Leslie isn't unduly worried about her, nor about Jock's drinking. She marries him, confident that love will conquer all.

The problems start when Jock continues to be extravagant after marriage and to party like a bachelor. When she's about to have his child, she catches him in a compromising position with Kitty and blows a fuse, crashing her car and losing the baby as a result. When he visits her in hospital, she tells him she's going to divorce him and go back to Bill. Will she? Everyone in the audience knows this won't happen. They know he'll get his act together and that Bill will be exiled to the place where all dull-but-nice suitors go when their Boston belles get tired of them.

And so it comes to pass. As time goes by, Leslie becomes a successful horse trainer. In the climactic scene we find her racing one of her steeds against one of Jock's. She can afford to lose but Jock can't, being up to his ears in debt.

As things work out, Kitty's horse wins and Jock thinks he's finished. But Maureen O'Hara would never leave a man like this in the lurch, would she? If Jock's horse won the race, he might have left her for Kitty, but women weren't like that in Hollywood in 1947. We know that O'Hara will bail him out because that's what women are good at in films, especially the kind of women played by Maureen O'Hara. They realize that men can occasionally have their heads on the wrong way, as when they court old flames when their wives become pregnant, but wives being wives should forget about this and even cheer on their errant husbands' horses when they're in competition with their own. Because men are good eggs basically, and if you play your cards right they'll come back to you.

Preferably with a winning horse. But if not, hey, you'll get by—especially with the love.

Scandals and Torments

After Rita Hayworth divorced Orson Welles, she had an affair with Howard Hughes and became pregnant by him. Hughes hated children and forced her to have an abortion. Hayworth wanted to have the child but Harry Cohn told her it would destroy her career. She gave in even though she felt such a career was already in dire straits since the *Lady from Shanghai* fiasco.

She then went on a jaunt to Europe and pursued similar romantic intrigues. She fell in love with Aly Khan, a millionaire playboy. Their whirlwind romance ended with Hayworth's third marriage but it didn't turn out any better than the previous two, Khan being pathologically unfaithful.

Hayworth made one last film before her trip to Europe, Charles Vidor's instantly forgettable *The Loves of Carmen*, with her old friend Glenn Ford. Afterwards she exchanged one form of misery for another as she went from the jadedness of movie culture to "an endless round of travel and empty socializing in the cafe society haunts of the Old World." By now, as Ford's son Peter put it, she had become "a spectator of her own life."[1]

Hayworth felt more like a trophy to Aly Khan than anything else. She resembled the gypsy dancer of *The Barefoot Contessa* (a role offered to her by Joseph Mankiewicz before Ava Gardner landed it): a noblewoman who ran a continual risk of losing herself. It didn't take a genius to divine the fact that Khan's high sex drive—he was alleged to have gone to bed with other women even during the week of their wedding—was going to guillotine any chance Hayworth had of domesticating him, and this is roughly what happened. It wasn't long before she realized she ran a poor second to his latest race horse or his latest casino.

The marriage to Khan saw the beginning of Hayworth being pestered by the press. This resulted in a camera-shy person becoming even more camera-shy. Hayworth took to entering and leaving hotels through back doors and basements, and she also learned to be more tightlipped with interviewers for fear of being misquoted. The price of being a love goddess, they say, is to be public property at all times. If so, it was a price she paid with interest. The ensuing stress led to her growing fondness for alcohol, and the beginnings of her unpredictable mood swings.

As the forties neared their end, so did many of the careers that had made the decade light up so brilliantly in its early years. Not only was Hayworth suffering, so were former icons Veronica Lake and Judy Garland. The problems undergone by both of these stars have been mentioned already but by now they seemed insurmountable. Lake made *Saigon*, the last of her four films with Alan Ladd, in 1948. By now the chemistry between the pair of them had totally burned out and the film reflected that. Also that year, Lake's mother took her to court to force her to increase the money she was sending her each week, from $200 to $500. It was an extortionate demand, and one based on a verbal agreement made years before, but the court ruled against her in a judgment that decimated her bank account even further than had been done by the spending of her former husband André De Toth.

Garland appeared in *The Pirate* but by now the mounting pressures exerted on her mind and body by the punishing regimen of the past decade made her, in the words of one writer, look "visibly strung out, barely in control of her voice and movements, and almost anorexic in her appearance."[2] Her degeneration mainly resulted from the diet pills to which she was still addicted. She was on other pills for everything from depression to insomnia and these caused erratic mood swings and paranoid delusions. At one point she formed the impression that her husband Vincente Minnelli, who was directing the film, had a sexual interest in her co-star Gene Kelly. The film flopped but MGM rushed her into two more, *Easter Parade* and *Summer Stock*. Once again the studio exhibited a profound disregard for her maladies; once again they tried to put out the fire of her depression by adding oil to it. Instead of sending her away to recover from the strain of overwork, they simply cancelled her contract. Garland reacted to this by attempting suicide. The following year, she and Minnelli divorced.

Every time one door closed, another one opened. In the absence of Garland, MGM turned its eyes to its new talent. One of the stars they were "developing" was Esther Williams, a swimmer whose dreams of winning a gold medal at the Olympic Games were shattered when the war broke out, resulting in their cancellation. As a second best she was given a contract by MGM, mainly on the strength of her aquatic skills. Williams made 26 films for MGM in a career dominated by the sight of her in a swimsuit. She demonstrated great pluckiness in her splashy histrionics but was also exploited, sustaining many injuries negotiating overly-ambitious stunts.

When she was making *On an Island with You* in 1948 in Biscayne, Florida, she fell into a four-foot-deep pit covered in palm fronds. She sprained her ankle and had to finish the film on crutches. A short time later, shooting a scene from *Pagan Love Song* (1950) she narrowly escaped serious injury when a wave tossed her from an outrigger canoe onto a sharp coral reef. When she made *Million Dollar Mermaid* for Busby Berkeley in 1952 she nearly broke her neck after performing a 50-foot swan dive from a cascading fountain, spending six months in a body cast afterwards. While all this was going on, Berkeley was sitting naked in a bathtub drinking martinis.[3]

Mickey Rooney attested to Williams' aquatic identity when he remarked, "I can't honestly say Esther Williams ever acted in an Andy Hardy picture, but she swam in one."

Williams herself droned, "All they ever did for me at MGM was change my leading men and the water in the pool."

Jane Wyman was typecast in a different way. In 1948 she won an Oscar for playing a deaf mute in *Johnny Belinda*. Afterwards she was offered innumerable roles featuring women suffering from physical maladies. Her "victim" status was evident in everything from *Magnificent Obsession* to *All That Heaven Allows*.

Irene Dunne was Oscar-nominated for George Stevens' *I Remember Mama* (1948) but she was a long shot. Dunne was a fine actress but is more or less a forgotten figure in Hollywood today. She once griped, "If a picture of mine is good, people will praise the director and the writer and the cameraman. But if it's bad they'll say, 'Irene Dunne's latest picture was bad.'"[4]

Ava Gardner was also pigeonholed, though not as obviously. She played a window statue that comes to life in *One Touch of Venus* (1948), a one-joke movie that did little but showcase her beauty. As was the case with so many other women in Hollywood's history, directors generally failed to look behind this to any acting talent that might have been buried beneath it. If women went to bed with Gilda and woke up with Rita Hayworth, they went to bed with Venus and woke up with Ava Gardner. If she hadn't looked the way she did, it's possible she would have been given the kind of character roles that went to stars like, say, Julie Harris or Mercedes McCambridge. But she didn't clamor enough for these. She just took the money (or, as she liked to call it, "the loot") and ran. (What most people didn't know was that she was very much a hoyden, as she proved in her later years when she struck up a friendship with "Papa" Hemingway, becoming one of his adoptive daughters like Marlene Dietrich and Ingrid Bergman.)

We've already seen how Gardner was manhandled by people like Artie Shaw and Howard Hughes throughout her career. Something similar happened to Harriet Frank, Jr., that year when she wrote the script for the Raoul Walsh western *Silver River*. Star Errol Flynn propositioned her one day, as he was wont to do with anything in a skirt. When she told him she wasn't interested, he expressed a wish to have her off the picture. This was not her first experience of being regarded as a sex object. In her early days in films she went into an office and the producer inquired, "How dare they send a Tootsie Roll in here to do this job?"[5]

The most shocking event of 1948 was the suicide of Carole Landis (she took an overdose of Seconal). Rex Harrison was having an affair with her at the time and it was he who found the body when he visited her house. Landis had just initiated divorce proceedings against her fourth husband but held little hope that Harrison would leave his then-wife Lilli Palmer for her. Before she died, she gave a chilling *résumé* of her life: "You fight so hard and then what have you got? You begin to worry about being washed up. You get bitter and disillusioned. You fear the future because there's only one way to go and that's down." Landis married a man twenty years older than her before she was even sixteen. Three more marriages followed but she never found happiness. "I was ex-wifed to death," she complained. "It might be the husband's fault, you know," she added.[6]

When she died she was practically bankrupt, having sold her house and car shortly before. She'd even dismissed her press agent because she had no money to pay him. Harrison had dinner with her the night before she died. It was rumored she was carrying his child, which would have contributed to her negative frame of mind. "I didn't notice the extent of her down-ness," he said defensively after her death, "I felt no guilt complex, no, none at all, but I did spend months afterwards going to psychiatrists, discussing the suicide with them, seeking the reason for it. The plain fact is that Carole had a death wish."[7]

Landis left a suicide note to her mother and another one to her maid. Many people claimed she wrote a third one to Harrison and that he removed it when he found her. It was also alleged that she was still breathing when he discovered her but he failed to call an ambulance, instead spending his time thumbing through her address book looking for the number of her private doctor in the hope of keeping a scandal at bay.

Harrison always played his cards close to his chest about the events of Landis' last night, obviously knowing he would have been at least partly blamed for her death if he revealed the full depth of his involvement with her. The fact that she returned all of his letters to her before she died he (conveniently) took to be a bountiful gesture on her part to spare him from the extent of that involvement. Was it, though? It could equally have been the anger of a spurned lover.

Was there a third suicide note? Lilli Palmer alluded to the existence of one in her autobiography, claiming policemen found one in her clenched fist but didn't release its contents to the public.[8] It's also curious that there were no pills found beside her body, nor any prescription for them anywhere in her house. Did she die somewhere else and, as would be rumored about Marilyn Monroe fourteen years later after she too died from a Seconal overdose, have her body then moved to her house? We'll probably never know for sure, but Harrison should have taken some blame for her death, as indeed he should have for the eerily similar suicide of his wife Rachel Roberts in 1980.

Harrison was remarkably good at rationalizing his way out of these situations. If he'd used the same energy in loving the women in his life as he did at forgetting about them when he was tired of them, they might have lived longer. (He didn't even mention Landis in his autobiography.)

Landis was besotted with him, pinning all her hopes on a life with him as her career went into remission, but Harrison was merely toying with her affections. When he realized how serious she was about him, he distanced himself from her. On the night before she died he told her he was interested in appearing in a play, *Anne of the Thousand Days*, in New York. For Landis this was probably the last straw.

On a website purported to be run by relatives of Landis, her niece Tammy Powell states that her family has never believed she committed suicide. "We're now 100 percent convinced Rex Harrison is to blame for her death," it states. "My grandmother Dorothy begged the police to investigate more but they refused. She hired a private detective. All he could tell her was that evidence was destroyed and people were paid off."[9] It goes no further than this, which leaves the website open to charges of conspiracy theories. Harrison, after all, had no motive for killing Landis—their affair was common knowledge despite his denials—and he's not around to defend himself about the accusations. But the story refuses to go away. (Harrison's next film was *Unfaithfully Yours*. He played a jealous husband plotting to kill his wife. Not surprisingly, Twentieth Century–Fox delayed its release.)

Another scandal that took place at this time involved Ingrid Bergman. Frustrated by the fact that her Hollywood career seemed to be stymied, Bergman fervently sought an alternative to it. When she saw Roberto Rossellini's *Open City* she was blown away by it and wrote to ask him if he might be interested in employing her for his next film, *Stromboli*. When he agreed to this, she went to Europe to meet him. They were immediately struck by one another and it wasn't long before they fell in love. Both of them were married to other people at the time but neither marriage was strong.

After Bergman arrived in Rome she told a reporter, "Nobody understood me in Hollywood. They didn't know how to treat a sophisticated European. They thought I was a good, ordinary person."[10] One suspects a certain degree of irony in her use of the term "good" here. She compared Hollywood to being in a cage: "They thrust the parts through the bars and you take what they give you." Except she didn't this time.

Ingrid Bergman became a "scarlet woman" after she had a child out of wedlock by Roberto Rossellini, who directed her in *Stromboli* (1949), pictured above. Her relationship with Rossellini resulted in a seven year exile from Hollywood.

On December 13, 1949, Bergman announced she was seven months pregnant with Rossellini's baby. That was the day her life changed forever as she became a figure of public outrage. She suspected the reason people reacted as they did was because of the image that had been built up of her by the studios up until now. "I'd played so many good girls— nuns and saints—and somehow I was put on a pedestal. I was used as a good example by the parents and suddenly this happened. We wanted [the baby] and that shocked the world." She had some people pleading her cause, like her friend Ernest Hemingway, but even this was fraught with danger. Hemingway couldn't be touched by Hollywood but a young Swedish actress called Marta Toren rose to her defense and was almost fired from her studio as a result.[11]

The situation now became inflammatory. Joseph Breen, the director of Hollywood's Production Code Administration, wrote to Bergman and told her a divorce from Lindstrom would cost her her career. Howard Hughes then leaked news of her pregnancy to the press to increase publicity for *Stromboli*.[12]

Bergman's fall from grace wasn't so much her own fault as that of the studio that made her "Saint" Ingrid. David O. Selznick had hired a press agent for her at the beginning of her career to shield her from the press, only releasing stories that highlighted her whole-some image. Her screen roles as heroine and love martyr in films like *For Whom the Bell Tolls* and *Casablanca* had fortified this, which meant that her love for Rossellini (while still being married to Petter Lindstrom) was always going to be a forbidden one. She was denounced both by church and state, dismissed as everything from a "free love cultist" to "Hollywood's apostle of degradation." Between 1949 and 1950 she received over 30,000 letters from the public castigating her. There were even calls for her films to be boycotted, or banned outright.

Most of the letters were abusive. They told her she was an evil woman, that she'd burn in hell for all eternity, that her baby would either be born dead or a hunchback. Rossellini advised her not to read them but she had to; it was "the only way I could find the letters from friends who were encouraging and supporting me."[13]

Bergman took most of the heat for the affair. It seemed to be forgotten that Rossellini was also a party to it, and also married. Did different rules apply because he didn't live in the U.S.? Or because he was a man and therefore not culpable for such marital indiscretions?

When Bergman went into hospital to have her baby, a journalist had his wife check into an adjoining room. He then asked a nurse to leave Bergman's door open "just a crack" to enable him to take a photograph of it. After the child was born, its father's name was listed as Roberto Rossellini but after "Mother" it said "temporarily unknown." Under Italian law she was still married to Lindstrom and had to have that label attached to her. As her husband, Lindstrom even had the legal right to take possession of the baby.[14]

She was denounced by women's clubs, church groups and (inevitably) the Legion of Decency. It was also expected that *Stromboli* would be banned in the U.S. and that both her career and Rossellini's would be destroyed. When the baby was born he was called Robertino. He was legitimized by a Mexican proxy divorce from Lindstrom and a Mexican proxy marriage to Rossellini.

Much was made of the fact that the woman running away from her husband to another man had been the smiling nun in *The Bells of St. Mary's* and that her most recently released film was *Joan of Arc*. It should also have been noted that she'd played a fallen woman in *Dr. Jekyll and Mr. Hyde* and *Arch of Triumph* and adulteresses both in *Casablanca* and *Notorious*.[15]

A part of her couldn't conceive—if that's not the wrong term—why people would turn against her. Wasn't it her own life? Shouldn't one's personal life be one's own business? Marriages broke down every day of the week. Was that not a fact in Hollywood and out of Hollywood? Rossellini's was over and so was hers. Why, then, did the fact that they formed a new alliance together, and had a child, suddenly become scandalous? Was it simply a question of red tape, the formalizing of the two divorces, before such an alliance was allowable in the public eye? To her it seemed a storm in a teacup: "Ilsa could be forgiven in *Casablanca*, Alicia could be forgiven in *Notorious*, but Ingrid in Rome could not."[16] What she didn't realize was that movies were one thing, real life another. Also, America wasn't Europe. A free spirit in one part of the world was a scarlet woman in another.

Stromboli was released in February 1950. As was expected, people stayed away in droves. Bergman's name was mud both in Europe and Hollywood and everybody seemed to want to rub her nose in it. A politician called Edwin Johnson even denounced her in the Senate, accusing her of "moral turpitude."[17] Her downfall seemed to be final.

Another actress who fell foul of the establishment at this time was Marsha Hunt. Hunt starred in the melodrama *Take One False Step* in 1949. The film was aptly named as she was blacklisted afterwards for alleged left wing sympathies. Having made 52 films between 1935 and now, she would only make three in the next seven years. In some ways it was a blessed release as she'd never been properly fulfilled in her career, playing what she called "sweet young drips" in film after film with only a change of wardrobe to distinguish one from another. This improved somewhat when she moved from Paramount to MGM but she always felt undervalued and underused, even in her later work.

The British actress Anna Lee appeared in *Prison Warden* in 1949 but it was the last film she would make for nine years as she was also placed on Joseph McCarthy's blacklist. The reason was markedly different than it had been for Hunt, her name having been confused with a woman called Ann Lee, who'd written a letter to a communist called Harry Bridges at that time. Anna wasn't made aware of the reason for her decade-long lay-off until she submitted a script to *The Loretta Young Show* in 1958. "The only Bridges I knew," the startled actress exclaimed, "was Lloyd."[18]

Judy Garland was supposed to star in *The Barkleys of Broadway* that year but insomnia and agonizing migraine attacks resulted in repeated absences from the set, and an eventual sacking. "They didn't even give me the courtesy of a meeting," she recalled bitterly, "They [just] sent me a telegram."[19] The film was tailor-made for Garland, being a virtual action replay of the previous year's *Easter Parade* in which she'd co-starred with Fred Astaire. They kept Astaire but replaced Garland with Ginger Rogers.

Less famous stars than Garland were suffering too. Audrey Totter appeared with

Clark Gable in a lame gambling drama, *Any Number Can Play*. "They were putting me in terrible films that damaged my star status," she complained. Most of her career was spent playing fallen women as if that was all she could do. Lionel Barrymore once told her that she'd never become a big star because she was too versatile and Hollywood felt threatened by that.[20] They preferred to have her play the same role over and over again with minor variations to keep her in her box. If Gloria Grahame was the poor man's Lana Turner, Totter was the even poorer man's Gloria Grahame.

Behind the camera, women still remained virtually invisible, or as invisible as Hollywood could make them. The screenwriter Virginia Van Upp divorced her husband in 1949, his career as a producer having been eclipsed by hers. When asked if she thought jealousy was the cause of the divorce, she replied, "I suppose so." From now on, she promised, she was going to marry her work instead. "I think that's safer," she ventured.[21]

Ida Lupino was exceptional in that she went behind the camera to direct as well as being a major league star. She directed *Not Wanted*, the story of an unmarried mother giving up her child for adoption. It was her directorial debut and she knew she wouldn't have been given the job if the original director hadn't fallen ill. That year also she set up a company called Filmakers with her husband Collier Young, which allowed her to produce and co-write scripts.

Lupino was the most high-profile female director Hollywood had up until now. Even though she was well known as an actress, it was still an achievement to be allowed behind a camera as a woman in 1949. Her trick was to play the "little girl" role. "You don't tell a man [your idea]," she advised. "You *suggest* to them." That meant saying something like "Let's try something crazy here. That is, if it's comfortable for you." Lupino referred to herself as "Mother" on sets to keep the atmosphere cozy. "Darlings," she'd say,

Women directors were thin on the ground in the 1940s which made it all the sweeter when Ida Lupino took on this role and managed to combine it with a career in front of the camera. Her "social issue films" never achieved the success they should have, probably because Hollywood wasn't yet ready to have a woman handle such themes.

"Mother has a problem. I'd love to do this. Can you do it? It sounds kooky, I know, but can you do this for Mother?"[22] By playing the defenseless female, she stooped to conquer.

Lupino directed a number of films

in the following years which had themes of great interest to women. In *The Young Lovers* (1950) she had a polio-stricken woman trying to have a normal sexual life while in *Outrage*, made the same year, she featured a woman struggling to deal with the after-effects of being raped. Film historians have accused some of these films of looking dated today but they were very controversial for their time. In 1949, sex wasn't an allowed theme, never mind pregnancy outside marriage or the trauma of a rape. She tried something different with *The Bigamist*, starring Edmond O'Brien as a man torn between his wife (Joan Fontaine) and lover (Lupino). The theme may have been controversial but the treatment was unfortunately too tame.

It's ironic that Lupino's women-oriented films didn't fare as well commercially as a straightforward thriller she later made, *The Hitch-Hiker* (1953). From this, one might draw the unfair conclusion that she didn't direct "women's pictures" well. A more likely cause was that audiences, particularly male audiences, may have been reluctant to praise women's pictures—especially those directed by a woman. The point is that she never came across as agitprop in her "issues" films. Of *Not Wanted* she stated, "It was a darned good idea we thought should be presented. The girl should be able to get sympathy from the family. Without being too 'message' we were trying to say, 'Don't treat her like she has some terrible disease. [She just] made a mistake.'"[23] In *Outrage* the ambition was to highlight the fact that rape victims often don't talk about their ordeal for fear they won't be believed.[24] Lupino wasn't interested in making films about women who sat in the corner in a docile manner. "I liked strong characters," she stressed. "I don't mean women who have masculine qualities about them." Instead she went for guts, "intestinal fortitude."[25]

Why were Lupino's films not more successful with male audiences? Maybe they felt they were going to be lectured to and therefore had negative preconceptions about them from the word go. People like Dorothy Arzner escaped this by making her films as neutral as possible. In our own time, Kathryn Bigelow seems to be doing something similar. The moral of the story seemed to be: Don't act (or direct) like a woman and you'll get places.

The Eisenhower Years

If the forties promised much for women but delivered little, the fifties promised little and delivered little. To that extent, it was at least less frustrating.

Hollywood didn't really know what to do with women after the war ended and people settled down to raise their nuclear families. Domestic harmony didn't conduce to exciting storylines so blandness was routinely served up. Fiery anti-heroines of the forties like Joan Crawford and Bette Davis gave way to the safer (if more ditzy) charms of Marilyn Monroe and her cohorts.

The Eisenhower years of the fifties ushered in a view of women that exiled Rosie the Riveter to home-sweet-home suburbia. The man went to work and the little lady took care of the kids until he came home. He might play softball with junior in the backyard, while Mom and daughter prepared dinner. Women in the Eisenhower era were expected to know their place, and that place was generally in the kitchen. As the old joke went, "Love begins when you sink into his arms, and ends with your arms in his sink."

In the fifties, new ideologies came to the fore. Censorial *diktats* were lessened but that didn't necessarily mean women were vouchsafed better roles. Often it was the opposite. American women seemed to retire into the background with the influx of European sex symbols. We were presented with the curvaceous delights of Gina Lollobrigida, the impossibly voluptuous Sophia Loren and the erotically enigmatic Silvana Mangano. Don Macpherson wrote: "Loren, Mangano and Lollobrigida stepped out of the war-torn back streets of Italy into the atomic age of bubblegum, television, nylons, pop music, drip-dry shirts and frozen food. Like their counterparts in America they flaunted sex as a consumer item, were supposedly capable of explosive impact, and catered for an infantile male obsession with large breasts."[1]

In such a dumbed-down milieu, any quality-studded women's films that came along were like the exceptions to prove the rule. In 1950 there were two that almost made up for what was lacking in the rest of the decade: *Sunset Boulevard* and *All About Eve*. In the former, Gloria Swanson played Norma Desmond, an aging diva trying to make an unlikely screen comeback. It was a wonderful role but not many women in Hollywood wanted it. Maybe they felt it was too close to home. Who wanted to be reminded of what they once were but couldn't be now?

Swanson gave the part everything, making it into a cross between poignancy and Grand Guignol, her hands clawing the air like talons as she sought desperately to recreate the glory days, waving to a parade that had passed her by long ago, in the words of her co-star "toyboy" lover, William Holden. The film was probably the best one Hollywood ever made about the mote in its own eye and it took an immigrant, Billy Wilder, to make it. He was castigated for doing so by those who feared anyone seeing the poison in the bottom of the industry's gold-plated goldfish bowl. Wilder was telling us that this was what happened to actresses past their prime. They were thrown on the scrapheap to sink or swim, or end up in a mental home like Desmond. Aging male stars could still play action and/or romantic roles but women of a certain age were put out on grass.

Fred Astaire had starred opposite Ginger Rogers in the thirties, Rita Hayworth in the forties and Cyd Charisse and Audrey Hepburn in the fifties. Nobody saw any disjunction in the fact that while he got older, his co-stars stayed the same age or became younger. Likewise with Cary Grant. Grant starred opposite Katharine Hepburn in the thirties, Ingrid Bergman in the forties, Grace Kelly in the fifties and Sophia Loren in the sixties. Swanson was allowed to romance the younger Holden in *Sunset Blvd.* but only for the sake of the plot, to make her into a pathetic or even perverted figure. Holden was nervous taking the part for this reason. Montgomery Clift refused it because he was seeing the older Libby Holman at this time and he thought people would notice parallels between the two relationships. It was okay to date an older woman, but one had to do it in a clandestine manner. (The fact that Clift was gay further complicated the situation.)

Desmond lives in a decaying mansion where an empty swimming pool beset with rats seems like an ideal symbol for her anachronistic status. A throwback to the silent era (her actual status) when stars had "faces," she towers over this cautionary fable like a deranged Colossus. Her most memorable line from the film occurs when Holden tells her she used to be big once. She replies that she still is: "It's the pictures that got small." Here she's speaking not only for herself but a generation of actresses who were put out to pasture before their time either because their looks faded or a younger star stole their place in the sun.

She gave the performance of her life and was nominated for an Oscar but she didn't win, the prize going instead to Judy Holliday for *Born Yesterday*. Why was this? Charles Brackett (the film's producer and co-writer) noted that too many of the voters had seen the film the previous winter so "all sense of timeliness was gone."[2]

Bette Davis played a Norma Desmond type in *All About Eve* the same year. (She'd left Warner Brothers because of the dearth of good roles available from that studio.) Margo Channing was in many ways her signature role and she essayed it like one to the manner born.

By now Davis had acquired a reputation for being "difficult," a euphemism for "bitchy." This wasn't true, the rumor coming about simply because she stood up for herself. She was well aware of the different perspectives of strong women versus strong men: "Men stars are confrontational right and left, yet it isn't even commented on. But with a woman a certain reputation develops.... By the time I was past forty I had a reputation as a sheer horror. [It was] totally unjustified but it caused many people to want not to work with me." This also applied to working with her behind the camera: "It became very fashionable to say you had directed me and survived. But later many directors admitted I was really a pussycat to work with."[3]

All About Eve has often been castigated for being ageist against women since it has Channing opting for marriage over career when she feels the years gaining on her. But as one writer pointed out, Channing doesn't really retire in the film. Instead she says she's dropping out of a play where she was playing a character twenty years younger than her. More importantly, she's still planning to tour with another one.[4]

Davis married her *All About Eve* co-star Gary Merrill after the film was completed but theirs was a tempestuous relationship. "He used his fists more than his mouth," she said of their years together, claiming the only time he touched her was to beat her up. Merrill's reaction to this taunt was to observe that the only thing Davis really enjoyed was "getting slapped around."[5] They were divorced in 1960.

Davis once complained, "My biggest problem in life was men. I never met one who could compete with the image the public made out of Bette Davis."[6] Merrill didn't fall into this category, their problems being of a different nature. According to Merrill, Davis was really married to her career all her life so no man had a chance. There's a certain amount of legitimacy to this view, though obviously it doesn't excuse his violence towards her.

Another man who was guilty of cruelty towards women (though he wasn't always aware of it) was Henry Fonda. "I'm not really Henry Fonda," he once said. "Nobody could have that kind of integrity." It was an honest appraisal of the disconnect between his actual identity and his screen persona. On April 14, 1950, Fonda's wife Frances, a depressive for many years, committed suicide by cutting her throat. It was her 42nd birthday. The actor's reaction was something less than empathetic: "I never dreamed [her depression] would be anything permanent. It was just a bore to have a wife who wasn't always well."[7] He was performing in a stage version of *Mister Roberts*

Bette Davis was one of the main standard-bearers for women's rights in films. Like Olivia de Havilland, she went on suspension to secure greater roles for herself and challenge the moguls, which often resulted in her being branded a "bitch." "Strong men are praised," she said, "but strong women are regarded only as *difficult*." Here she's pictured in one of her favorite roles, Margo Channing in *All About Eve* (1950).

at the time and didn't even cancel that evening's performance after hearing the news. Eight months later he married Susan Blanchard, whom he'd been seeing before Frances died. He told his children Peter and Jane that she'd died of a heart attack.

Peter took the news worst. The following January, as Fonda and Blanchard were honeymooning in the Virgin Islands, they received word that he'd had shot himself in the stomach and was in serious danger of dying. Fonda was furious at having to cut his honeymoon short. Peter pulled through but never talked about the incident. Nobody knows if it was accidental—he was playing with a rifle at the time—or "a ten year-old's half-conscious attempt at suicide."[8]

Jane blamed her father for many of her problems in later years, like bulimia and her generally poor self-image. What she called "the disease to please" afflicted her as she came to believe that only if she was perfect did she deserve the right to be loved by him. Because her father came from a generation where men didn't express their feelings, she was never sure how high she rated in his affections. She worked out some of those grievances when she co-starred with him in the film *On Golden Pond* in 1981 but while she was growing up they were a chronic source of frustration to her. They also affected her relationships with the other men in her life, from Roger Vadim through Ted Turner and even Tom Hayden.

Fonda disapproved of his daughter not only for her sexual permissiveness but for her political views. He once told her that if he discovered she was a communist, he'd turn her in to the government himself. Years earlier, when she stood before him one day in a bikini, he remarked that it looked tight on her. She took this to mean he thought she was fat, and her ensuing sensitivity caused her to develop bulimia. As far as Fonda was concerned it was a throwaway remark, the kind any father might have made, but he never really took the time to get to know Jane when she was growing up, immersed as he was in his work.

It would be a few years down the road before Jane Fonda became a leading light in women's causes or an iconic figure in movies. For now, more lightweight ventures seemed to hold sway. Betty Hutton played Annie Oakley in *Annie Get Your Gun* but Judy Garland would have been much better in the part. She'd been given it before Hutton but had disagreements with the film's original director, Busby Berkeley, and they continued with Berkeley's replacement, George Sidney. As was the case with the previous year's *The Barkleys of Broadway*, she was sacked, and not with dignity either. "They decided to fire her on a Friday afternoon," recalled producer George Schlatter, "before a long weekend and when everybody had gone home."[9]

Evelyn Keyes fortified her noir reputation with *The Killer That Stalked New York* but some offscreen drama in her love life meant it didn't go too far after that. Kirk Douglas had expressed a romantic interest in her but Harry Cohn disapproved of the "no-good bum" and barred him from the lot after he visited Keyes.[10] Cohn told Keyes he was going to leave his wife for her but Keyes said she wasn't interested in him. This sent him into a frenzy and he "froze" her career as a result. "I didn't get certain parts that I wanted," she revealed afterwards. "I'd [just] get the same level of parts that I'd had before."[11] Cohn was used to getting his own way and didn't take rejection lightly.

At the same time as Cohn was lusting after Keyes, so was Howard Hughes after Jean Simmons. He'd just bought her from the British movie tycoon J. Arthur Rank after becoming entranced with her in *So Long at the Fair.* The fact that she was already married (to Stewart Granger) didn't seem to bother him. Rank made a handsome profit on the deal but didn't tell Simmons this. She learned of it from her agent Bert Allenberg, who told her Hughes had signed her up for seven years, a prospect that was galling to her.

When she met him for dinner, he spent most of the evening ogling her breasts and making lewd comments, apparently oblivious to the fact that Granger was also present. Simmons fended him off as politely as she could but Hughes didn't like to be refused anything. When she told him she had her heart set on appearing in *Roman Holiday*, he blocked her from it. Instead he had her play a batty murderess in *Angel Face* in 1952. To gain further revenge he advised Otto Preminger, the film's director, to treat her "as badly as he wanted."[12] Preminger didn't usually need encouragement to bully actresses and this gave him an extra spur. The film was a horrendous experience for Simmons and she often fled the set in tears.

Afterwards she tried her best to escape Hughes' clutches but he told her she was committed to him for the seven years and that he'd sue any other studio that tried to employ her within that time period. Simmons claimed the contract only tied her to three pictures and told him she'd take him to court if he tried to hold on to her after these. Everyone advised her to back off for fear he'd destroy her career entirely but she held firm, strongly supported by Granger.

Granger's anger with Hughes at this time was so great, he fantasized about killing him, even working out the way he was going to do it. He decided he'd pretend to leave town, thereby drawing Hughes's spies after him. He would then give them the slip and return. At this point Simmons would ring Hughes and ask to see him at her house. When he arrived, she'd take him out onto the terrace which looked out over a cliff. She would then scream, as if Hughes was attacking her, and Granger would rush out of hiding and push Hughes off the cliff. Thankfully for all concerned, Granger didn't put his plan into action. His decision to abandon it wasn't caused by altruism but rather the simple fact that Hughes "wasn't worth going to the gas chamber for."[13]

Hughes produced *Where Danger Lives* in 1950. It was a fairly typical actioner with a destructive woman at its core, Faith Domergue. He repeated the formula the following year with *My Forbidden Past*, this time with Ava Gardner as the demonic woman. Both films had Robert Mitchum as the dupe. Hughes proposed marriage to Gardner during the latter film despite the fact that she was engaged in a torrid affair with Frank Sinatra at the time, and he himself involved with both Terry Moore and Jean Peters. (He eventually married Peters.)

Sinatra's desire for Gardner was so intense, he pretended to shoot himself one night in an effort to woo her, the bullets from his gun going into a pillow instead of his head. Gardner forgave him but pointed out that a slight problem with them becoming romantically involved with one another in the long term was the fact that he was still married to his first wife, Nancy. Sinatra told her he was going to divorce Nancy but one night Gardner ran into Lana Turner at a party and Turner told him she'd had an affair with

Sinatra too and he'd used that line on her. When push came to shove, he went back to Nancy.

Gardner became a hate figure in the media when she started dating Sinatra. She received letters addressed to her as "Bitch-Jezebel-Gardner." Nuns in schools asked their pupils to pray for Nancy. The Legion of Decency threatened to ban her movies. Everyone seemed to forget that it was Sinatra who was the married one, not she (she was divorced from Artie Shaw by now). It was like a rerun of the media frenzy surrounding the affair between Ingrid Bergman and Roberto Rossellini. The thinking was: Only women could sin.

Sinatra did eventually divorce Nancy for Gardner and they married in 1951. It was a storm-tossed marriage, characterized by tempestuous rows followed by equally energized reconciliations "in the feathers," as Gardner put it. "We were always great in the bedroom," she recalled. "Our arguments usually started on the way to the bidet."[14]

Hughes continued to pursue her even after she married Sinatra. He also had a coterie of starlets under his control at this time. These he kept on small salaries, but he denied them the freedom to work for anyone but him. Like Hugh Hefner's *Playboy* bunnies at a later time, they were largely kept in seclusion, with only the vague promise of a career keeping them from breaking away from him. They rarely met him and on the odd occasion that they did, they had to be bathed with antiseptic soap beforehand. They also had to wear white gloves when shaking hands with him because of his obsession with hygiene.

Their daily routines were rigid. They had to rise at seven and immediately take showers before they put on their makeup. Afterwards a maid brought them breakfast. At eight o'clock a driver took them to the studio where they had acting and dancing lessons. In the afternoons they rested or watched TV. They were allowed to shop once a week but no more. In the evenings they went to restaurants Hughes specified, with men he chose. Even the food they ate was decided by him. Their families were only allowed to see them by appointment. If they ran from the cars in which they were being driven to classes, they were forcibly brought back. Their drivers were ordered to drive at a slow pace, and to decelerate to two miles per hour when going over bumps on the road for fear the jolting might cause the starlets' breasts to sag. Many of the drivers were chosen because they were gay and therefore not dating material for them. If they were "straight," Hughes had detectives examine their every move in case they might "steal" one of his potential lovers.

As well as wooing, or trying to woo, Ava Gardner, Jean Simmons, Terry Moore and Jean Peters, Hughes developed a fascination for Elizabeth Taylor after seeing her in *A Place in the Sun* (1951). Never a man to hang about, he told his lawyer Greg Bautzer to go to her mother and tell her he wanted to marry her and that he was prepared to pay her $1 million for the privilege. Bautzer, amazingly, agreed, and put the proposal to Taylor's mother. When she heard it she exclaimed "Tax free?" amidst peals of laughter. Taylor herself is alleged to have said she wouldn't have been interested in Hughes because "His socks stink."[15]

Hughes didn't forgive Taylor for this, nor anyone else who didn't do his bidding. He generally plotted revenge on his enemies and was so rich and powerful he was usually able to gain it. He got back at Simmons by refusing to loan her out for *Roman Holiday*, a part she dearly wanted, as mentioned. Instead it went to Audrey Hepburn. The film made her famous overnight. Dismissing notions that American audiences wouldn't accept a flat-chested leading star, she turned their eyes upwards to her incredibly beautiful face. Before Hepburn, unless a young actress had a 38- or 40-inch bust, she was usually destined to play "the *ingénue's* friend."[16] Hepburn changed that, opening the floodgates for a different type of sex symbol.

No longer did a woman have to be voluptuous with heaving bosoms. No longer, according to Billy Wilder, would directors have to "invent shots where the girl leans forward for a glass of scotch and soda"[17]—or, in the case of Jane Russell in *The Outlaw*, a pail of milk.

William Wyler, *Roman Holiday's* director, was initially thrown by Hepburn's lack of cleavage. "If you don't mind me saying so," he advised, "I think you should be wearing falsies." Hepburn replied, "I am!"[18]

Wyler also made *Detective Story*, the tale of a detective (Kirk Douglas) who can't accept the fact that his wife (Eleanor Parker) once had an abortion. The film boasted a fine debut performance from Lee Grant and she received an Academy Award nomination. Her career capsized afterwards when she spoke out against the McCarthy blacklist and, more dangerously, refused to implicate her husband Arnold Manoff as a communist sympathizer. Her marriage to Manoff was on the rocks but she still stuck by him. The upshot was that she was cast into the Hollywood wilderness for over a decade. It was 1964 before she managed to secure some occasional TV roles. Three years later she got a small part in *In the Heat of the Night* after being cleared of all charges against her. Her sad exclusion from movies in the interim period was a terrible indictment of the flimsy "evidence" upon which someone with her great talent could be rendered unemployable.

Eleanor Parker was nominated for an Oscar for *Detective Story* but lost out to Vivien Leigh's Blanche Du Bois in Elia Kazan's *A Streetcar Named Desire*, a film that grabbed most of its headlines for Marlon Brando's towering performance as Stanley Kowalski. He was electrifying, to be sure, but in Tennessee Williams' play the relationship between Du Bois and her sister Stella was pivotal. Kazan highlighted Kowalski instead, sidelining the tensions between Blanche and Stella (played by Kim Stanley) in favor of those between Stella and Stanley. At the end of the film, Stella tells Stanley never to touch her again, another contravention of the play, which ended with her in Stanley's arms. The censors demanded this. Stanley had to be "punished" for raping Blanche and Stella wasn't "allowed" to forgive him.[19]

The following year Maureen O'Hara appeared in her most famous film, *The Quiet Man*. She thought she deserved an Oscar nomination for it, and indeed was informed by Anne Baxter that her name had been put forward, but that she was "knocked out of the box" by John Ford, who seemed to have had an inexplicable resentment for her, despite having used her in so many of his films.[20]

While the film allowed her more opportunities for feistiness than many of her earlier efforts, it also seemed to condone her being dragged across a field by her male co-star John Wayne, and also kicked in the rear end by him. She got on very well with Wayne and made many films with him. It didn't seem to bother her that he came out with statements like, "I don't mind what kind of job a woman has so long as she has the dinner on the table when her man comes home." In fact, this is precisely what she does at the end of *The Quiet Man*: She prepares dinner for him while he and her brother (played by Victor McLaglen) engage in frivolous fisticuffs. The film might appear as innocuous whimsy to us but there's an unsettling undercurrent which seems to predicate a kind of "sex for sale" ethos in Irish marriages. (O'Hara is only willing to give Wayne his conjugal rights if he "buys" them with a dowry.)

There was a similarly coy finale in the Bette Davis-Barry Sullivan drama *Payment on Demand* that year. Davis felt the film sanitized itself by having herself and Sullivan, her alienated husband, opt for reconciliation instead of the original version of the script, which had him walking out on her. She felt that was more realistic, and also thought the original title should have been preserved: *The Story of a Divorce*. But Howard Hughes wanted the ending sugarcoated. Davis begged him to change it but he was relentless. "Doesn't every woman want a roll in the hay?" was his estimation of matters.[21]

With people like Hughes holding the reins of filmmaking, what chance had women to make any kind of an impact, even women like Bette Davis? Susan Hayward seemed to encapsulate the sexism of the time with her quip on a Biblical epic she was currently making with Gregory Peck called *David and Bathsheba*. Asked what she thought of it, she replied, "I'd like it a helluva lot better if it was called *Bathsheba and David*."[22]

Hayward was having problems in her marriage with Jess Barker by now, and there was more marital friction among other stars. Hedy Lamarr married the restaurateur Ernest Stauffer in 1951 but divorced him the following year, claiming he'd been physically abusive. Lucille Ball married the Cuban playboy Desi Arnaz and this was also a volatile marriage. Their savvy business sense saw them take charge of Desilu Productions but behind the scenes they argued fiercely, often resulting in physical fights. Arnaz was also a philanderer. When *Confidential* magazine ran a story about him being involved in a *ménage à trois* because men should have "as many girls as he has hair on his head," Ball hit the roof.[23] The couple finally divorced in 1960.

Doris Day married Marty Melcher on April 3. "It should have been April 1st," she remarked ruefully afterwards. Her choice of husbands fell far short of her choice of movie roles during her life. Melcher adopted her son Terry, whom she had by Al Jorden, her first husband, and Marty became a successful film producer and a beloved ally to Day. Otherwise, though, the marriage was a disaster. Melcher robbed Day blind as a result of his involvement with her business manager Jerome Rosenthal.

Veronica Lake finally left André De Toth, the parting appearing to coincide with the decline of her career. Things were now so bad that she had to go to Mexico to get a job. The film was called *Stronghold* and it disappeared rapidly from screens. Her time in Mexico was more notable for a piquant experience she had one day while attending a bullfight. In the course of it she heard the crowd shouting out "Veronica! Veronica!" She took a bow to acknowledge the cheers but nobody noticed it. It was only afterwards she learned that a "veronica" was a technical term for a matador's flourish. The incident was a sobering reminder of her failing status. After *Stronghold* failed to do any business, she slid into obscurity with the words, "The hell with you, Hollywood, and fuck you too."[24] They were heartfelt. The town had never been interested in expanding her range, she knew, just her image. "For a time," she reminisced sadly, "my hair was more famous than myself."

Teresa Wright made *California Conquest*, a routine western she had to do because her previous film, *The Men*, bombed and she needed the money. Her co-star was Cornel Wilde and the director was Lew Landers. One day Landers came up to her and said, "I want you to put on a bit of makeup. It's because Cornel is prettier than you are."[25]

Grace Kelly had her first major role in *High Noon* in 1952. She didn't have a heaving bosom or a plunging neckline but she still set pulses racing. Neither did she have much to do in the film, at least until the last scene where she proves an unlikely ally to Gary Cooper. John Wayne felt the film was un–American and un-macho. He didn't like the fact that

Grace Kelly saved Gary Cooper's life in *High Noon*, which caused John Wayne to berate Cooper for allowing himself to be rescued by a "mere" woman. Her ice-cool sexuality exploded off the screen but her career ended prematurely when she became a princess and retreated to a life of empty luxury under the dominating influence of Prince Rainier in Monaco.

Cooper got no support from his townsfolk, or the fact that he had to rely on a woman to save his life in the end. Wayne's friend John Ford droned, "All she did was shoot a guy in the back. Cooper should have given her a boot in the pants and sent her back East."[26] It was as if she breached some hidden male code by rescuing him.

Kelly was demeaned in a different manner when Cooper—who had a romance with her off-set—said, "She looked like she could be a cold dish with a man until you got her pants down and then she'd explode."[27] Alfred Hitchcock also had this view of the self-styled Ice Queen and it was a quality he exploited in the films he made with her in later years.

Bing Crosby met Kelly during the making of the film and began an affair with her, despite the fact that his wife Dixie Lee was terminally ill with cancer. After Dixie died, Crosby ignored the traditional mourning period and dated stars Rhonda Fleming, Mona Freeman and Kathryn Grant, eventually marrying Grant. His indiscretions were hushed up by the press because of his huge popularity. The fact that he was a "grieving" husband (at least on the surface) also added to the public's sympathy for him, as did the fact that

Dixie had been an alcoholic. Whatever her faults, they seemed minor compared to those of her husband. Crosby even agreed to travel to Europe to make a movie as her death drew near, returning only a week before she died. He played the role of victim in their relationship but as Dixie droned once, "If you're married to a Crosby, you've got to drink."[28] He seemed more interested in playing golf than ministering to her, or indeed to the children he had by her. After her death he grew further away from them. His son Gary wrote a corrosive account of growing up under his iron discipline.

Another abused woman was the then-rising starlet Marilyn Monroe. Publicists concentrated on her breathy voice, her "horizontal" walk, her half-closed eyes and half-opened mouth. The story of her orphaned childhood as Norma Jean Baker made people feel protective of her; women wanted to be her and men wanted to bed her: "It was as if the absence of family had rendered her attainable."[29]

Monroe made a number of movies in 1952, including *Don't Bother to Knock* and *Clash by Night*. The latter starred Barbara Stanwyck, who was bemused by the manner in which Monroe used her body to get attention. "With that kind of equipment," she laughed, "who needs to be able to act?" These were sentiments that would be echoed more by men than women in the coming years.

At the beginning of her career, Monroe was a sexual plaything for the aging Fox executive Joseph Schenck. Afterwards she was commandeered by Harry Cohn, who treated her with equal dismissiveness. "Harry," she derided, "just told you to go to bed without even saying hello."[30] When she met the baseball star Joe DiMaggio, he took her away from the casting couch and into the marital bed. He probably treated her with more respect than any other man she would ever meet but they weren't compatible.

Monroe loved DiMaggio but couldn't live with him, his obsessive neatness driving her up the walls. As Sheilah Graham observed, "Everything on his dressing table was arranged in alphabetical order: A, aspirin; B, brush; C, comb, etc. The maid would go in to make up his bed and it was already done." In contrast, one could find Monroe "by following the trail of her stockings, her bra, her handkerchief and her handbag, all dropped as she went."[31]

The 19-year-old Debbie Reynolds became famous overnight with *Singin' in the Rain* in 1952 but her success wasn't attained without a struggle. She literally worked her socks off, Gene Kelly making her dance until her feet bled, which caused her to remark years later, "*Singin' in the Rain* and childbirth were the two hardest things I ever had to do in my life."

Myrna Loy appeared in *Belles on their Toes*, a sequel to the highly-successful *Cheaper by the Dozen*. By now her character was a widow, a woman so involved in raising her flock on her own that she has to refuse an offer of a second marriage. The film fed into Loy's "homemaker" persona. This dogged her since the Thin Man movies, ignoring the fact that she'd been much more besides this at the onset of her career when she showed she could do fiery, self-willed women in *The Squall* (1929), *Rebound* and *Consolation Marriage* (both 1931).

Rita Hayworth's marriage to Aly Khan broke up at this time and she returned to Hollywood, making *Affair in Trinidad* and *Miss Sadie Thompson*, neither of which pulled up any trees. It was generally believed that much of her magic had disappeared in the four years she'd been in Europe with Khan. She now married the crooner Dick Haymes. Haymes visited her on the set of the latter movie, which was being filmed in Hawaii. Since he was an Argentine citizen and hadn't informed the authorities about his visit to Hawaii, he had immigration difficulties. A rumor went out that Hayworth married him for no better reason than to solve these. No sooner had they gone to the altar than he was taking her over like Ed Judson and Orson Welles once had. He vetted her movie scripts, her costumes, even the style of her hair. As was the case with the other men, she allowed herself to be manipulated. This infuriated Harry Cohn. He felt his authority was being usurped and set about replacing her. "Screw her," he said with his customary ruthlessness. "We'll make a new star."[32]

Divorce from Khan left Hayworth cash-strapped, which meant she wasn't able to bargain contractually with Cohn as she'd done when she was at the top of the celluloid tree. Khan was a reckless spender but his profligacy didn't extend to being generous in the divorce proceedings. Hayworth didn't care about money as long as she got custody of her daughters so she went lightly on him here.

Hayworth was slated to appear in the Biblical extravaganza *Joseph and His Brethren* in 1954 but the film was shelved after she walked off the set. Her nerves were shot and the marriage to Haymes wasn't going well. Cohn seemed to relish her frustration. "When you came here you were nothing," he told her, "All you had was a beautiful body and Harry Cohn. Now you just have the body." The marriage to Haymes ended after he punched her in the face one night at a Hollywood party. "I stood by him as long as he was in trouble," she said, "but I can't take it any more."[33]

Hayworth could have had a career revival in Fred Zinnemann's *From Here to Eternity* but the role she was interested in went to Deborah Kerr. Kerr was in familiar mode as "the other woman." Donna Reed also starred. Both women received Oscar nominations but this was really a man's film, the women acting as kinds of added extras to the military action. Reed morphed from the prostitute of James Jones' novel to become Montgomery Clift's innocuous girlfriend.

Kerr was more steamy than usual as a married woman cavorting with Burt Lancaster in the surf, the image of the water lapping around them on a beach being one of cinema's most iconic ones. Joan Crawford muttered after attending the premiere, "I was glad to see Deborah finally getting fucked after so many years of trying!"

Zinnemann hadn't wanted Reed in the film and flattered Clift in their scenes together, giving him most of the closeups. Reed was outraged and went to Harry Cohn, demanding that the scenes be re-edited. She was relieved when he came to her rescue on this score but after the film was released and she won an Oscar for it, he assigned her to westerns and B-pictures. She instructed her agent to organize her release from Columbia on a matter of "life and death."[34]

Frank Sinatra also won an Oscar for the film. As was the case with Reed, it was for a supporting role. But it revived his career, which was on the ropes at the time, both in movies and music. Legend has it that a horse's head was found in Harry Cohn's bed to "persuade" him to give the part to Sinatra (as per a scene in *The Godfather* believed to be based on this anecdote) but it's more likely it came about due to the intervention of Ava Gardner, who put in a word for him with Cohn's wife Joan, with whom she was friendly. Sinatra had told Gardner how much he'd wanted the role when he visited her on the set of *Mogambo*, crying on her shoulder about his problems. After she gave him her support and his career rose again, he grew more distant from her. "Frank was always more lovable when he was in the dumpster," she believed. "When he got out of it he could cut you dead."

Clark Gable fell in love with Grace Kelly on the set of *Mogambo* and she was attracted to him too but the age gap between them made a long-term relationship impossible. John Ford directed the film, treating Kelly and Gardner in the bullish way he did most of his female stars. "Don't you have any goddam instinct, Kelly?" he bawled. "We're doing a movie, not a goddam script!" She took the abuse but Gardner didn't, giving him back the "colorful" words he used on her and adding some more of her own that weren't in the Bible. He preferred this approach, even when she stormed off the set in a rage.[35]

One day after a botched take, Gardner remarked that it was a real "fuck-up." Ford roared back at her, "Oh, you're a director now. You know so fucking much about directing. You're a lousy actress but now you're a director. Well, why don't you direct something? You go sit in my chair and I'll go play your scene."

Gardner found Sinatra equally volatile but what really broke up her marriage to him was his infidelities. She often heard elevator boys in hotels saying things to him like, "Oh, Mr. Sinatra, the last time you were here it was with Miss X," referring to one of his other conquests. "Once you lose your faith in what the man you love is telling you," Gardner reflected, "there's nothing left to save."[36]

This marriage wasn't the only one to go belly-up that year. So also did Marilyn Monroe's to Joe DiMaggio. In this case the catalyst was the famous scene Monroe did in *The Seven Year Itch* where she allowed her dress to billow up around her before a throng of people as the air from a subway vent blew up at her on Lexington Avenue. DiMaggio never recovered from this and a few months later instituted divorce proceedings. Monroe said afterwards of him, "He didn't talk to me. He was cold. He didn't want me to have friends of my own. He watched television instead of talking to me." And in a more general vein, "My marriage to Joe was a sort of friendship with privileges. I found out later that marriages are often no more than this. And that husbands are chiefly good as lovers when they're betraying their wives."

Vivien Leigh's marriage to Laurence Olivier had also started to fall apart. Olivier was losing interest in her as her psychological problems worsened. These necessitated her having electro-convulsive therapy, an experience that numbed her both physically and emotionally. Olivier wasn't empathetic. He moved further and further away from her in her hours of need.

The third marriage to reach crisis point that year was that of Susan Hayward and Jess Barker. Barker could never come to terms with the fact that she was a bigger earner than he was and one night during the summer of 1953 they had a vicious argument. Barker had asked her for a loan of $3,000 to invest in oil shares in Texas and she refused, telling him she wanted a divorce.

He told her he wouldn't give her one "because you're a good meal ticket" and when she became enraged at this, a heated argument started. Barker struck her and she ran from the house into her garden screaming, "Don't kill me!" Barker then threw her into their swimming pool and, according to Hayward, held her head under the water for so long she thought she was going to drown. When he finally let go, she went back into the house and dialed the police.

Barker left the house the following morning and she began divorce proceedings against him. He always insisted he loved her, and that the fight that night was caused by both of them being drunk. They reconciled temporarily but never lived together again. When she told him he'd be getting $100,000 after a "quickie" divorce, he replied, "Is that all?"[37] He tried to claim half of her fortune in the divorce hearing but his ploy failed miserably, resulting in him getting nothing but the family station wagon. The work-shy actor hardly deserved even this. She also imposed a restraining order on him.

Hayward attempted suicide during the filming of *I'll Cry Tomorrow,* distraught over the divorce from Barker and his threats to sue for custody of their twin children. She washed down a handful of sleeping pills with grapefruit juice and gin one night and phoned her mother afterwards. It was probably a cry for help. She didn't tell her what she'd done but ended the call with one of the lines from the movie she was shooting, "Don't worry, Mother, you're taken care of."[38] Her mother rang the police and when they got to her house they found her unconscious on the floor. She was rushed to a hospital in an ambulance and had her stomach pumped. She was in a coma for the next 24 hours, only narrowly escaping death.

Marilyn Monroe would die in similar circumstances some years later. She now appeared in *Gentlemen Prefer Blondes,* playing one of her familiar dumb blond roles, this time the gold-digging Lorelei Lee, a character created by Anita Loos. Loos was a lot more intelligent than she let on, preferring to write tame scripts for fear anything else would disturb the stability of her personal life with men. "I learned very early to keep my mouth shut about my literary life," she said, remembering one beau she dated who "didn't want to believe I was an authoress; it turned me into some sort of monster."[39] A subsequent marriage to John Emerson was equally infelicitous, Emerson often demanding that his name be put on her screenplays as co-author even though he had no hand, act or part in them.[40] Emerson was diagnosed as schizophrenic in 1937 after an incident where he tried to strangle her. He was admitted to a sanitarium, where he spent the last twenty years of his life.[41]

The Lipstick Sex

In 1953, Simone de Beauvoir published *The Second Sex*, a book which became a kind of Bible for women who felt they'd been ground down for too many decades and had finally found an eloquent spokesperson. De Beauvoir saw society's obsession with female glamour as a way of objectifying women and keeping them down. She defined elegance as "bondage."[1] Her language was eccentric but her points struck home. It was time to let the genie out of the bottle, women realized, time to let the spirit soar. Her book was read avidly by women hungry for equality. But Hollywood continued along its merry way of keeping them down, either overtly or covertly.

This was also the year Alfred Kinsey shocked America, if not the world, with his survey of the sexual habits of the country's young women, which threw up the statistic that over half of them had had sex before marriage. And it was the year Hugh Hefner brought out the first edition of *Playboy* magazine, a publication that offered "the pleasures of sex without the burden of family."[2]

Hefner was a failed cartoonist, an *Esquire* copywriter who put his life's savings into the magazine. He didn't even date the first issue, unsure of whether there would be a second. Family values were still sacrosanct at the time and his flouting of these in favor of a culture of loose morals was treading on thin ice. But when he chose Marilyn Monroe as his first centerfold, there was no going back. What hot-blooded man could resist her generous curves, her invitation to men to partake of them? Set against a blood-red backdrop with her left hand stroking her golden curls, she had "nothing on but the radio." The comedian Mort Sahl joked that, as a result of her effrontery, a whole generation of men grew up believing women folded in three places and had staples in their navels.

Hefner's ideas of male and female roles were almost primeval: "The man goes out and kills a saber-toothed tiger while the woman stays at home and washes out the pots." Further, "No sane woman would really want equality." The magazine promoted women as accessories for bachelors who were generally discarded "either when she reaches age 25 or before that if she exhibits any intelligence." The only thing Hefner shared in common with feminists was an approval of the right to abortion. His celebration of women's right

91

to liberal sex wasn't regarded as feminist because *Playboy* usually portrayed it in a way that made women acquiescent to men.

Pornography became "respectable" as a result of *Playboy*. In years to come, models would cavort on the tops of Lamborghinis in bondage gear to make this also respectable, and in tune with the hormonally-charged male's careerist aspirations. With the aid of *Playboy*, men could fantasize about the fact that women who were airbrushed to within an inch of their lives could be theirs for a few dollars. Bachelors with a small amount of disposable income felt suddenly empowered as Miss February looked out at them from the glossy pages, legs apart and wearing nothing but a smile.

Diana Dors was marketed as a British version of Monroe. "I'm paid large sums of money," she crowed, "because my name is linked with mink, fast cars and pink champagne." Did such a wonder of nature need to act as well? The studios thought not and put her in a brace of vehicles designed to increase the blood pressure of male audiences rather than their consciousness. Joan Collins was another British import with the right statistics and the mandatory "Come hither" look. Sometimes referred to as Britain's answer to Ava Gardner, she appeared in edgier material than Dors. Collins was the hard-drinking girlfriend of a boxer in *The Square Ring*, a teenage prostitute in *Turn the Key Softly* and a thug's pregnant girlfriend in *Cosh Boy*. Often billed as "The Coffee Bar Jezebel," her sweaters in these roles were more stretched than her talent. The formula was simple: Beauty plus cleavage equals box office. The ability to act was an optional extra.

At the other end of the scale we had polite girls like Doris Day. Day de-sexualized the film noir blond and made her virginal. Suddenly the shadows of the forties were gone, replaced by day-glo (Day-glo?) colors and pastel shades that fitted an age of staid conformity. To this extent her surname (changed from its original Kappelhoff) was apt: Day had followed night just as family values had replaced the *louche* abandon of her sultry forbears.

She seemed to readily accept her squeaky-clean image even if she tried to parlay it into screwball tomboyism with *Calamity Jane* (1953) or leaven it with straight drama in *Love Me or Leave Me* (1955). In films like these she gave vent to an ebullience sorely lacking from the vapid "sex comedies" she made with Rock Hudson (which weren't all that funny, and had precious little sex). Day was a better actress than she was given credit for, as was evidenced by films like *Love Me or Leave Me*, but she was shoehorned into a plenitude of vapid sitcoms that played into her all-too-easy delivery of bland one-liners.

Don Macpherson summed up her appeal: "Doris Day was one of those fixtures of the American home in the early fifties. Outside was the cruel world of the Korean War and the atomic bomb; inside was an advertisement from *Good Housekeeping* with Doris in the kitchen—blond, bobbed and as pert as a kitten."[3] Because of her sunny disposition and wide-eyed jocundity, any pretensions towards something of more moment was buried under the frothy song-and-dance routines.

Grace Kelly was a much bigger threat to men. Ray Milland fell head over heels for her on the set of Alfred Hitchcock's *Dial M for Murder* in 1954. Milland was married for thirty years at this time but that didn't stop him straying in the past and neither would it now. Kelly was 25 years younger than him. His wife Mal had given him a long leash, knowing only too well that Hollywood wives "had the choice either to look the other way or marry an average guy who worked from nine to five."[4] His affair with Kelly eventually broke up his marriage.

Kelly scooped up an Oscar for her next film, *The Country Girl*, her win making an also-ran out of Judy Garland, who'd played one of the most challenging roles of her career in *A Star Is Born*. Garland played the wife of self-destructive James Mason but in real life it was she herself who was self-destructive, causing Roger Ebert to remark, "The film is about Garland, played by Mason." By now her pill-popping past was showing even more on her face but she worked as hard as ever, even when the film had to be re-shot after a month when it was decided to make it in CinemaScope. Some of the crew walked off the set in anger. Garland didn't but was still blamed for the spiraling budget. "I'm a little tired of being the patsy for the production delays on this film," she groaned, "That was the story of my life at Metro when I was a child actress. When some problem came up and they couldn't lick the delay, it was always blamed on the star. Whoever was responsible figured that the star could get by without a bawling out."[5]

George Cukor, who directed the film, exploited her traumas to "improve" her performance. To this end he reminded her of her "joyless" childhood, her career low points, her disastrous history with men—though yet just thirty, she was already into her third marriage—and her "chronic insecurity."[6] Nobody can guess how much worse these reflections made her feel. All that seemed to matter to him was getting a good movie out.

She was an odds-on favorite to win the Oscar that year but Kelly, the "new kid on the block," stole it from under her nose. Garland was devastated. She was in hospital on the night of the ceremony, having just given birth to her third child, but it seemed more like a funeral than a birth to her after she learned she'd lost out. Her husband tried to console her by saying, "Baby, fuck the Academy Awards, you've got yours in the incubator."[7] It was a sweet thought but the blow hit her too hard for her to be able to think that way. In some sense the film became her valediction to the screen. Afterwards she developed phobias on movie sets. She was probably suffering from post-natal depression but the term hadn't even been coined then. For the rest of her life, with some minor exceptions, she would return to Broadway, her first love, to earn a crust. "The only time I ever felt accepted or wanted," she sighed, "was when I was on stage."[8] The days of plenty were over. From now on she'd be singing for her supper.

In the same year on a different set, the similarly self-destructive Dorothy Dandridge appeared in her best-known film, *Carmen Jones*, becoming a role model for black actresses by landing the coveted role. She had a torrid romance with Otto Preminger, the film's director, during the shoot but his passion for her didn't extend to him showing her any special favors, as he proved when he had her singing voice dubbed by Marilyn Horne. "Don't show kindness," Preminger advised Dandridge, "or people will construe it as weakness." To her, this seemed like jungle law. "What a key to Hollywood success," Dandridge surmised. "What frank self-revelation. Suddenly I realized why many men were at the top of Hollywood and why many women retained and maintained their queen roles. They were tough."[9]

Dandridge welcomed her investiture into the "Ivy League" status of white stars on Hollywood's totem pole but feared her presence there was always going to be temporary, that the fashion for equality might dissipate as suddenly as it appeared. She saw herself as a "white black" woman. "What was I?" she asked at the height of her fame, "Was I too light to satisfy Negroes, [but] not light enough to secure the screen work [and] marriage status available to white women?"

After *Carmen Jones* Dandridge was typecast in this kind of role. She wasn't allowed to spread her wings and by the end of the fifties, as a result, her career was effectively over.

Ida Lupino's career also went downhill in the fifties. This was partly due to the breakdown of her marriage to Collier Young. After they divorced he decided to wind up Filmakers and go into film distribution instead. She disagreed strongly with this decision but she was outvoted. Her view was proved right when the new company failed. "We weren't very wise to step into a field we didn't know too much about," she concluded.[10] Afterwards she went into television for a fraction of her old salary. On the strength of *The Hitch-Hiker* she got work on shows like *Have Gun, Will Travel* and *The Twilight Zone*, shows one would have associated more with men than women. Her fight to avoid genre stereotyping was fought too well because, "I'd always done women's stories and now I couldn't get one." Frank Price, the executive producer of *The Virginian*, eventually came to her rescue, allowing her to inject a "sentimental" element into the series.[11]

Lupino was one of the few to escape the studio straitjacket. Other actresses did what they'd always done, either trying to buck the system or trying to survive within its constraints. Jane Russell appeared in *The French Line* (1954), a dull comedy romance that gave her little opportunity to do much except exhibit her bust in 3D. It was another Howard Hughes production tailored for the same viewers who oohed and aahed

Apart from some brief career highlights like *Carmen Jones*, Dorothy Dandridge failed to make a mark on Hollywood or strike a proper blow for black women in an industry run by white men. Like Susan Hayward, Doris Day and so many others, she fell prey both to the manipulation of men both outside and inside the film business, resulting in an early death that may well have been suicide.

over her in *The Outlaw*. The following year Hughes paraded her breasts yet again, this time in *Underwater!*, to see how they'd look plunging out of a bathing suit. There were no complaints from audiences about them but the film itself, like its two predecessors, went nowhere fast.

Maureen O'Hara's troubled relationship with John Ford reached its nadir that year on the set of *The Long Gray Line*. Ford had been a thorn in her side right through her career, his grudging respect for her acting talent leavened by a tendency to demean her both personally and professionally, probably as a result of a sexual desire for her which he knew he could never realize. Before the shooting of *The Quiet Man* he sent her love letters but he later said of her, "That bitch couldn't act her way out of a brick shithouse."[12]

She put up with him because of his genius but he went too far on the set of *The Long Gray Line*, greeting her each day with revolting comments like, "Did herself have a good shit this morning?"[13] To her brother Charles he referred to her as "that whore sister of yours."[14] He had another brother of hers, Jimmy, put in jail in Mexico on a trumped-up charge of smuggling jewelry. When his sexual frustration reached a peak, he took to drawing penises on a piece of paper in front of her as another means of harassment. He also broke into her house one day and stole a number of her records, for reasons best known to himself.

O'Hara was instrumental in the closure of *Confidential* the following year when she sued the magazine after it published a story alleging that she flirted with a "south of the border sweetie" while married to Will Price. *Confidential* also alleged that Marlene Dietrich "played both sides of the street" in her affections, accusing her of having had gay relationships with Claire Waldoff, Mercedes d'Acosta, Jo Carstairs and a Parisian lesbian called Frede. A few months later, in another issue of the magazine, Lizabeth Scott was tarred with the same brush.

Today it may appear trendy for actresses like Anne Heche to veer from men to women but in 1955 there was a certain notoriety attaching itself to being part of Hollywood's "sewing circle," as stars like Greta Garbo and Katharine Hepburn well knew. The fact that Scott wasn't married, and hadn't especially been noted for her dalliances with men, further fed the gossip mills. *Confidential* also claimed that the police had found her name in a call girl's book of clients. This took the story in a different direction, and Scott didn't help matters by saying that she liked wearing male cologne and sleeping in men's pajamas—though she never openly professed herself to be gay.[15]

Confidential had plans to "out" Rock Hudson at this time but its editor, Robert Harrison, held back on this. To protect his image, Hudson married Phyllis Gates, the secretary of his agent Henry Willson. Willson was gay and had been one of Hudson's former lovers.

Gates thought he loved her and was naive enough never to suspect he was gay throughout their marriage even though there were many warning signs. After the wedding he refused to wear a ring, claiming it would be awkward having to keep removing it for movie roles. After they exchanged vows, Gates wanted to call her mother to tell her the news (they'd held a secret ceremony to avoid a media storm) but Willson went, "Oh no, you've got to call Hedda [Hopper] and Louella [Parsons] first. They'll still have time to make the home editions."[16] She could hardly have asked for a clearer indication of the reason for the marriage.

Hudson dominated Gates right through their married life, playing the media game with the "sob sisters" who photographed them in their so-called married bliss. Behind the scenes Hudson told Gates to give nothing away about her private misery. "If Hedda or Louella or Sheilah [Graham] come up to you at a party," he warned, "be polite but don't say anything. Talk about the weather or clothes or anything. But don't give them anything they can quote."[17]

Hudson himself fed such columnists the soundbites they craved, gushing, "Now that I have Phyllis to share life with, I'll never have to experience that bottomless pit of loneliness again. It's a very comfortable feeling." Such "comfort" was fortified by the fact that he had everything his way. He even demanded she leave her agenting job as soon as they married: "I wouldn't let her do anything outside [the home] even if she wanted to. When I got married it was my idea to have a home and a wife [in that] home."[18] The fact that such sentiments were accepted by the public was a testament not only to Hudson's boorishness but an era where women's second class status was accepted without a by-your-leave.

Hudson also had a violent streak. One time when the pair of them were on vacation in Italy they fell into the company of an Italian man to whom Hudson seemed to be attracted. When Gates referred to him as "a fruitcake," Hudson struck her across the face. After he did so, she remembered a previous incident where he'd put his hands around her neck and started to choke her after an argument they'd had. "I could kill somebody sometime," he said to her. "I have an uncontrollable temper."[19]

Hudson's friend Tony Curtis espoused similar attitudes to the "little ladies" of his ken. In August 1955 he wrote an article in *Photoplay* in which he purported to give advice to women (whom he referred to as "the lipstick sex") about how to treat the men in their life. If such an article were written today it would be laughed at, its sexual politics somewhere to the right of Genghis Khan. But at the time it was par for the course.

Entitled "Be a Doll for a Guy," it started off by stating that all women were alike. "They want to marry, to run a home and to have children. For this reason, it's much simpler for a girl to find a satisfactory mate than it is for a man." Men, on the contrary, were competitive. They wanted to travel, to accomplish things, to be successful. This was born out by the "traditional family story of the son who goes off to make his fortune while his sister stays at home, looks after the parents, marries and has her own family.[20]

So men went out to jobs and women stayed at home minding the babies and running the house. (Considering Curtis was married to Janet Leigh, who'd had a more thriving career than himself when he met her, this was an amazing precept.) However, "Some jobs don't permit a guy to make his own decisions so it's doubly important for him to have some authority in his home." In other words, if the boss kicks him around in the office, he has to come home and, as it were, kick the wife around to maintain his authority.

If a girl was beautiful, Curtis continued, she should accept the fact that this was just an accident of birth and not think it gave her any special entitlements with men. It wasn't only plain girls who had to be nice to men to "get" them; beautiful ones should also be.

If a boy rejected a girl, she shouldn't act the martyr or drool, rather just accept that it was in the nature of things, men being men. The notion that a man could love his sweetheart forever was a myth "fostered by novels which bring the old boyfriend back on the scene after twenty years in Africa—still unmarried, still infatuated."[21]

If a "doll" was lucky enough to be marched up the aisle by the man in her life, Curtis continued, she had to submit to his desires. He "allowed" her to spend afternoons with her friends but nights had to be reserved for her knight in shining armor. When it came to money, the husband should have the "controlling vote" because he was the guy who had to go out and "pop" for it. Curtis wrote this at a time when he was putting pressure on Leigh to give up her career, or work only with him.

It may amuse us to read sentiments like this today, and we know that Curtis was indeed a loving husband to Leigh, even if that love didn't last forever. He came from an era when sexist ideas were in vogue but it's still something of a shock for us to see them being trotted out here so blatantly like something from a woman's country club catalog of the thirties. Had he not heard of the suffragettes? An even more disturbing fact is that nobody thought to complain about the article, or see anything untoward in it.

Speaking of "dolls," Elia Kazan directed *Baby Doll* that year, and got much heat as a result. Carroll Baker played the title role. She became famous, or rather infamous, overnight while Kazan tried to fight off the censors who saw her premature sexualization as heralding the end of civilization as we knew it. Carol Dyhouse put her finger on the nub of the issue: Little girls were less scary to men than adult women and thereby more easily objectified and repressed. "Baby dolls," as a result, "segued into the image of the 1960s 'dollybird,' undercutting any assertiveness associated with women's role in the 'youthquake' of the decade."[22]

The fact that the film wasn't very good was forgotten in all the brouhaha surrounding it, as could have been said of *The Outlaw* some years before. Here the robust sensuality of Jane Russell was replaced by the Lolita-like sultriness of Baker as the thumb-sucking child-woman of the Deep South. She found it difficult to outgrow the role in later years despite giving solid "character" performances in *Giant* and *The Big Country*. She felt *Baby Doll* ruined whatever chances she might have had of diversifying herself in movies. "I'm still called Baby Doll," she said in her later years. "It's like my middle name. I wouldn't mind so much if, like Marlene Dietrich, it had been the Blue Angel or something." The sobriquet became even more disquieting when she attained grandmother status: "If I take my little grandson somewhere and they call me Baby Doll, I'm not going to like that very much."[23]

Apart from career frustrations, Baker also had a troubled private life to contend with. She was raped by her first husband and sexually molested by Jack Warner and another producer, Joseph Levine, suffering two nervous breakdowns as a result. To regain her health she had to distance herself from her acting. "The more I exposed myself," she revealed, "the more I turned off personally. That flagrant, unnatural whorishness I was [portraying] seemed to harden my own state of frigidity." Such qualities were on display in films like *Something Wild* and the biopic *Harlow*. It bled off the screen to such an extent that when she made *Mister Moses* in 1965, an African Masai chief reportedly offered to buy her for 150 cows, 200 goats ... and $750.[24]

Kim Novak was another star who strained at the leash to be seen as something more than eye candy. Critics scoffed at her when she first came into movies, making fun of her "smoky" voice, her "expressionless" eyes, her apparent obliviousness to what was going on around her. In retrospect maybe we should see this as an attempt on her part to underact. Maybe she was trying so hard not to fall into the "over-the-top" trap of stars like Diana Dors that she did too little.

Novak's real name was Marilyn. Obviously this couldn't be retained because of Marilyn Monroe but she fought hard to keep the Novak. She was marketed as a second-string Monroe, as was evidenced by an exchange between Harry Cohn and Jerry Wald after her initial screen test. "I can't hear what she's saying," Cohn complained, whereupon Wald remarked, "Don't listen. Just look."[25]

As a model she was Miss Deep Freeze, and when Kim Novak became an actress she carried that *noli me tangere* appeal to her screen performances as well. She endured rough treatment under directors like Joshua Logan and studio bosses like Harry Cohn but she never let Hollywood beat her, right up to the Oscar ceremonies of 2014 where, in her eighties, she railed against the bullies who denied her the right to use Botox to improve her appearance.

Cohn made it his business to dominate Novak from the outset, anxious not to allow her the same amount of leeway he'd given Rita Hayworth. For starters he insisted she live at the Studio Club, a YWCA-sponsored rooming house for young actresses where there was a curfew in force, much like a college dorm. When she gained weight here he bound her to a strict diet. Her social life was also strictly monitored. She was only allowed to date at weekends, a guard being placed outside the door of the Club to ensure she didn't try to sneak out. He addressed her as "Novak," often referring to her as "that fat Polack."[26]

She got her breakthrough role in *Picnic* (1955) opposite William Holden. Joshua Logan, the film's director, had objected to her being in it. He hadn't much confidence in her range, exhorting a co-star in a test scene to "Get some emotion from her any way you can, short of rape." She was so terrified of Logan she refused to come out of her dressing room one day, causing him to storm in and physically drag her out. "Now, goddamit, you act!" he roared at her.[27] He also insisted on souping up her sensuality—as if this could be avoided. As he put it himself, "Trying to hide what she's got would be like trying to hide an elephant in a phone booth."[28]

"I get tired of just being told I'm pretty," Novak complained in one scene, and the comment might have also been applied to her life outside movies. She started her modeling career as Miss Deep Freeze and went on to reprise that image in a number of films that played up those *noli me tangere* qualities she possessed in such abundance.

Rosalind Russell played a small but significant role in *Picnic* as a schoolteacher worried about becoming an old maid. Afterwards she had problems with salary and billing. When she told her agent she wanted bigger and better roles, he shot back, "What do you mean you want such-and-such? You just played a third-rate part."[29] This was a blinkered attitude as the character she played in the film was superior to many other ones who might have had more lines. But that was the way the business worked. To get her salary back to where it had been before *Picnic*, she had to do *Auntie Mame* on Broadway, a role that was like "falling off a log" for her in comparison to the challenge of this one.[30]

Later that year Harry Cohn loaned Novak out to make *The Man with the Golden Arm*, a deal that netted him $100,000, none of which went to her. She was earning $750 a week at this time. When she shot *Jeanne Eagels* the following year she was only given $15,000 for making the movie. After she found out that her co-star Jeff Chandler was getting $200,000, she was livid. She threatened to walk off the picture if she didn't get a raise but Cohn refused to budge. He put her on suspension but she then found a new agent who forced Cohn into a salary hike for her. "You had to fight him every inch of the way," she said.

Novak started dating Sammy Davis, Jr., at the end of the year. Cohn blew a fuse because of Davis' color, telling her the relationship could kill her career in the blink of an eye. Novak refused to break it off with Davis, and Cohn ended up getting a heart attack.

James Bacon saw Novak's relationship with Davis as being a conscious act of rebellion against Cohn's cruelty: "She always said he treated her like a piece of meat." Davis was rebelling too—against the prevalent racism of the time. As a result of their forbidden love they became co-conspirators, drawn together, as Davis put it, "by the single thing we had in common: defiance." Novak agreed, saying, "I was a gentile raised in a Jewish neighborhood, always being shoved in the snow or having rotten pies pushed in my face, so I identified with him as a minority."[31]

When *Confidential* got hold of the Novak-Davis story, Cohn realized it was time to act or else he might lose his precious star. He's alleged to have had some gangsters drive Davis into the desert one night and threaten to blind him if he didn't stop seeing Novak. For her sake as well as his own, Davis agreed to this. To deflect the attention from Novak, Davis was encouraged to marry another black person, Loray White, in a quickie ceremony and then divorce her. He did this, going on to marry the Swedish actress Mai Britt. (Britt was white but not as high-profile as Novak so this was "permissible.")

Novak was listed as the top female star in Hollywood by *Box Office* in 1956 but Cohn took the credit for this, insisting that her success was due to the films she was in rather than anything she herself brought to them. "Any girl who gets six pictures like Novak got has got to be a star," he bleated. This was to misread the situation. It was no more a representation of the true picture than Josef von Sternberg's allegation that he "was" Marlene Dietrich some decades before. In the same way, Cohn liked to think that he was the brains behind Novak. But as Danny Peary rightly remarked, "No one invented Kim Novak but Kim Novak." When her films failed she was blamed for the lapse but when they were hits Cohn took a bow.[32] Irene Dunne had a similar experience, as we saw. Indeed, David O. Selznick claimed the same "ownership" of Jennifer Jones. It was as if his wife was, in the words of Bill Horrigan, "little more than a photogenic mannequin around whom the proud husband could mount expensive productions."[33]

Marilyn Monroe watched Novak's career (and private life) unfold with interest. She too had an excess of "advisors" telling her who she should and shouldn't date and what movies she should and shouldn't make. The pair didn't quite become friends—there was too much rivalry for that—but they empathized with the way each of their careers were managed … and mismanaged.

When Monroe married Arthur Miller in 1956, it was dubbed the union of Hour-Glass and Egghead. Everything had to be encapsulated in such shorthand. There could be no middle ground, no emotional vulnerability on his part or intellectual pretensions on hers. The question remained: Could an industry that created her as a cheesecake accommodate her latter incursion into things literary? Hardly. Even less digestible was her announcement that she wanted to play Grushenka in *The Brothers Karamazov*. How could someone who posed for *Playboy* have such gall? The only way it could be achieved, according to one wit, was if the "Brothers" were played by Groucho, Harpo and Chico.[34]

Few were inclined to take Monroe's intellectual ambitions seriously. If she was spotted carrying a heavy volume of European verse under her arm, her colleagues sniggered. One evening during a conversation, she dropped the name Abraham Lincoln and one of the people in the company went, "My God, she's met everyone!"[35]

"In Hollywood they never ask me my opinion," Monroe grunted, "They just tell me what time to come to work."[36]

Miller arrogantly thought he could "save" Monroe, either from herself or the system that was crippling her, but he didn't have much time for her mind, speaking of her as a casual acquaintance rather than an intimate. "I don't know how to talk to her," he complained, "but I find her overwhelmingly attractive."[37] As though that made up for it.

In *Bus Stop* Monroe gave one of her more "mature" performances, but there were so many preconceptions of her as the dizzy blond by now that few noticed. After the movie wrapped, she met Indonesia's President Sukarno in L.A. at her 30th birthday party. She'd heard he was a great admirer of hers and after she met him she realized why. "He couldn't stop looking down my dress," she recalled with amusement. "You'd think with five wives he'd have enough." Apparently he hadn't.

Monroe was already tiring of Hollywood and would soon snap as a result of its pressures. Gene Tierney was at this stage already, though for different reasons. The strain of her broken marriage and her handicapped daughter was so bad, she couldn't conceal it any more. When she made *The Left Hand of God* in 1954 she found even the simplest scenes a struggle.

Her co-star, Humphrey Bogart, helped her through her duress but after the film wrapped she refused further contracts, knowing she wouldn't be able to do justice to them. The studio failed to understand her problem and suspended her. The media were also cruel, plaguing her with phone calls. One night as she sat in a nightclub, a reporter spotted her putting her gloves on and taking them off repeatedly for no reason like somebody in a psychiatric ward. He wrote about the incident in a New York newspaper, thereby bringing her distress into the public arena. This had negative repercussions both for her mindset and career.[38]

The Left Hand of God was the last film Tierney made for seven years. "My departure from Hollywood was described as a walk-out," she said. "Nobody realized I was cracking up." She had no trouble playing movie characters, she claimed: "When I had to be myself my problems began."[39]

Gene Tierney's career—and life—were blighted by the fact of her having a disabled daughter. She fought bravely against the psychological problems this caused, but few in the film industry were empathetic to her plight or did enough to rehabilitate her.

She signed herself into a sanitarium in 1956 and spent the next three years battling her demons. Like Frances Farmer a decade or so earlier, she received diagnoses that were often rudimentary. She was also, again like Farmer, the recipient of multiple electric shock treatments which did her much more harm than good. She suffered headaches and vomiting bouts from it and also partial amnesia so whatever short-term relief she gained from it was more than outweighed by the side effects.

In one of the sanitariums in which she was confined, the Institute for Living in Hartford, Connecticut, she was placed in a locked room no bigger than a prison cell and with bars on the windows. Michelle Vogel painted a grim picture of this supposedly rehabilitative center in her biography of Tierney:

> She could only manage to get one finger underneath the window and raise it not more than an inch without the confines of the bar stopping it from going any further. It was the middle of winter, icy cold outside and blazing with artificial heat inside.

Gene's claustrophobic feelings of being locked in were making her even hotter. She would sit huddled by the window, lifting it to its one-inch limit as she sucked in as much of the cool air from the outside as she possibly could.[40]

Anyone viewing the world of films from the sidelines could have been forgiven for thinking that the whole glorified edifice was beginning to crumble. Grace Kelly even deserted it: She left Hollywood in 1956 to marry Prince Rainier of Monaco. His princely domain became more like a prison than a haven to her in her later years when she was prohibited from making a return to Hollywood by royal decree. It was perhaps naive of her to imagine she could combine the two lifestyles but those who met her in later years sensed a longing in her for the heady energy of the world she left behind, even if she was loath to admit this. Instead she constructed a bubble of diplomacy around herself to camouflage a lonely heart.

She fell in love with Rainier, and he seemed to love her too, but there was a political motive behind the wedding because Monaco was in dire financial straits at the time. His requirements for his princely bride also seemed far from passionate: She had to be able to cook, to arrange flowers, and to set a "beautiful" dinner table. Kelly was tired of the glitz of Hollywood but was the bland luxury of Monaco any better? Rainier wouldn't allow any screenings of her films in the palace and also forbade palace visitors to take photographs or even ask for her autograph.

Before she went to the altar with him, *The Chicago Tribune* wrote: "She's too well bred to marry the silent partner in a gambling parlor." After the marriage started to spring a leak, Trevor Howard was even more blunt in his assessment of it: "Grace thought that by leaving Hollywood to become the wife of a fat prince in a tiny country owned by France she would find some greater destiny. Instead it was the beginning of the end for her."

Changing of the Guard

As was so often the case in the world of films, when one beauty queen departed the scene, another one took her place. From the moment Brigitte Bardot appeared in *And God Created Woman* in 1957, one was aware of an almost electrical charge hitting film theaters.

Bardot had a different attitude toward life than most American actresses of the time, and a different attitude toward men. "I wasn't made to live with just one man," she announced, "I'm a girl who must be allowed to do as she pleases." Hollywood sat up and took note of this brazen hussy from France who had the audacity to set her own agenda, blurring the divide between eroticism and seduction with pouty arrogance. She was a new kind of sex symbol, one more disdainful than Monroe but also more inflammatory. For the next ten years in greater or lesser degrees, men would undress her with their eyes, their attention glued to the screen even when her films failed to hit the target.

Monroe appeared in *The Prince* and *the Showgirl*, a regal comedy set in England and featuring her opposite Laurence Olivier, who also directed the film. Olivier was infuriated by her wide-eyed expressions, her lateness on set, her "blowing" of lines. He saw all this as a diva-like determination on her part to upstage him. A man who was always theatrical even in his films, he didn't seem to understand that she was playing to the camera rather than to the gallery here, which meant that in the finished performance she looked much more at home than he, despite (or because of) his august credentials. Teaching her how to act, he claimed, was "like teaching Urdu to a marmoset.[1] But he shouldn't have tried. She knew much more about it than he did from an instinctive point of view. She also matched him for repartee. One day when she was late on set, he snorted, "Why can't you get here on time, for fuck's sake?" She replied, "Oh, do you have that word in England too?"[2]

Who else but Monroe did Hollywood have to preserve itself against the European challenge of Bardot, or the British one of Diana Dors? Jayne Mansfield was being groomed to bring up the rear, as was Mamie Van Doren. Dors appeared in *The Unholy Wife* in 1957 and *I Married a Woman* the following year. Her co-stars in the films were Rod Steiger and George Gobel respectively and she was unhappy with both of them. "I should have had

Bill Holden or Cary Grant," she announced. "I had to carry the whole burden myself and the pictures fizzled out [as a result]. I was a sex bomb all right, with the accent on 'bomb.'"[3]

Van Doren had only one line in Josef von Sternberg's aviation drama *Jet Pilot* (made in 1950, released in 1957). Or rather one word, "Look!" This seemed to sum up how Howard Hughes, the film's producer, felt about her. Van Doren moved from RKO to Universal with this parting salvo: "I don't think the studio executives [at RKO] quite knew what to do with a blossoming young sexy actress. They were really [just] dedicated to exploitation. I had great aspirations as an actress but when they looked at me they saw the blond hair and they made me into a dumb blond." One day Hughes asked her if she was a virgin. Van Doren had a good answer for him: "You'll never know." Others weren't as brave because they knew they had too much to lose.

Hughes was now married to Jean Peters. It was one of the strangest marriages in film history, not only on account of his phobias about health and hygiene but also because of the iron grip he kept on her life. His paranoid control of her meant that he didn't even allow her to go shopping. She wanted to have a child by him, which may have been her main reason for marrying him. But he'd had a vasectomy two years previously, something he concealed from her before the marriage. She divorced him in 1970, not having seen him for over three years before that.[4]

Brigitte Bardot brought a saucier form of sex appeal to the screen than her Hollywood counterparts. She also knew when to walk away from movies when the time came, exchanging "the cruelty of men," as she put it, for "the love of animals."

Jayne Mansfield appeared in *The Girl Can't Help It* in 1956, her performance imitative not only of Marilyn Monroe's breathy voice but also her hoochy-coochy walk. In the same year, though, she appeared in a film which made one think that if she hadn't been marketed so crassly as a second string Monroe she might have had some chance as a serious actress: *The Wayward Bus*, based on the John Steinbeck novel of the same name. While it struck the wrong note in many scenes, it was a welcome relief from her other work, where she spent most of her time shoving her breasts in people's faces.

Apart from *The Girl Can't Help It*, today Mansfield is most noted for *Will Success Spoil Rock Hunter?* The latter film went on to develop a certain cult appeal thanks to her lubricious charms but even by their own standards neither of them seem much up the ladder from locker-room humor about women. Mansfield colluded in her packaging. "How can I put it?" she asked, "Two girls put on a dress. One girl will look just like a pencil, the other like a highway. With my kind of figure it's difficult not to look like a road."[5]

According to Martha Saxton, she suffered from having a 40-inch bust. "There was nothing else she could be but sexy," Saxton contended, "and there was no way anyone could respond to her but sexually. She was at the mercy of men's approval. She suffered from a host of cultural myths about weak, childish men needing strong, powerful women. The older Jayne got, the younger she dressed and talked, as if only through infantilism could she be treated like a real woman."[6]

Hollywood's obsession with breasts continued with Sophia Loren, who co-starred with Alan Ladd in *Boy on a Dolphin*. She played a skindiver (emphasis on the "skin") and director Jean Negulesco missed few opportunities to exhibit them suitably moistened. Ladd was uncomfortable with her towering over him, though, telling people that acting with her was "like being bombed by watermelons."

Joan Collins was partnered with Richard Burton in another nautical venture of the time, *Sea Wife*. She played a survivor of a torpedoed ship. He pursues her romantically, unaware she's a nun. He pursued her off-camera as well. When she spurned his advances, he turned to various other members of the set to add to his boudoir scalps. "Richard," she said to him one day, amazed at his insatiable sexual appetite, "I do believe you'd screw a snake if you had the chance." He replied, "Only if it was wearing a skirt, darling. It would have to be a female snake."[7]

In the summer of that year, a number of stars including Lizabeth Scott and Dorothy Dandridge sued the scandal sheet *Confidential* for trashing their reputations with lurid tales about their private lives. The Dandridge story claimed she allowed herself be seduced by a white musician in the woods behind a Nevada resort. She won a settlement of $10,000. Scott had also been defamed in the magazine, as already mentioned. She starred in *Loving You* that year as Elvis Presley's press agent but her career was slowing down and the film was very obviously a Presley vehicle. The fact that she was twelve years older than him didn't help, especially when romance intervened in their relationship. (A 34-year-old man with a 22-year-old woman wouldn't have been a problem.) Though still a relatively young woman, she saw the writing on the wall. From now on, all she would probably be offered would be "character" parts. Even in her prime she was never given leverage to expand, all too often cast as a homewrecker or murderer, a low-rent Lauren Bacall.

Unlike Barbara Stanwyck, Bette Davis and others who moved to television after their film careers dried up, Scott decided to call it a day after *Loving You*. "There comes a time," she said, "when living in the limelight, the impersonalization of your personality, becomes so offensive that you finally say, 'I've had it.'"[8] She made just one more film years after *Loving You*, the third-grade *Pulp* (1972), but by now she was, like Norma Desmond, waving to a parade that had long passed her by.

Scott was sad to hear of the death of Humphrey Bogart that year, having enjoyed working with him in *Dead Reckoning* in 1947. Bogart's fame extended well beyond his death. The hardbitten hero who came out with statements like, "I never met a dame who didn't understand a slap in the mouth," even became a sex symbol, the "dames" apparently forgiving him for his occasionally boorish lapses. The downside of his posthumous fame was that it had an adverse effect on Lauren Bacall, whose career up to now had been well-nigh inextricable from his.

"Being a widow is not a profession," she argued, but she found it difficult to outgrow the persona she developed under Bogart, that of the self-composed woman with her eyes cast downward, giving off the signal that she was happy with her own company but could possibly be won over if the right man came along. "If you want anything, just whistle," she'd advised him early on. He was good at doing that but in his absence she found it difficult to convince people she wasn't as confident as she made out on screen.

"I've had that problem all my life," she told chat show host Michael Parkinson. "I'm looked upon as a woman who's in total control of every situation." Because she'd lived so long in the public eye, everyone felt they knew her better than she knew herself. "It's very tough to walk into a room," she told Parkinson, "and have someone decide what you're all about."[9]

Bacall started seeing Frank Sinatra after Bogart died. They even became unofficially engaged to be married but when she leaked this to the press he called it off. She was devastated at his reaction, seeing her disclosure as little more than a minor infraction—Sinatra would do the same to Juliet Prowse a few years later. But as time elapsed, she began to see the upside of being dumped by the Chairman of the Board. "Frank did me a great favor," she concluded. "He saved me from the disaster our marriage would have been. But the truth is that he also behaved like a complete shit."[10] To protect others from being stung like she was, she issued this general piece of advice to stellar widows: "Don't sell the house ... and don't sleep with Frank Sinatra."[11]

Sinatra had settled into a tame movie niche by now. In 1957 he played a nightclub singer with ambitions to run his own club in *Pal Joey*. The film teamed him with Rita Hayworth and the actress whom Harry Cohn had groomed to replace her, Kim Novak. The cruelty of putting them together was typical Cohn. Hayworth accepted the role of the older woman graciously but it can't have been much fun gazing at her heir(ess) apparent each morning on the set, looking that much fresher, that much younger, that much more in demand.

Hayworth also made *Fire Down Below* that year. Ava Gardner was the first choice of director Robert Parrish but when he couldn't get her he settled for Hayworth. One day shortly after shooting began she was sitting near a cameraman who was taking an inordinately long time to set up a scene. One of the producers passed by, not realizing she was within earshot. "Why the hell are you taking so long?" he roared at the cameraman, "No matter how long you take, she ain't gonna look any younger." Hayworth was so upset at the jibe that she ran to her dressing room in tears.[12]

Some of the lines in the script seemed to have an ironic relevance for Hayworth herself, as when she tells co-star Robert Mitchum, "I'm all worn out. I've been passed from hand to hand. I've lived among the ruins. Armies have marched over me."

After shooting was completed she became dejected about the way she was branded by the moguls up to now: "They put you into pigeonholes. They see you as who you were, and that's it.... I'm not an old star. I'm an actress."[13] Maybe in her own mind she was but in the eyes of those with cash register brains she was a product that was fast approaching the Last Chance Saloon.

Hayworth had one last great part to play: Delbert Mann's *Separate Tables* (1958) had her as the world-weary ex-wife of Burt Lancaster and gave her an opportunity to do some real acting rather than simply charming her way into men's hearts. It also introduced her to her fifth husband, the producer Jim Hill. Buoyed by the film's success, she went back to Columbia in search of similar types of roles but unfortunately she couldn't find any.

She made mediocre films like Columbia's *They Came to Cordura* and Fox's *The Story on Page One* as the marriage with Hill went the same way as all the rest.

Every time she married, it was with a newfound hope, the victory of optimism over experience, but her marriage to Hill was the unhappiest of all: "He would come in, go straight to his room and wouldn't even talk to me all night." When she was preparing for her divorce, her lawyer asked her if she could remember what day she married him. She replied, "I can't even remember what *year*."[14] In a different context, after being asked how many husbands a career woman should have, she was equally witty with her interlocutor: "At least six, I would imagine," she informed him, "but it's difficult for me to say since seventeen has always been my lucky number."[15]

As Hayworth sailed into the sunset, another new star was being born. Otto Preminger picked Jean Seberg from hundreds of young stars who'd auditioned for the part of Joan of Arc in his forthcoming movie on the life of the saint. His choice was surprising considering he didn't seem to like her very much. When he first tested her

Jean Seberg underwent cruel treatment at the hands of Otto Preminger, who directed her in *Saint Joan* (1957), pictured here, and her life ended tragically after a series of persecutions by the media.

for the role, he insulted her: "You're a ham and a phony. You can't act and you will never be able to."

Shooting of the film started in London in January 1957. Both of them were staying in the Dorchester Hotel, Preminger occupying an apartment directly above Seberg's. He exerted an almost military style control over her, supervising what she wore, what she ate and even what she said. He told her what time to get up in the morning and what time to go to bed at night. He was an ersatz father figure who alternated between bouts of affection (these seemed mainly designed for the press) and temperamental outbursts. Seberg described him as "the world's most charming dinner guest and the world's most sadistic director."[16]

He admitted he gave Seberg a hard time on the movie. "I didn't help her to understand and act the part," he admitted, "Indeed I deliberately prevented her, because I was determined she should be completely unspoilt."[17] His quasi–Method logic was uncharacteristic. (It was also misplaced, as one would have had to search far and wide to find somebody as "unspoilt" as Seberg was then.)

His mistreatment of her reached a crescendo during the scene where the saint was burned at the stake: The flames of the fire actually scorched her and caused her to scream out in pain. Was Preminger in search of realism or simply a way to assert his authority over the callow young star? Perhaps a bit of both. Her hair was singed and her fingers blistered. He eventually shouted "Cut" and she was placed on a stretcher and covered with a blanket. "I smell like a burnt chicken," she told people standing by.[18] Preminger put it all down to a bad accident—an air bubble had caused it, he insisted—but those who'd witnessed his aggressive attitude to her up until this had their doubts. For all concerned it was an experience best forgotten. "I was a better actress the first day I auditioned for Otto Preminger than all the time we worked together," was Seberg's eventual summation of it.[19]

To add insult to injury, reviewers lacerated it. Said Seberg afterwards, "I have two memories of *Saint Joan*. The first was being burned at the stake in the picture. The second was being burned at the stake by the critics."[20] Considering the way she'd been abused by its director, how did she gird her loins to return to the scene of the crime with *Bonjour Tristesse*, another Preminger offering, the following year? A sense of masochism seemed to be the only explanation.

He obviously hadn't mellowed in the interim. For a scene which called on her to look like she'd been swimming, he had one of his assistants to pour buckets of water repeatedly over her head as he insisted on interminable retakes. What came to be known as the "torture by water" scene was accompanied by his repeated demands for her to smile as she was being doused. In the words of Preminger's biographer, the call to smile was so fierce it was more akin to a request for her to "cut her throat."[21]

A different kind of liquid torture was practiced that year by Alfred Hitchcock when he made Kim Novak jump into the freezing waters of San Francisco Bay over and over again to get the "right" suicide shot of her character in *Vertigo*. In future years Hitchcock would demonstrate even worse cruelty towards another actress, Tippi Hedren. Commentators have speculated that much of this was down to frustration over the fact that he couldn't persuade his prime heroine, Grace Kelly—whom he now referred to as "Princess Disgrace"—to make a screen comeback.

Susan Hayward won an Oscar for *I Want to Live!* in 1958, gushing afterwards, "I finally climbed on top of the dung heap,"—a testament to her own fighting skills and the venality of a business she both loved and hated. As often happened with Oscar winners, her career went downhill afterwards with clunkers like *Woman Obsessed* and *Thunder in the Sun*. She felt her days of glory were numbered but she was philosophical about it: "I don't miss Hollywood at all, not even my psychiatrist."[22]

Her attitude wasn't surprising. The business had been hard on her, and merciless when she was below par. Also, Howard Hughes had recently paid Darryl F. Zanuck $1 million to lend her to him for his overblown epic *The Conqueror*, featuring John Wayne in one of his most embarrassing roles as Genghis Khan. Hayward hated the movie. She begged Zanuck to release her from it but her pleas fell on deaf ears. He threatened her with suspension if she refused to do it. Because she was going through a divorce, she needed the money, so she gritted her teeth and went ahead with it. When she died of cancer some years later, people speculated that the location of the film (near a nuclear weapons testing site) could have been a contributory factor to her contracting the disease. Many other cast and crew members who worked on it, including Wayne, would also succumb to cancer.

David Niven won the Best Actor Oscar that year for *Separate Tables*, denying, among others, Paul Newman for *Cat on a Hot Tin Roof*. Newman was believed to be disgruntled that his wife Joanne Woodward had beaten him to the award, having won it the previous year for *The Three Faces of Eve*. Newman and Woodward married in 1958 and theirs became one of the few star marriages that went the distance in a town notorious for marital splits.

Newman liked to say, "Why fool around with hamburger when you can have steak at home?"[23] He imagined that placed Woodward on some sort of pedestal but her (entirely justifiable) reaction was, "I don't like being compared to Paul Newman's meat." She may not have liked it but it seemed to be a genetic weakness of men to see women in this light. What made matters worse was the number of them who didn't seem to see anything wrong with it.

Gina Lollobrigida appeared to happily inhabit the "sex object" box. She flaunted her curved eyelashes and gravity-defying figure in films like *Fast and Sexy* (1958) and *Go Naked in the World* (1960), the very titles indicative of the manner in which the former model seemed to have foregone any ambitions to be a "serious" actress. One always felt her only chance to dovetail her sexual appeal with material of some quality would have been in her native Italy. In the sixties she became even more frothy, but nobody was complaining, least of all the male voyeurs who salivated in the aisles.

The exploitative director Russ Meyer made *The Immoral Mr. Teas* in 1959 and it became something of a *succès de scandale*. He followed it up with a string of pornographic offerings, the titles of which were self-explanatory: *Eroticon, Europe in the Raw*, etc. Many of them featured women as sexual aggressors and men as their helpless victims. Most had scenes of sex in outrageous places—in canoes, up trees, behind waterfalls, etc. Meyer liked to say, "If I can't have a lady with big tits, I'd rather play cards."[24] He found an unlikely advocate in Roger Ebert. Ebert displayed an uncharacteristic lack of judgment by agreeing to co-author *Beyond the Valley of the Dolls* with Meyer in 1970. This was a film which would probably have been discarded with Meyer's other offerings some years before but now the boundaries between underground and mainstream were being whittled away, for better and/or for worse. Worse because films of bad taste were given prominence; better because many of the old taboo topics were now common currency.

Which was *Room at the Top,* one wondered? It was a brilliantly made film but it fed into many of the stereotypes about the battle between the sexes that one hoped had long been laid to rest by now. It was described as one of the "Angry Young Men" films of the time but maybe "Pregnant Young Woman" might have been a more appropriate term. Pregnant unmarried women seemed to be the central plot plank of so many kitchen sink dramas of this period, especially British ones like *A Kind of Loving* and *Saturday Night and Sunday Morning.* All too many of them seemed to revolve around the fact that the woman in question was "up the suff." She had a "bun in the oven" outside wedlock and the man in her life had to be dragged kicking and screaming to the altar or else "have something done about it"—the film world's euphemism for an abortion.

Room at the Top was different from other "problem movies" in the sense that it wasn't so much about sex as careerism. It was, however, guilty of sexism in the way it treated Laurence Harvey's romance with "cougar" Simone Signoret. Signoret was allowed to be free with her sexuality because she was European and therefore liberated but she also had to die at the end of the film so Harvey could marry his English rose, the bosses' daughter, and climb the corporate ladder.

Richard Burton made the epitomic "Angry Young Man" movie in *Look Back in Anger,* co-starring his old friend and lover Claire Bloom. She still carried a torch for him but whatever hopes she may have had of rekindling their romance were dashed when she walked into his dressing-room one day and found him making love to Susan Strasberg. Burton was also sleeping with another member of the cast, Mary Ure, at this time, while still being married to his first wife Sybil. Bloom felt totally humiliated.

Sybil always feared Bloom would end her marriage to Burton. She suspected he'd been sleeping with her on and off for years, as he had—both with her and another array of women—but she was content to put up with this kind of behavior as long as he came home to her afterwards. In the end it was Elizabeth Taylor rather than Bloom who took him away from her. They met on the set of *Cleopatra* (1963) and had a whirlwind romance, Taylor leaving Eddie Fisher to hook up with him. Fisher had earlier ended his so-called fairy tale marriage with Debbie Reynolds for Taylor. At times it appeared to be a form of musical chairs, reading the gossip columns about who was bedding who, or for how long.

By now the studio system was on its knees. It was almost destroyed by *Cleopatra,* for which Taylor had been paid $1 million, an astonishing sum by any standards, especially for a woman. She took it in blithe revenge for all the years women received paltry salaries in contrast to their male co-stars. "If someone is dumb enough to offer me a million dollars to make a picture," she argued, "I'm certainly not dumb enough to turn it down."

Ben-Hur had cleaned up both at the box office in 1959, sending out the message that an epic with a man in the lead was more likely to succeed than one with a woman. But of course Hollywood knew that anyway. What madness had possessed the moguls to offer Taylor such money? Frustration at the failure of *Cleopatra* would make Hollywood leery about sackcloth-and-ashes films from now on.

Marilyn Monroe's demons were now starting to make their appearance on the set of *Some Like It Hot*, Billy Wilder's madcap cross-dressing comedy in which she played the character of Sugar Kane opposite Jack Lemmon and Tony Curtis. She received high praise for her performance but it was tainted for her by the mechanics of the plot, which had Lemmon and Curtis in drag. She was offered the part of Sugar Kane, she contended, because only she could be dumb enough not to notice that Lemmon and Curtis were men in drag rather than members of an all-girl dance band. She seemed to take her frustration at such stereotyping out on both Lemmon and Curtis, not to mention Wilder, and by the end of the shoot—much protracted due to her tantrums—all three of them were livid with her and vowed never to work with her again.

Those more sympathetic to Monroe's behavior were aware that a miscarriage, a nervous breakdown, an impending divorce, fairly constant insomnia, chronic addiction to pills and a terror of aging were all responsible for her blowing of takes. The writer Joan Smith clicked on a more practical reason for her discomfiture on the set of the movie: The 1920s time-frame in which it was set. "This was a crude device to make the most of Marilyn's curvy, feminine figure," she argued. "While the other female characters and her male co-stars, who are required by the plot to spend much of their time disguised as women, appear in straight up-and-down flapper dresses, Marilyn's costumes are completely out-of-period and skin-tight, so much so that she couldn't sit down between takes. The dresses were not only ludicrous but lethal: a matter of weeks after filming ended she lost the baby she'd been expecting."[25]

Wilder was unmoved by this and continued to blame Monroe's tantrums on sheer selfishness. He joked to an interviewer: "I'm the only director who ever made two pictures with Monroe. It behooves the Screen Directors Guild to award me a Purple Heart." Arthur Miller wasn't amused by the comment and fired off a telegram to him, castigating him for his ill treatment of his wife on the set. At the end of the day, he argued, "She did her job and did it superbly."[26]

Dorothy Dandridge, whose sensitivity mirrored Monroe's in many ways, made *Porgy and Bess* in 1959. It was directed by the notorious Otto Preminger. By now their affair was over and Preminger showed little warmth towards her, if anything treating her more cruelly than he would have done a stranger. The film was a hit but Dandridge married a white man, Jack Denison, the same year and her career declined as a result. Hollywood wasn't yet ready for an ebony-ivory marriage and she was boycotted by casting agents. "Everything changed the day we were married," she said afterwards.[27] She started to drink to excess as a result of her marital problems and was constantly asking her doctor for pills to help her sleep. She was also short of money at this time, largely due to poor investments. She was so cash-strapped she had to take her brain-damaged daughter Harolyn out of private care and have her put into the State Hospital, which broke her heart.

Everything suddenly seemed to be up for grabs. The love goddesses of the golden age of cinema were winding down and a new and brasher breed squeaking through. If Hayworth and Monroe were going, who would replace them? And if the major studios were terrified of the investment required for big-budget movies in case it wasn't recouped, where would the blockbusters of the future come from?

Television administered another blow to the studios. The "eternal rectangle," that demonic Cyclops placed in the corner of the suburban living room, became a miniature cinema. "Why go out and see a bad movie at enormous expense," asked Sam Goldwyn, "when you can watch a bad movie at home for nothing?" Billy Wilder added, "Film directors at last had an art form they could look down on." But beneath the humor there was grimness. The moguls knew their days were numbered. Would they be missed? Maureen O'Hara thought they would. "Those old boys worked you like slave-drivers but they loved movies," she contended, "unlike the new breed." She was referring to the young Turks who were lining up to occupy their vacant thrones, the accountants with their sharp suits and sharp brains who knew nothing about history but a lot about profit.

In the future the studios would be bought by conglomerates, oil companies. Directors would be more politically correct in their dealings with women but they would have less natural warmth towards them. Some of them would even evince a feminist credo. They wouldn't beat their chests like a Gable, or squash grapefruits in molls' faces like a Cagney, but would they be men?

The times, they were a-changing. It was the era of easy riders and raging bulls. Where were all the real men? "Hollywood men are either married or doing your hair," according to Doris Day. And what about the "real" women? Where were they? Were they in the long grass or buried behind the latest holy grails of cinema, the special effects?

And where, indeed, was our old friend, the woman's movie? "A woman's movie," Oscar Levant believed, "is one where the woman commits adultery all through the picture and at the end her husband asks her to forgive him." This sounded like a post-feminist attempt at a joke. But was it where things were headed? If it was, women might have even more to fear from the bland sixties than the moribund fifties, the war-torn forties, the censored thirties or the pre-vote twenties. They'd gone from suppression under the Code to near-dominance with women's liberation but were now stuck in a kind of limbo of irrelevance. Would they survive the new era? Maybe they needed more rebels. The "tough broads" and *femmes fatale* had often belonged to B-movies. Was there a female Dean or Brando on the horizon now that the lights of stars like Bette Davis and Joan Crawford had dimmed?

Woman's lib was everywhere but was it in the movies? If Doris Day was the cinema's biggest star, it hardly looked like that. Day was taking the place of Marilyn Monroe, a sex anodyne filling in for the real deal. The world had passed from monochrome to color but instead of opening up new horizons, it only emphasized the richness of the old ones. Where was Norma Desmond when we needed her?

They really did have faces then. But what did they have now—facelifts? Oh brave new world that had such people in it.

A terrible beauty was born.

The Swinging Sixties

The sixties was the decade of rebellion, against even Hollywood itself. Glamour became almost a dirty word as women sought to define themselves outside that ambit, but quality roles were few and far between. Alfred Hitchcock made his most famous film *Psycho* in 1960, his killing of "Mother" in the film being seen by some as a metaphor for the destruction of the family. The heroine, played by Janet Leigh, was murdered a quarter of the way through the movie, which was unheard of at the time, and would be unusual even now. But then actors were "cattle" for Hitchcock—actresses even more so.

Elvis Presley came out of the army in 1960 and embarked on a decade of brain-dead movies that were an insult not only to the women who danced around him in various stages of undress, but also his own limited talent. He was never going to be Hollywood's greatest actor but he evinced a certain insolent power in the pre-army *King Creole*. If he continued in this *King Creole* vein, he may have gone some way to realize his childhood ambitions of earning the respect of his heroes, Marlon Brando and James Dean. Instead he settled for 30-plus sex-and-sand offerings where he was content to dally with innumerable identikit women to whom he crooned insignificant ditties before he bedded them. Or after. (Or even during.)

Mary Ure won an Oscar nomination for a fine performance in Jack Cardiff's adaptation of D.H. Lawrence's *Sons and Lovers* but her life afterwards was tempestuous, largely due to her affair with Robert Shaw, by whom she became pregnant while being married to the playwright John Osborne. She divorced Osborne to marry Shaw, but Shaw was more focused on his own career than hers and preferred her in the role of wife-mother than rival star. He seemed to be more comfortable in the marriage when she was pregnant. She appeared in some movies with him in the mid-sixties (*The Luck of Ginger Coffey* in 1964 and *Custer of the West* in 1966) but these were thankless roles. This was also reflected in their respective salaries. For *Custer,* Shaw got $350,000. She had to make do with $50,000.

Bette Davis now divorced Gary Merrill. Maybe the surprise was that it took so long for them to split up. When they did, she reiterated an old refrain: "He was a macho man, but none of my four husbands was man enough to become Mr. Bette Davis."[1]

Both Davis and Merrill were unfaithful in their ten-year marriage. Merrill believed it failed because of Davis' domineering personality while Davis put the problems down to him. They should have rewritten the words in the wedding ceremony, she suggested, and turned them into "In sickness and in hell."[2]

Davis had acquired her hawk-like image more as a result of her screen characters than any scandal in her private life. "Until you're known in my profession as a monster," she proclaimed, "you're not a star." She certainly seemed like one. Brian Aherne cackled, "Surely nobody but a mother could have loved Bette at the height of her career." Tom Sholes rowed in with, "Bette got most of her exercise by putting her foot down."[3]

Such barbs pointed to the double standard at the heart of Hollywood. "A man has to be Saddam Hussein to be called ruthless," Bette Midler suggested, "but all a woman has to do is put you on hold." Doris Day echoed that. If a man did something silly, she observed, people said, "Isn't he silly?" but if it was a woman they said, "Aren't *women* silly?"[4]

Marilyn Monroe began the new decade with *Let's Make Love*. Various co-stars had been suggested for her for the movie but they dropped out like flies amidst tales of her increasingly demented behavior. Yul Brynner was in the running for a while, then Rock Hudson, then Cary Grant. Eventually Yves Montand took the role. Monroe fell for him but couldn't win him over from Simone Signoret. Their affair damaged both her heart and her pride.

In *The Misfits* (1961) Monroe was given the most challenging role of her career, and one which captured both her sweetness and depth. As Roslyn she got a chance to play a real woman and still display her little-girl-lost vulnerability. Clark Gable became a father figure for her and Montgomery Clift a soulmate. "Monty is the only person in Hollywood more messed up than I am," she joked. How ironic that a film which could have launched her on a new career path—and which was bequeathed to her by her now alienated husband Arthur Miller, who wrote the screenplay—would be her last completed one.

By now she was alienated from Miller. Neither did she get on with John Huston, the film's director. "He treated me like an idiot," she remembered, using phrases like "Honey this" and "Honey that"—terms not likely to appeal to a woman who spent her life trying to crawl out of the doll's house Hollywood constructed for her. Huston had a lot of trouble with Monroe's fragile state of mind on the film, and also with her constant lateness, but he didn't help matters by his attitude. In a scene where she kisses Gable from her bed, she wanted to do it topless to show her naturalness with him. Huston agreed to let her drop the bedsheet from her but shot it from behind her, droning dismissively, "I've always known girls had breasts."[5]

Posterity would see this as one of the strongest roles she ever played but she had a different view of it. "I'm not a dumb blond this time," she sighed. "I'm a *crazy* dumb blond. And to think Arthur did this to me."[6]

Maybe her negative feelings about Miller as a man influenced her view of his writing. One has the image of her lying alone in her bed fearing the passage of time or, her huge dread, mental incarceration like her mother, as he worked in his study. He always claimed he tried his best to get on her wavelength but neither he nor his friends properly understood her. She said the latter treated her "like a dull sex object with no brains," and that they talked to her "like a high school principal would to a backward student."

She overdosed on pills during *The Misfits* and was taken to a hospital to have her stomach pumped. The incident affected Gable profoundly and was believed by some to have contributed to his death shortly after shooting finished.[7] This was an unfair assumption. If anything hastened his death, it was the grueling scenes he performed with the horses near the end of the film. This was something Huston was always defensive about: He insisted a stunt double was used for them. It was easier to blame Monroe for his death. Gable's wife also partly blamed her. Monroe didn't go to his funeral for fear of tongues wagging about a rumored romance between them.

Her spirits sank after *The Misfits*. Most people were aware of her personal traumas at this time but there were career ones as well. She'd like to have played the lead in *Breakfast*

By the time she made *The Misfits* (1961), Marilyn Monroe was an accident waiting to happen. Here she is with her friend and co-star Montgomery Clift, of whom she said, "He's the only person in Hollywood more messed up than I am." Debates still rage about whether she could have been saved if men were kinder to her or the industry more understanding of her erratic ways.

at Tiffany's and Truman Capote also believed she'd have been ideal for his "lady of the night" but Hollywood went for a more sanitized treatment, having Audrey Hepburn play her as a society lady instead—a betrayal of the book.

Hepburn was nominated for an Oscar for her performance but was beaten by Sophia Loren for *Two Women*. Loren owed much of her success to the fact that she refused to conform to Hollywood's idea of what the "perfect" woman should be. An early screen test cameraman huffed, "She is quite impossible to photograph. Too tall, too big-boned, too heavy all around. The face is too short, the mouth too wide, the nose too long."[8] Loren didn't see herself as being classically beautiful but she resisted attempts to change her. "I have a long face," she said. "I have a big mouth, but maybe the ensemble of so many irregularities makes me a person who doesn't look like anyone else. I [avoid] the banality of being the perfect beautiful face and the perfect beautiful body."[9] By refusing to be streamlined, she stayed as she was, snubbing her (long) nose at surgery. She decided not to have it straightened or to have her face "done." As for her voluptuous figure, instead of falling prey to the later fad for near-anorexic shapes, she cooed, "Everything you see I owe to spaghetti." She turned a potential defect into a boast and by doing so made careers possible for other "big-boned" women as well.

As well as seeking a role in *Breakfast at Tiffany's*, Monroe also wanted to be in Billy Wilder's *Irma La Douce*. Wilder gave the idea some thought, despite what she'd put him through on *Some Like It Hot*. "You know how it is," he quipped to a reporter. "You hate your dentist when he's pulling your teeth but the next day you're playing golf with him again."[10] But Monroe was abusive to Wilder's wife one night on a phone call and that killed off her chances.

Shirley MacLaine got the part but it wasn't one of her more memorable roles. She was better playing "the other woman" rather than a jobbing prostitute. She'd donned the call girl gear so many times now, she joked that producers didn't pay her in the regular way any more; instead "They leave it on the dresser."[11] In a more serious vein she said the reason she played these parts so many times was because "they're the only good ones being written in Hollywood these days. There are no other parts for women. And the reason is that men feel more comfortable writing about hookers. Hookers represent no threat in this male-dominated industry. Maybe I'll write myself a role of a madam who runs for the Senate and wins."[12]

By now Wilder seemed to be losing his touch, or repeating himself too much. "Unless she's a whore she's a bore," he said once, calling attention to his own limitations.[13] Could one not have too much of a good thing? Or even a bad thing?

MacLaine was more downbeat in William Wyler's *The Children's Hour*, a film he'd already made under the title *These Three* in 1936. By now the relaxation of censorship allowed him to approach the theme of lesbianism more openly, as Lillian Hellman had done in her novel, but not as openly as he would have liked. Even though the word "lesbian" isn't uttered in the script, it was still an achievement to make a film about this topic with two such high-profile stars, MacLaine and Audrey Hepburn. In another way this made it safer for the studio. Both MacLaine and Hepburn were mothers in real life. Would an unmarried—or "unmaternal"—actress have accepted the role, or been offered it? It's unlikely.[14]

Wyler was blocked from advertising the fact that the film was about lesbians because of the dictates of the time. Publicity posters for it described Hepburn and MacLaine as "different" from other women to hint at their proclivity but in interviews Wyler had to say the film was really about gossip. He also had to make MacLaine die for her "sin" at the end. Her suicide was "essential for heterosexuals in 1961" because "the only good lesbian is a dead one."[15]

MacLaine liked working with inflammatory material. Despite having had a "small town, middle American WASP" upbringing, she had a social conscience as well as artistic ambitions. Her father used to call her "a missionary in a skirt" in a pejorative manner. He believed the best way to conduct one's life was "never to upset the apple cart, to observe the status quo and not make any noise, because it upsets the neighbors." MacLaine broke out of that mold time and again in a versatile career, becoming a spokesperson for women's rights as well as a fine actress. In the forties and fifties, she said, women weren't allowed to have sex on screen even if they were married because of the Hays Code. As a kind of surrogate sop, stars like Barbara Stanwyck, Katharine Hepburn and Joan Crawford got to play women judges, women politicians, women mayors and women scientists. After more liberal attitudes came in and the Code became a thing of the past, all the sexual doors opened but now the posts of judges, politicians, mayors, etc., were re-appropriated by the men: "Men were running the studios, men were writing the scripts and men were the directors. They put us back in the bedroom and we haven't been judges or politicians or mayors since."[16] It's an interesting way of looking at it.

Having said that, MacLaine was never stuffy about women's rights. She managed to keep friendly with an overtly macho organization like Frank Sinatra's Rat Pack while still holding to her principles. "I want women to be liberated," she grinned, "and still be able to have a nice ass and shake it."[17]

The Children's Hour, whatever compromises it made, had ripples. In its aftermath, the willingness to tackle gay themes spread to Britain as well. In *A Taste of Honey* (1961) Rita Tushingham is impregnated by a black sailor who deserts her. She's then aided through her pregnancy by a gay man. Agnes Varda directed *Cleo from 5 to 7* (1961), using the storyline of a French singer facing death to launch a broadside against a world that depersonalized women. It was also a tale of female bonding. Why, Varda asked, were most films that dealt with bonding themes invariably male-oriented? "There are always stories about virile male friendships, Brando and Nicholson, Newman and Redford and so on, but not about friendships between women. The women are always motherly or tarty."[18] Varda liked to emphasize the fact that even though she was a woman, a feminist and a filmmaker, that didn't necessarily make her "a feminist-woman-filmmaker." "Filmmaking is filmmaking," she declared, "Do you ask a man who doesn't have hair if he considers himself a bald filmmaker?"[19] No, he's just a filmmaker who happened to be bald."

Rita Moreno now won an Oscar for playing Natalie Wood's sister in *West Side Story*. By now she was well and truly fed up playing "Latin spitfires," having been locked in this groove almost since her arrival in Hollywood. "I played all these roles the same way," she admitted, "barefoot with my nostrils flaring." Her demeanor was always the same too: "Hoop earrings, off-the-shoulder blouses, teeth gnashing—those were my trademarks. The blouse and the earrings would get transferred from studio to studio and it became known as 'The Rita Moreno Kit.'" She struggled with this kind of ethnic pigeonholing for most of her early career but after *West Side Story* she knew she'd reached the end of the line and she moved to Britain afterwards in an attempt to diversify herself.

Her private life was no less mercurial. For years she was engaged in an on-again, off-again affair with Marlon Brando. She adored him but he wouldn't commit to her. The relationship reached meltdown when she attempted suicide in his house after he forced her to abort their child. Events like this, coupled with some serious substance abuse and diet issues, landed her in therapy for many years. Miraculously, she came out the other end.

Women continued to struggle against typecasting and age issues. They were slotted into grooves and dispensed with when they became "irrelevant" to the studio's needs. When their beauty faded, they were quietly retired or pushed into negligible cameo roles. As Lana Turner saw things, "It used to be that when an actress reached thirty she was considered almost washed up. We started by playing girls who only married at the end of the picture. We didn't play wives. That came later. But the most dreadful thing was when a star had to play a mother. That was the beginning of her professional end."[20]

Grace Kelly was asked to play the quintessential mother, the mother of Jesus Christ, in *King of Kings*. Prince Rainier, however, vetoed the idea. It wasn't the first time she asked him to allow her to return to the screen but he was intransigent. Their discussions, wrote Jane Ellen Wayne, "again ended with boisterous arguments or Grace's retreating into a shell."[21]

To console herself she invited her old co-star Cary Grant to visit her with his wife Betsy Drake. She met them at the airport. The next day Rainier was furious to see a photo of her in the newspaper kissing Grant. He was so jealous of her relationship with Grant that he forbade his staff from watching *To Catch a Thief* in the palace's cinema. He sulked right through Grant's visit to punish her.[22]

Gail Russell died in August 1961 after losing a lengthy battle with alcoholism. Her life had also been blighted by her friendship with John Wayne. Wayne's wife Esperanza cited her as co-respondent in their divorce but Russell always denied having slept with him. The publicity created by the case affected her career adversely, eventually resulting in the over-sensitive actress having to go to a sanitarium to be treated for her growing addiction to alcohol. When she came out, she continued drinking. She was arrested for drunk driving on a few occasions, one of them resulting in a suspended prison sentence. The divorce case didn't hurt Wayne's career at all, Hollywood customarily punishing women more than men in situations like this.[23] She was only 36 when she died. Her body was being discovered in her apartment surrounded by empty vodka bottles. "I didn't believe I had any talent," she confessed once. "I was afraid, [though] I don't know exactly of what."[24] It was probably just life itself.

By this time Veronica Lake had also succumbed to alcohol abuse. Her money having totally disappeared, she took a job as a barmaid in desperation. She didn't think she'd be recognized but she was, and the story reached the media.

So the great Veronica Lake was in the gutter. She tried to pretend she was only filling in for a friend but few believed her. She received letters from all over the world, many of them with money enclosed, and was touched by their kindness. But her pride wouldn't let her keep any of it. Her situation made one wonder why there wasn't some organization in Hollywood to help people like her who'd given so much pleasure to so many filmgoers. Two years later she parodied herself in a Broadway role, *Best Foot Forward,* playing a fading movie queen. In 1965 she was arrested for drunkenness in Galveston, Texas.

Vivien Leigh played a fading beauty falling into the arms of a young lover (Warren Beatty) in *The Roman Spring of Mrs. Stone* but the film wasn't a pleasant experience for her. Her nerves were bad, she was losing her looks and Laurence Olivier was gone from her life. Olivier married Joan Plowright when it was being shot, which upset her concentration greatly. She cried her eyes out during her most significant love scene with Beatty, unable to comprehend the fact that she'd finally lost Olivier for good.[25] Her 20-year marriage to him had been dissolved in just 28 minutes the previous year.

She tried to put a brave face on things. Asked how she felt, she wished Olivier and Plowright "all the happiness in the world" but inside herself she was gutted, the last nail having being put in the coffin of the most important relationship of her life.[26] Men could find second relationships at any age, it seemed, while women could only have "Roman springs" on celluloid.

One day during the shooting, Leigh announced she was going to have some electric shock treatment. She said this, according to the film's screenwriter Gavin Lambert, "with no more fuss than someone with a headache asking for an aspirin."[27] By now she accepted the need for it in her life. Whether it did her any good or not was another question.

In *Roman Spring*, Leigh got to speak the line, "I lived a long time in a very flattering, very artificial, very insincere kind of world—the world of an actress." It could equally have been applied to herself. Lady Diana Cooper believed the most difficult part Leigh ever played was "her own life's part," which is probably true.[28]

The same could have been said of Marilyn Monroe, a woman much younger than Leigh but suffering the same inner hell. Monroe was also going through marital stress. Her divorce from Arthur Miller was finalized on January 20, 1961, the same day as John F. Kennedy's inauguration. This was to avoid publicity. She then made a will, leaving 75 percent of her estate to Lee Strasberg. *The Misfits* proved to be a box office disappointment as well as a critical one, which depressed her. She had a breakdown at a New York Hospital complex and was consoled by Joe DiMaggio and her therapist Ralph Greenson, who advised her to distance herself from her entourage.[29] Too many people had been running her life for her, he thought, and it was time to shout *stop*. But already it was too late.

For a time there was a rumor that Frank Sinatra would marry her but he seemed more interested in her as one of his playmates, like Shirley MacLaine. She was too "high maintenance" for him for a lengthy commitment. She spent a lot of time now at his Palm

Springs home, hiding her face (and sagging bustline) under a striped parasol as she dreamed of JFK, not realizing that he was also only interested in her as a diversion. Rejected in love once again, she ran to Greenson, to Paula Strasberg, to pills. But none of them could quell the demons within her for long. When she began work on a new movie with Dean Martin, the ominously-titled *Something's Got to Give,* she was absent from the set more often than she was present. Her decision to fly to New York to sing "Happy birthday" to Kennedy at Madison Square Gardens in the middle of one of her "sick breaks" was one of her last cries for help.

Kennedy distanced himself from her afterwards, as he distanced himself from Frank Sinatra after Sinatra's Mafia connections became a political hot potato for him. Robert Kennedy, his more diligent brother, was a factor in this decision. But Robert was happy to have him "donate" Marilyn to him, if we're to believe the Monroe legend. And then to dispense with her after she'd served her "function" with him. She said she felt like a piece of meat as she was tossed between them.

Back on the set of the movie, the patience of director George Cukor was wearing thin. One day she decided to bare all for a swimming pool scene. She was supposed to wear a flesh-colored bikini but chose instead to go nude, which meant the intended scene was replaced by a voyeuristic display for the crew. Images of this were beamed around the world. It was as if she were reverting back to the girl who'd done the *Playboy* centerfold for Hugh Hefner when she was a nobody. Things were ending as they began.

When Miller saw a photo of her in this guise in *Life* magazine he feared for her. "It seemed to me," he wrote, "that she had a grin of willed insouciance quite different from the genuine joy with which she had shown off her glorious body years before." Were all her years of travail for this, he wondered? "That photograph, meant to celebrate the return of the old carefree Marilyn, was overcast with a kind of doomed coolness for me, as though she had given up trying to cease being the immemorial prey."[30]

She celebrated (if that's the word) her 36th birthday soon afterwards but was sacked from the film, the studio's patience having been worn out with her repeated absences from the set. She was also sued for $500,000. Lee Remick was chosen to replace her in the movie but Martin loyally stood by Monroe and refused to make it with Remick. There was no recourse now but to shut down production completely.

In late June, Monroe joined Sinatra for the opening of the Cal-Neva Hotel in Lake Tahoe. Here she descended deeper and deeper into a mire of pills and booze as she cavorted with the Rat Pack. "She wanted back into the fairy tale," wrote Nick Tosches, "but there was really no way back." Monroe took a fatal overdose of Seconal on August 4, sending shock waves around the world.

The columnists who had haunted her in life weren't content to leave their pens down after she died. Rumors of murder proliferated and thus began a running debate that has lasted to the present day. Was she taken out by the CIA? The FBI? The Mafia? Even Eunice Murray, her mild-mannered housekeeper, became a suspect for a time. Why did Ralph Greenson and Murray have to batter down her door to reach her body when she never locked doors? Had someone else been in the room to administer the fatal dose of pills?

An autopsy showed her colon was bruised. Had somebody given her a Seconal enema to prevent an *exposé* she was rumored to be planning about the Kennedy brothers?[31]

Further rumors suggested she had a "little red book" and was planning to spill the beans on certain people before she died. The most outrageous conspiracy theory suggested she was linked to a plot to kill Fidel Castro. Many writers speculated that Peter Lawford was in her house on the night she died and removed her body from it, and also other "evidence" that could have incriminated him and the Rat Pack in her demise.

If there were less conspiracy theories, any one of them might have been easier to believe. People's willingness to embrace them suggested there didn't have to be too much proof to service the feeding frenzy of the gossip presses. But sometimes, as Sigmund Freud once remarked, a cigar is just a cigar. It's probable that she simply overdosed on Seconal— not intentionally, but maybe not unintentionally either. She had, after all, tried it before. And Hollywood was a very dismal place to be when she looked in the mirror and didn't see Marilyn Monroe any more, or when the body parts that made her the world's most adorable sex symbol started to go south.

Noël Coward wrote in his diary the day after her death: "Marilyn Monroe committed suicide yesterday. The usual overdose. Poor silly creature. I'm convinced that what brought her to that final foolish gesture was a steady diet of intellectual pretentiousness pumped into her over the years by Arthur Miller and 'The Method.' She was, to begin with, a fairly normal little sexpot with exploitable curves." This narrow view of her was shared by many.

Sinatra thought the Kennedys might have been involved in her death because she was a political liability. Sinatra's valet George Jacobs felt this was a convenient belief for Sinatra to hold because it absolved him of his own complicity in her demise.

Jacobs believed Monroe loved Sinatra much more than either of the Kennedys and dearly wanted to marry him: "He was her guardian, her lover, her friend, her soulmate. She trusted him more than anyone else in her life except her shrink."[32] He thought Sinatra was eaten up with guilt at having thrown Monroe to the Kennedys when he didn't want to have anything to do with her.

Miller refused to go to her funeral, giving as his reason the interesting comment "She won't be there."[33] He was sad about her death but not surprised. "There were always new doctors willing to help her into oblivion," he sighed resignedly.[34] To have survived she would need to have been either more cynical than she was or even further from reality. "Instead she was a poet on a street corner trying to recite to a crowd pulling at her clothes."[35]

Did Hollywood kill Monroe or, as Billy Wilder alleged, did Monroe "kill" Hollywood? "This industry," she once said, "should behave like a mother whose child has just run out in front of a car. But instead of clasping the child to them, they start punishing [it instead]."[36] In her case the child-woman had just run out in front of her last car and paid the price.

What did her death prove—that she couldn't hack fame? That Norma Jean Baker could never become Marilyn Monroe and survive? That she subjugated herself so much to men's needs that once the day came when she couldn't fulfill those needs—either on celluloid or in the boudoir—she had no relevance in life any more? "People had a habit of looking at me as if I were some kind of mirror instead of a person," she wrote in her autobiography. "They didn't see me: they saw their own lewd thoughts. Then they white-washed themselves by calling me the lewd one."[37]

Norman Mailer believed sex with her would have been like ice cream: "She would ask no price."[38] He meant it affectionately but from a more ominous viewpoint the observation taps into the collective male view of her as public sexual property, the wet dream upon which sex-starved men could nurture their movie-fed fantasies. Joan Smith wrote of her as "a child's afternoon treat, cheap and quickly consumed." Her image, for Smith—the pointy breasts and wiggling walk—"take on a tinge of terror for women who understand the meaning of her spectacular success. By turning herself into an icon of female passivity she had studio bosses, directors, sportsmen, intellectuals, politicians and princes at her feet. Her popularity represents a rejection of mutuality in sex in favor of a pattern of male dominance and female submission." When she died, as far as Smith was concerned, that submission was both final and glamorous. Men could now "own" her because she was a static entity that could never challenge their dominance. They would continue to slaver over her image on screen without the fear of her three-dimensional existence becoming an issue or a threat: "After all, isn't pedophilia next to necrophilia?"[39]

Her life was riddled with questions. What if her mother hadn't been locked up in an institution? What if she hadn't been illegitimate? If she hadn't been a child bride? What if she found someone to love her for herself rather than her image, or to "cure" her? What if she didn't need curing? If she'd had children instead of abortions? If she hadn't been at the behest of studio bosses who had the morals of alley cats and the consciences of racketeers?

According to the perceived wisdom, every model wants to be an actress. Maybe Monroe was the first who wanted to be a *Method* actress. Perhaps that was the rock she perished on. "Hollywood," she once said, "is a place where they'll pay you $50,000 for a kiss and fifty cents for your soul. I know because I turned down the first offer enough and held out for the fifty cents."[40]

Life After Marilyn

"It was tough for women to last in films," wrote Jeanine Basinger. "Those who ran the studios and operated the star machine knew only too well that the beautiful female stars they were manufacturing were going to lose popularity sooner than the males. If a female star could last for a decade she really paid off. If she could last for two decades she was a phenomenon. If she lasted longer than that she was a miracle."[1]

Such a woman was Bette Davis, who cheated time—and studio tyranny—by reinventing herself. Around the time of Monroe's death, the consensus in the film industry was that Davis was a busted flush. Her recent films hadn't done much business and her forthcoming, *What Ever Happened to Baby Jane?* seemed like a desperate leap into gothic excess.

Hollywood had various ways of dealing with aging actresses, as we've seen. It either put them out on grass, gave them minor parts as mothers and grandmothers, or aunts, or "friends" of the lead. But with Davis, and her *Baby Jane* co-star Joan Crawford, we witnessed a new phenomenon: The transformation of an aging woman into a *monster*.

Davis was happy to do whatever it took to make the film a success. She was less vain than Crawford and more willing to reinvent herself if such a transmogrification would revive her career. She'd been a chameleon all her life anyway. In this sense she had less to lose than Crawford with *Baby Jane*, Crawford having molded her image primarily on glamour. "Bette's best chaperone is her face," Crawford had rasped once had rasped once—unfairly, because at her best Davis was a very attractive woman whereas much of Crawford's allure came from a bottle or a makeup man. But the makeup men on *Baby Jane* were going to be her avowed enemies.

Davis was never vain. "I have eyes like a bullfrog," she confessed, "a neck like an ostrich and limp hair. You just have to be good to survive with that equipment."[2] Especially in an industry dominated by appearance. "Hollywood always wanted me to be pretty," she said, "but I fought for realism."[3]

Baby Jane had a kind of decayed charm, Davis chewing the scenery while Crawford metamorphosed herself from the camp bitch-goddess of the fifties into a decidedly more scary one. But she couldn't match Davis, which served as a reminder that she'd always lagged behind her in versatility. This was apparent like never before now that they were sharing the screen; there was nowhere to hide. Davis emerged with the Oscar nomination, not Crawford.

Director Robert Aldrich had a tough time raising the budget for *Baby Jane*. The financiers went, "Those two old bags? Recast this film and we'll give you any amount of money you want."[4] He refused to do this, which meant he had to shoot it on a shoestring. It was made in three weeks.

Because Davis got so little up front, she made a fortune out of the residuals when it became a box office smash. Buoyed by its success, she then made the bold move of trying to build on it by offering her services via a tongue-in-cheek ad in *Variety*. It went like this: "Mother of three, 10, 11 and 15, divorcée, American, thirty years of experience as an actress in motion pictures, mobile still and more affable than rumor would have it, wants steady employment in Hollywood. (Has had Broadway.) Bette Davis, C/o Martin Baum, G.A.C. References upon request."[5] It was so much in character that one had to commend her. Margo Channing was alive and well, even if temporarily "resting."

Davis had spent the better part of her career trying to avoid being typecast but after *Baby Jane* she allowed herself be put into *Hush ... Hush, Sweet Charlotte* (1964). *The Nanny* (1965) and *The Anniversary* (1967), all of which featured the "new" Bette Davis; *Baby Jane* may have revived her career but the price she paid was too high for some. "I am a star," she announced, "my name goes above the title." Myrna Loy's reaction to this comment was, "Yes, she is a star, and a great one, but is it worth playing all those demented old ladies to maintain that status?"[6]

Davis and Crawford weren't the only aging stars forced to shift gear to keep their careers going. Barbara Stanwyck had to as well. In *Walk on the Wild Side* (1962) she was cast as a lesbian. Ergo, she had to be the villainess of the piece, a "sly dyke" in the words of one viewer. The twist is that she's married to a man. Her husband is disabled. Alison Darren felt this "cleverly confirms a commonly held belief that lesbians are frigid, and that their relationships with women are safely spiritual rather than basely carnal."[7]

Gene Tierney was another aging star glad of a marginal role in a film at this time. Otto Preminger cast her in *Advise and Consent* against the wishes of studio execs who saw her as uninsurable because of her history of mental illness. Preminger's reputation as a bully was counterbalanced by kind gestures like this. It was Tierney's first time on a movie set in seven years and kickstarted a mini-revival for the much-loved actress who, like so many other beauties, was sidelined for far too long for far too little cause.

Stars like Tierney were content with the scraps thrown them by former friends, but at the coalface of the industry a new breed of woman was emerging: more visceral, more charged. The demise of Monroe left a vacant throne and various types of sex symbols sought to occupy it.

One such was Ursula Andress, who was apotheosized by the image of her walking from the sea in the James Bond movie *Dr. No.* She wore a bikini that showed off her huge hips and heaving bosom and Sean Connery, as Bond, looked on approvingly. In future years many other equally curvaceous Bond Girls would seek his approval by peeling off their clothes. Many of them would sleep with him and some would try to kill him afterwards, like human embodiments of praying mantises. They were usually exotic types with faces and figures to die for—literally. Meanwhile Connery saved the world. He couldn't allow sexy women to stop him in his mission, could he?

Men who read *Playboy* (Connery often gave interviews to this publication) and who liked guns and girls (if not in that order) thrilled to the mixture of sex and danger. Our trusty hero dispatched another megalomaniac with some tart one-liner and then went back to his luscious lovely for dessert—presuming she was one of the few trustworthy ones who liked "Meester" Bond for himself. And the world continued to spin on its axis, free once again of the threat of a mushroom cloud.

No matter what Andress did afterwards, she lingered in viewers' minds as a mermaid-like vision of Everyman's sexual fantasy. "When she rose from the sea," one writer suggested, "most men probably thought she lived down there, donning her bikini only for visits to dry land."[8]

Bond girls set feminism back an eon and so did many of the other kinds of films being made at this time, even those based on ostensibly feminist material. Natalie Wood appeared with Tony Curtis in *Sex and the Single Girl* (1962), a film which shared little but the title of the Helen Gurley Brown book on which it was based. Brown was a kind of neo-feminist in the Mae West vein. She believed women should use their sex appeal to get ahead and in that way not be "mouseburgers." Feminists approved of her idea that women should be empowered but hardly by the way she advised going about it. She had a lot of pragmatic advice to unleash but the film was little more than a spoof designed to cash in on her name and her book. In the end, it did neither.

Curtis fell in love with Christine Kaufmann on the set of *Taras Bulba* the same year and left Janet Leigh, his wife for over a decade, for her. Kaufmann was only a teenager at the time, prompting Curtis to crow, "I wouldn't be caught dead being married to a woman old enough to be my wife."[9] His marriage to Leigh had been built up as a fairy tale one in the press but now Prince Charming vamoosed. Other so-called fairy tale liaisons, like that of Eddie Fisher and Debbie Reynolds, had also ended by now. It always seemed to be the man who walked out, trading in his spouse for a younger model. In Fisher's case that was Elizabeth Taylor. But this marriage, like the Curtis-Kaufmann one, would also collapse.

Marlon Brando shared a room with Curtis when they were both starting out and also shared his insatiable appetite for women. Brando played Fletcher Christian in the glossy remake of *Mutiny on the Bounty* in 1962. Dubbed *The Mutiny of Marlon* by some, it had Brando reportedly sleeping with every Eurasian–looking woman he could find on the set and contracting gonorrhea as a result.

He'd often described himself as a sex addict. His biographer Peter Manso thought this was caused by a fundamental disrespect for women that went back to his feelings for his mother, who was an alcoholic. Brando loved her but as she sank deeper into the abyss of alcohol and loose living he lost respect for her. Manso described his subsequent satyriasis as "a repetition of maternal rejection, a childhood hatred of Dodie as a 'whore,' and his own adult promiscuity with easy women who became substitutes for the despised yet longed-for mother. Self-loathing lay at the heart of the dilemma."[10] The more often women fell at his feet, the less he seemed to respect them. He told an interviewer that being famous opened all the doors for him: "There's no chick I can't have if I program it right and time it right. They all fall for the movie star bit."[11]

The parts that were being written for actresses seemed to underline such chauvinism. "The rule is that women have got to wind up with [a man] in the end," Shirley MacLaine believed. "It was the same during the years of the big women stars like Bette Davis and Rosalind Russell. All of them suffered the same fate. The first part of the film established them as strong, capable women. Then the man was introduced and the next thing you know the strong woman fell into the arms of the stronger hero."[12]

Foreign actresses suffered from this strain as much as American ones. Leslie Caron was regarded as "hot stuff" by male audiences but they failed to appreciate her attempts to become a serious actress when she played a woman trying to cope with an unwanted pregnancy in *The L-Shaped Room*. Claudia Cardinale had a similar problem. Because of her previous sex symbol status, she found it difficult trying to appeal to the arthouse audience in Luchino Visconti's *The Leopard* (1963) opposite Burt Lancaster. When the film premiered, all a certain member of the audience could say was, "When is Lancaster going to screw Cardinale?"[13]

Ava Gardner starred in *The Night of the Iguana* the same year and received some of the best notices of her career but John Huston, who directed her in it, couldn't seem to see anything beyond her physique. His attitude to her was, "Don't worry, sweetheart, just stand there and look beautiful. That's all you have to do."[14] One was reminded of Hedy Lamarr's "It's easy to be glamorous. All you have to do is stand still and look stupid." Lamarr married her sixth husband that year, this time opting for a divorce lawyer. ("How convenient!" chirped a member of the congregation.) Lamarr saw it differently: "Some women have affairs but unfortunately I marry my men. It's funny that a woman can have 25 affairs and nobody says anything but if she has six husbands she's terrible. I guess I'm just a homebody."

Ageism also continued to be a problem for actresses. Tony Richardson directed Edith Evans in *Tom Jones*, a rumbustious ode to male carousing in 18th century Britain. He seemed to reflect the sexist slant of the film when Edith Evans asked him pleadingly, "I don't look seventy, do I?" He replied, "No, love, you don't. Not any more."[15]

Cary Grant appeared opposite Audrey Hepburn in the thriller *Charade*, the age disparity between them cleverly negotiated by a plot device that had her as a widow. By now, as one writer pointed out, Grant was seven years older than Bette Davis when she played the "demented drone" of *What Ever Happened to Baby Jane?* but nobody batted an eyelid as he romanced Hepburn here.[16] In fact sometimes it seemed as if the more the years gained on Grant, the younger his screen lovers became. His May-December celluloid dalliances were bitter pills to swallow for the women whose careers jack-knifed when they even approximated his vintage.[17]

Hitchcock made *The Birds* that year. For this he recruited newcomer Tippi Hedren— probably because the final scenes were so grueling, no established actress would have done them. Speaking of the most difficult week of shooting, she recalled, "By Thursday I was noticeably nervous. By Friday [the crew] had me down on the floor with the birds tied loosely to me with elastic bands which were attached through the peck-hole in my dress. One of [them] clawed my eye and that did it. I just sat and cried."[18]

For an entire week Hedren had to endure having live seagulls thrown at her in confined spaces. Sometimes she was told to lie on the floor as frantic birds were tied to her arms and legs with nylon threads and elastic bands. She described it as the worst week of her life.[19]

The bruised and battered actress vainly tried to process what was happening as the feathered creatures hovered about her, feeling she was being used as a guinea pig for Hitchcock's experiments. In the end she considered herself lucky not to have lost an eye.

Hitchcock developed an obsession with Hedren during the making of the movie, even having his assistants stalk her at one point. He did his best to supervise what she wore and ate and drank and also tied her to a contract he seemed to have little interest in developing.[20] Why did he do all this? In Hedren's view, it was because he liked to take someone who was in control of her life and slowly break her down.[21]

Insult was added to injury after filming was completed when Hitchcock sent a gift of a doll to Hedren's six-year-old daughter Melanie—subsequently to become the actress Melanie Griffith. On the surface this looked like a kind gesture but the doll was dressed in the same green suit her mother had worn in the movie, and had her hair coiffed the same way as well. More ominously, the box in which Hitchcock sent it was made of wood rather than cardboard. Was it meant to represent a coffin? Was the Master of the Macabre sending out a subversive message to Hedren that she was "dead" as far as he was concerned? Asked about Hitchcock's behavior in this regard years later, Griffith fumed, "He was a motherfucker. And you can quote me."[22]

Tippi Hedren was plucked from obscurity by Alfred Hitchcock to star in *The Birds* in 1963, his previous blond heroines now having departed the scene. He took advantage of her rookie status to impose all sorts of humiliating demands on her both before and behind the camera. The memory of those experiences affected her long after her career—which was shortened by Hitchcock's machinations—ended.

Considering the physical and mental pain meted out to her, it's incredible that Hedren signed up for another film with Hitchcock the following year. It may not have been as ostensibly pulverizing as *The Birds* but it had a creepy undertone. In *Marnie* she played a kleptomaniac opposite Sean Connery. The subtext involves Connery having a desire to catch her stealing and then "rape her on the spot," something Hedren wasn't apprised of prior to filming.[23] By now Hitchcock had started to show a romantic interest in her, pampering her with gifts of champagne and flowers between takes. He was also alleged to have propositioned her in her trailer, and to have informed her that she'd appeared in his dreams as a love object.[24]

When Hedren became engaged to be married—to her agent Noel Marshall—Hitchcock was beset with jealousy and cooled in his attitude towards her. When she asked to be excused from the set for a few days in January 1964 to pick up a film award, he refused. An argument ensued between them, culminating in her demanding to be released from her contract with him. Again he refused, this time threatening to destroy her career if she went against him. At this point she made a joke about his weight and he exploded with rage. Referring to his weight was an unpardonable sin with Hitchcock, especially in front of others. One could blithely discuss murder and vivisection with him until the cows came home but his girth was another matter entirely. A war of attrition now began.

Hitchcock continued to tie Hedren to him contractually while informing other directors who sought her—including François Truffaut—that they couldn't have her. He told them she was busy with projects when in fact she wasn't doing any acting at all. Hedren claimed Hitchcock cheated her out of a career as a result of these lies, depriving her of productive work when she was at her peak. When he finally released her, she knew her window of opportunity had closed.

A different type of abuse was visited upon Ava Gardner when she starred with George C. Scott in *The Bible* (1966) and thus began one of the most horrendous periods of her life. It was characterized by Scott's repeated physical abuse of her, something she was ill-equipped to deal with, having come from a culture that seemed to endorse that kind of behavior in her native North Carolina. As her friend Stephen Birmingham put it, Gardner emanated from a "redneck" environment where men routinely beat up on women: "If you weren't happy with what your wife or your girlfriend did, you let her have it, you slammed her across the face. So I think she thought that was part of the way men and women interact."[25]

Like many abusers, Scott was charming when he was sober. This was what threw Gardner off guard when they first met. It wasn't until they went to a hotel in the Abruzzi mountains to shoot some exterior shots that she saw his dark side. After being out to dinner with him one night he took her back to his room for a nightcap and all hell broke loose as his furies began. He rained punches on her from all angles for no reason and she was too stunned to react like most other women would, i.e., by running for her life. Instead she tried to reason with him, which only brought more punches.

The following morning her bruised face was all the evidence anyone needed to guess what happened but she told nobody. Scott apologized profusely to her and she bought it, which was another mistake: "Only much later in life did I discover that this kind of abject apology is very much the rule from the sort of men who beat up women."[26]

Her third mistake was continuing to meet Scott socially even though she knew what he was capable of. She went out to dinner with him and even listened to proposals of marriage from him. One night he looked as if he was going to erupt again but John Huston, the director of *The Bible*, had by now employed some "heavies" who escorted him home before he could do any damage. She didn't have any more trouble with him on the set but after the film wrapped she ran into him in London and again agreed to go to dinner with him. When she got back to her hotel she bade him goodnight and shot up to her room but he followed her and banged on the door. When she refused to answer it, he bashed it in. A few moments later he was holding a broken bottle at the throat of her roommate and demanding to know where she was. By now she was hiding in the bathroom. She managed to escape from it through a transom window. Some security men took Scott back to his apartment but once he got there he trashed it. He ended up spending the night in a jail cell.

Ava thought she'd seen the last of him by then but one night not too long afterwards, as she sat with friends in a bungalow attached to the Beverly Hills Hotel, he paid her another surprise visit, smashing his fist through a back door and descending on her with wild declarations of love: "He wanted to marry me. Why wouldn't I marry him? If he couldn't have me, he was going to kill me." Afterwards he hit her so hard she fell to the floor. Then came "more blows, more anger, more threats." He sat astride her with a broken bottle in his hand: "He was kneeling across me, waving the jagged edges of glass in front of my face with one hand and hitting me with the other. Telling me he loved me and smashing a fist into my eye." As she began to fear for her life, the phone rang. He allowed her to answer it, amazingly, but did so with the warning, "One wrong word and I'll kill you." It was Gregory Peck's wife but she didn't tell her what was happening.[27]

After she put down the receiver she thought of a plan to escape him. "Listen, honey," she said, pretending she wasn't afraid of him, "You're in bad shape. You have to have a doctor." He allowed her to ring a friend of hers, Bill Smith, who came around and injected him with a sedative. By now Gardner had a detached retina in one eye and a badly bruised cheek but her ordeal was nearly over. When a friend called Bappie arrived and threatened to hit Scott with a poker, he stood up slowly and walked out of the room. And out of Gardner's life. She never saw him again. Every time one of his films was shown on television afterwards, she shook all over and had to turn the set off.[28]

Another star who had romantic problems at this time was Romy Schneider. She appeared in the harmless comedy *Good Neighbor Sam* in 1964. It wasn't exactly a plum role for the German beauty but she looked on it as a way to get to Hollywood, having spent most of her career in Europe up to then. When she got back to her Parisian apartment after shooting finished, however, it was empty. She'd been living there for five years with the actor Alain Delon at this point. Delon deserted her without warning, going off with the model Nathalie Barthelmy. All he left her was a short goodbye note ("I am in Mexico with Nathalie. Best, Alain") and some faded red roses.

Devastated, Schneider took to pills and drink to try and cope. "I am nothing in life," she said, even though people saw her as "everything on the screen."[29]

A complex person, she did nothing by halves. She was as obsessive about love as she was about acting and when she became a mother she threw herself into that whole-heartedly too. But when something went wrong in her life, she couldn't take it, being too sensitive. She was also distrustful of Hollywood and its fake values. An incurable romantic who always thought she'd have been happier if born in an era of "waltzes and men who kissed my hand," instead she inherited the crassness of someone like Delon who seemed to regard relationships as temporary arrangements to be abandoned at will.

Schneider spent most of her youth in Germany but liked Paris better when she moved there, which alienated her German fans. "I don't feel I have any nationality," she revealed. "Passports should be abolished."[30] Though she was under contract to Columbia at the time of Delon's departure, the studio didn't know what to do with her, her fiery nature challenging them too much. "I suppose they weren't used to imported actresses being difficult," she reflected.[31] In Germany she'd worked with directors like Otto Preminger and Luchino Visconti but now she was reduced to light comedies like *Good Neighbor Sam*. It was better than some of the pap Columbia put her in but still not where she wanted to be.

The break with Delon increased her frustration. After they split she still continued to wear a ring he gave her, either to embarrass him or because she wanted it as a keepsake of the time they had together. "Some people wear a ring to show they are married," she huffed, "I wear one to show I am not."[32]

Pina Pellicer, a Mexican actress unknown in Hollywood, was another sensitive soul who suffered at the hands of men. Marlon Brando put her into his western *One-Eyed Jacks* (1961) and had an affair with her at this time as well, something Pellicer never really got over. A nervous young woman capable of bursting into tears on the flimsiest of pretexts, her fragility made her ideal for the film but when the cameras stopped rolling such fragility ate into her private life.

Brando was sleeping with other women besides Pellicer during the making of the movie. He had trysts going with another cast member, Katy Jurado, his on-off girlfriend France Nuyen and a Chinese woman who had interviewed him in the recent past, Lisa Lu. This was all too much for Pellicer. She went back to Mexico after the film concluded but couldn't settle. She made two more movies and then, after an alleged lesbian relationship with an older woman, took her life in December 1964.

Was Brando in any way responsible for her death? In the view of his biographer Peter Manso he was. Manso alludes to some discussions Brando had with Pellicer about suicide when she conveyed her dark feelings to him. "I don't think he told her to go kill herself," the publicist Walter Seltzer surmised, "but there may have been an idea planted. The gossip was that he encouraged it. Not by simple suggestion but overtly—'There is a way out.'"[33] It seems unfair to accuse Brando of this but a significant number of women involved with him committed suicide: Gia Scala, Pier Angeli, his former secretary Susan Slade, his daughter Cheyenne. Other women in his life attempted it and survived: Rita Moreno, his wife

Anna Kashfi, even his mother. Why did so many women end, or try to end, their lives after affairs with the actor? Manso posited this theory: "Brando was often attracted to emotionally fragile women [but] after drawing them in he would resent their dependency and break with them. Realizing that their affair would never lead to marriage [or even] any kind of commitment, his women seemed bent either on ending it all or recapturing his attention by any means at their disposal."[34]

Rachel Roberts also committed suicide due to an inability to deal with the breakdown of a relationship. She married Rex Harrison in 1962 but her fragile temperament made the relationship rocky. She never really outgrew the tag of being "the fourth Mrs. Rex Harrison," a title he seemed to enjoy conferring upon her. After he won an Oscar for *My Fair Lady* (1964) she put her career on hold for him, an unwise decision. She took to drink and became over-possessive of him afterwards, becoming increasingly insecure when he showed attention to other women.

Roberts made her first suicide attempt in 1964, washing down a handful of Seconal with gulps of brandy after an argument with Harrison. It was really a cry for help but it set the tone for their future together, which was largely comprised of drunken bouts of wild exhibitionism by Roberts. An increasingly more frustrated Harrison tended to ignore them.

Stars like Rachel Roberts, Pina Pellicer and Romy Schneider let their hearts rule their heads and suffered the consequences but a new type of thinking about men and marriage was making its appearance in Hollywood now. It was personified chiefly by Jane Fonda, who'd adopted the European sense of liberalism after becoming involved in a relationship with the French director Roger Vadim. Fonda was also politically aware, which annoyed the kind of men who liked women "in their place."

Fonda traveled to Russia on a "fact-finding" mission in 1964 but not too many people were interested in the reformed nymphet. "Who cares?" was the most common reaction. "American people want to know about her sex life, not how noble she thinks the Russians are."[35] Not too much had changed in Hollywood's cultural landscape since the time of Frances Farmer, who'd evinced similar "red" traits in the 1940s.

Later in 1964, the newspaper *The Sun* wrote sneeringly about the "new style star" who refused to be "trapped into marriage" with Vadim.[36] Fonda huffed, "What I fear about marriage is being possessed. Nobody belongs to anybody. Why can't we learn that?"[37] No wonder they called her the American Bardot.

Fonda trained to be an actress in New York and had much more fulfilling roles there. After she came to Hollywood "The roles I played gave me no outlet for expression. I was being marketed as a future movie star. We were all off the assembly line."[38] At her first screen test she wore falsies because Jack Warner told her, "You'll never become a movie star if you're flat-chested."[39]

Fonda moved in with Vadim in 1965 despite her concerns that he was a controlling man with a checkered history of bedding beautiful women like Brigitte Bardot and Catherine Deneuve and then leaving them. Or was it the other way around? Sean French wrote: "Far from being a bullying Svengali, he was more comparable to a male stick insect who turned his lovers into famous stars before they bit his head off and moved on. He made them into new women, and generally the first thing the new woman wanted to do was to leave Roger Vadim."[40]

Fonda's father, Henry, berated her for living with Vadim without being married to him. She thought this was rich coming from a man with a well-known reputation for carousing himself. According to Fonda's son Peter, his attitude on this score "blew our minds."[41] Once again the double standard between what was allowable for men and women made itself manifest. Highly-sexed men were "macho" but highly-sexed women either "loose" or nymphomaniacs.

The doublethink was also apparent in films. *In Repulsion*, Roman Polanski dealt with his highly sexed heroine by making her psychotic as well, as if this was the only way audiences could accept her nymphomania. It would be a motif repeated often in the forthcoming years, right up to *Looking for Mr. Goodbar* in 1977.

Jane Fonda was both beautiful and talented but still had to fight to break out of the shell imposed by men like her father and Roger Vadim, an early Svengali figure who directed her in the sci-fi sex spoof *Barbarella* (1968).

A different type of free spirit was played by Julie Christie, who supposedly epitomized the freedom of the "swinging" sixties, British-style, as an ambitious model in *Darling*. Dirk Bogarde says to her in one scene, "Your definition of sexual fidelity is being in bed with one man at a time." Was this liberalism or tawdry excessiveness? Christie won an Oscar for her performance.

The Best Supporting Actress Oscar was won that year by Shelley Winters for *A Patch of Blue* but it came at a price. When she showed the statuette to her husband Tony Franciosa later that night, she recalled, he "took one look at it and I knew my marriage was over." Like many men, Franciosa couldn't accept the fact that his wife's career outstripped his. Winters joked afterwards, "In Hollywood all the marriages are happy. It's trying to live together afterwards that causes all the problems."[42] She had a bemused attitude to Hollywood's denigration of women as well. Informed that a casting director she was going to see about a film role was probably going to tear her dress off, she joked, "No problem, I'll wear an old dress."[43]

Winters wasn't the only star having marriage problems. Kim Novak married her *Moll Flanders* co-star Richard Johnson but was divorced the following year. "Married women," she remarked glumly, "look more like spinsters than single girls. It's a frigid look born of having to go to bed night after night for thirty years with a man they can't stand." At least now she wouldn't have to worry about that. The same year, Hedy Lamarr divorced her sixth husband, claiming he'd threatened to hit her with a baseball bat.

Dorothy Dandridge divorced Jack Denison in 1963 after being bankrupted by him as well as abused psychologically. She went through a lot of depression afterwards and was found dead in 1965 in her West Hollywood apartment. She was only 42 years and had just two dollars in her bank account.[44] For many it was an inevitable last chapter to her troubled career, Hollywood having washed its hands of her when she married Denison, not yet being ready for an inter-racial marriage, as it proved in its attitude to Kim Novak and Sammy Davis, Jr., a few years before.

Was it suicide? The coroner's initial verdict was that she died of an embolism but later research pointed more towards the fact that she overdosed on the drug she was taking for her depression. After a promising career that saw her pave the way for black actresses everywhere, a recurring problem with drink and money—the latter causing her to reluctantly commit her handicapped daughter Harolyn to state care—probably tipped her over the edge.

Another Dorothy, the gossip columnist Dorothy Kilgallen, was also found dead that year, setting off a flood of rumors that she'd been murdered. Conspiracy theories abounded. Kilgallen had been of the belief that John F. Kennedy's assassination wasn't the work of a lone gunman. She had in fact interviewed Jack Ruby, the man who shot Lee Harvey Oswald, one of the few reporters to have been granted an audience with the shady nightclub owner. Had he told her of FBI involvement in Kennedy's death? Or indeed in the death of Marilyn Monroe? Nobody would ever know but the circumstances of her death were mysterious. When police found her she was propped up in bed with a book in front of her but she didn't have any glasses on. Her notes on Ruby and Kennedy were also missing. The cause of death was given as alcohol and barbiturate poisoning. Had somebody forced her to take the lethal drink? (A water glass laced with barbiturates was found beside her bed.) Many people had been in her room before the police got there but no charges were ever levelled at any of them. One thing police did know was that she'd made many enemies in Hollywood, most notably Frank Sinatra, as a result of her forthright columns.

The Sexual Revolution

Sex was everywhere you looked in the sixties. Some directors behaved as if they actually invented it. Now that everything was out in the open, most available orifices seemed to feature gratuitously in every other film. In pre–Code films there was at least some subtlety in the delineations but now it was vulgar and largely dull. And yet this was where the work was, so people tapered themselves to demands.

Women were the main losers in such a culture. By the mid-sixties, female screenwriters were so desperate to keep some kind of a career going that many of them went downmarket into (s)exploitation ventures to earn a buck. In 1966, Stephanie Rothman directed two Roger Corman movies, *Blood Bath* and *It's a Bikini World*, the titles themselves giveaways. The first was a beatnik vampire movie, the second a beach movie for which Corman instructed her to feature lots of nudity. He gave her "creative control" over both ventures—a term one should perhaps use advisedly in such a context. She made a vague attempt to rescue the latter by having her male character disavow his macho credential to attract the woman in his life (Deborah Walley) but this was a very small oasis in a very large artistic desert. Rothman went on to produce films like *The Velvet Vampire* and *Group Marriage* in the seventies, the titles again reflective of the material contained therein. "I was eager to try every genre offered to me," Rothman admitted, sounding very much like a woman who'd fallen in love with her chains.[1]

Another compromise was undergone by Barbara Eden. Eden starred in the TV sitcom *I Dream of Jeannie* which ran from 1965 to 1970, its chief ambition seeming to be the display of the scantily-clad Eden's sensuous figure. The question of whether to show the genial genie's navel or not seemed to consume as many column inches as the series itself, which had her cast opposite a pre–*Dallas* Larry Hagman. Eden is more remembered for this than her film career, which failed to stretch her in any discernible direction. Her first audition set the tone of what was to follow: A Warner Bros executive told her she was pretty but not sexy enough. "They want sex in this town," he informed her as he looked her over, following up by showing her a photograph of his daughter and saying, "This is what they want—big tits."[2]

The trend continued on the big screen. *In One Million Years B.C.* (1966) Raquel

135

Welch more resembled a high-class model who'd just emerged from an L.A. beauty salon than a prehistoric damsel in distress. Her bikini was torn enough to suggest some rough living but the curves were those of a Pilates guru. Struggling with dinosaurs must have given her the kind of muscles modern people had to pay to acquire. Welch was the first (only?) prehistoric sex symbol who looked like she worked out. She referred to her considerable physical attributes as "the equipment" and one can see why. Where was the vulnerability of a Monroe, the allure of a Hedy Lamarr? This was *Playboy* centerfold fare, a woman with everything in the right place but someone who, either despite this or because of it, failed to raise the body temperature of those who believed a woman's main erogenous zone was between her ears.

George Masters referred to Welch as "silicon from the knees up," while Andrew Sarris didn't even believe she existed: "She's been manufactured by the media merely to preserve the sexless plasticity of sex objects for the masses."[3] Welch complained that directors were trying to bury her in a "sea of C-cups" in the ensuing years but most of the time she seemed complicit in this.

It's unlikely she would have had the talent to become a great actress even if she didn't have the body she had but it didn't help. Her father wanted her to study Shakespeare and was upset to see her in bikinis. She told him she was going in a different direction: "Well, Dad, what can I do? This is the way it happened." Once "the equipment" arrived, she allowed herself to become its victim. This played into the hands of those who were only too happy to exploit it for their gain. Of course Welch gained too, at least

Raquel Welch displays her pneumatic curves to some effect in *One Million Years BC* (1966). Her bikini here seemed to be designed by some kind of prehistoric couturier. She was far too sexy to be taken seriously by directors and unfortunately colluded in this herself, rarely threatening to give a performance.

in her bank balance, but she avoided challenges. She didn't, for example, allow directors make her look dowdy like, say, Grace Kelly in *The Country Girl*. Or, years later, Charlize Theron in *Monster*. The thinking of the time was that if you looked a certain way, you would be put into "that kind of picture."

Rita Hayworth teamed up with her old friend Glenn Ford for *The Money Trap* in 1966. She didn't look glamorous any more but in a strange way that made her even more beautiful, the sadness of her countenance giving her a bittersweet elegance. Her last scene called for her to be thrown off the roof of her apartment house, which was almost like a metaphor for the decline of her career. She spent all day having her face blooded and muddied but by 7 p.m., having also ingested a fair amount of champagne with her makeup man George Masters, she was deemed to be too unrecognizable to be filmed. Perhaps mercifully, her dead body wasn't shown in the final cut.

Hedy Lamarr wrote her autobiography *Ecstasy and Me: My Life as a Woman* that year, having employed various ghostwriters to aid her, but she was incensed when the book finally hit the shelves, insisting that it wasn't the same as the text she approved. She sued the publisher and the team of ghostwriters for what she claimed was a barrage of half-truths and untruths regarding her sexual life.

Soon afterwards she was arrested for shoplifting. The detective who caught her insisted on pressing charges because it wasn't the first time she'd seen her pilfering. Was it a plea for attention on the part of the faded star? An attempt to garner publicity for a comeback film she was making called *Picture Mommy Dead*? Both theories were possible. Lamarr behaved very strangely in court when she was replying to the charges and this continued outside the courtroom as well. When a TV reporter asked her if she was feeling well, she replied, "Yes, you know my son is six feet four."[4]

In the next few years she took two men to court for allegedly raping her. Both cases were thrown out and both plaintiffs counter-sued her for damaging their reputations. "For many people over fifty," Lamarr once declared, "litigation takes the place of sex." It seemed to be the way with her. She was bored and had no career and the litigation seemed to give her some kind of thrill. Most bizarrely, she sued Mel Brooks for having a character called Hedley Lamarr in his spoof western *Blazing Saddles*. Was she simply looking for money from such actions or were they motivated by a need to be in the spotlight? Maybe, like Norma Desmond, she feared aging and the oblivion that came with it. Women in Hollywood, as was often remarked, aged in dog years.

Sophia Loren turned thirty in 1964, which was young for a man in Hollywood, but not for a woman: "The world press descended on me to ask how it felt to be middle-aged. I felt like a national institution starting to crumble at the edges."[5] Some time later, in a *Playboy* interview, Paul McCartney called Jayne Mansfield "an old bag." The comment was particularly hurtful in view of her frequent exposure in that magazine in times gone by. She took it hard and if she didn't need an excuse to over-drink (she usually didn't) this gave her a gilt-edged one. Mansfield was the grand old age of 32 at the time.

Maybe 32 was old for a woman but for a man it was positively juvenile. Even fifty was young for Frank Sinatra in 1966, the year he married Mia Farrow, a woman—or girl?—

thirty years younger. Dean Martin quipped, "I've got Scotch older than her." Eddie Fisher weighed in with, "Frank didn't have to buy Mia a diamond ring. He gave her a teething ring." Ava Gardner was more cruel when she said she always knew Sinatra would end up in bed with a boy—a reference to Mia's svelte figure and close-cropped hair.[6]

Sinatra saw the marriage to Farrow as an opportunity to rejuvenate himself. He wore a Nehru jacket and love beads to try and become part of the emerging hippie movement. But he looked faintly ridiculous as he combed what remained of his natural hair over his scalp. They were a mismatch from the word go. He continued his bachelor lifestyle and made few attempts to make her a part of it. One night he was spotted gambling in Las Vegas with the Rat Pack while she sat alone in a corner telling a friend, "He doesn't see me at all." He came over to her at 3 a.m. and said just three words to her: "Go to bed."[7]

Other stellar relationships of the late sixties were equally problematic. Lee Marvin separated from Betty, his wife of many years, with the blunt valediction: "This is nothing personal but I don't want to be married any more." (He was now consorting with Michelle Triola, who would launch a palimony suit against him in the future). Betty's stunned reaction was, "I wish you told me this four children ago."[8] Liza Minnelli married a gay entertainer in March 1967 only to find him in bed with another man three weeks later. It was almost like history repeating itself as Minnelli's mother, Judy Garland, also seemed to have the unfortunate knack of marrying men of dubious sexuality.

Gig Young divorced his wife Elaine in a bitter case that saw him going so far as to deny that his own daughter, Jennifer, was his. For Elaine the divorce was something of a culture shock, a rude awakening to Hollywood's skewed value system. "[For] the first couple of months," she recalled, "I needed to go to a psychiatrist. It was wonderful being Mrs. Gig Young. I could walk into a restaurant [when] we didn't have a reservation and they'd sit us down and fifty people could be waiting." But after they divorced, "I'd go to a builder, a doctor, [and] they'd make me wait two hours." When she went to auctions she was also charged more for furniture than when she was with Gig, "so I was paying more when I wasn't Mrs. Young than when I was." She realized that in former years they sold him material cheaply because they liked having movie stars around.[9]

Another marriage that was showing signs of strain: Rachel Roberts and Rex Harrison. Roberts had always been wild but she started to display signs of psychological instability when Harrison was making *Doctor Doolittle* in 1967. A woman who abhorred the "rich, wasteful" lives of the Hollywood elite, her Welsh bluntness always seemed about to explode, with or without the alcohol upon which she was becoming increasingly dependent.[10] Her tragedy was that she fell in love with a man who epitomized that very rich and wasteful ethos, which meant that her left-wing pronouncements were always going to fall on deaf ears in this marriage. Roberts was nursing a cancer-stricken father at this time so Harrison's hyperbolic prattling to animals in *Doctor Doolittle* seemed even more asinine to her.

Harrison was so concerned about Roberts' growing instability that he "allowed" her go back to work, feeling it would get her mind off herself. They appeared together in the French farce *A Flea in Your Ear* but unfortunately the activity of acting together increased tensions between them instead of easing them.

Harrison gave much more attention to his co-star Rosemary Harris on the set than to Roberts. "Rex was always nicer to his leading ladies than his wives," Roberts reflected. "They got the pleasant public face. The wives got the cold reality. If we hadn't been shackled together he'd have flirted with me on the set, just for appearances, for his credentials. Those get more important as a man gets older. Rex was always afraid of being past it."[11]

The year 1967 was a fruitful one, especially for two landmark movies, *A Fistful of Dollars* and *Bonnie and Clyde*. On the surface *A Fistful of Dollars* was simply a Europeanization of the Western hero, a genre movie given a quasi-operatic overlay with Sergio Leone's stylish tricks and a predominance of atmospheric closeups serving to camouflage the paucity of plot. When one looked closely, the Man with No Name (and precious little dialogue) was really just an Italian John Wayne, and the film's plot wasn't much more sophisticated than those silent movies where the hero rescued a maiden tied to railroad tracks as a train approached. If burning down a whorehouse was Raoul Walsh's idea of a tender love scene, as Jack Warner once opined, Leone's equivalent was Clint Eastwood blowing away everyone who looked sideways at him before rescuing the silent, sultry Marianne Koch from their grisly clutches. Once again the woman's role was to be rescued, not to be a quote unquote Real Person.

One expected a more generous treatment of women in *The Fox*. Based on a short story by D.H. Lawrence, it tackled the theme of lesbianism in a shallow manner. Sandy Dennis plays a woman who seems to be in love with Anne Heywood but after Keir Dullea shows up, Heywood falls for him and then Dennis dies. The plot resolution is almost perfect: "One lesbian is killed, the other cured."[12]

Dennis is more determinedly lesbian in the film than Heywood, therefore she has to die. This makes it possible for Heywood to go straight and consummate her love for a man. After Dullea arrives on the scene, the moral order is returned. That wasn't the way it was in the book but Hollywood has rarely been renowned for adapting literary works for the screen and this was no exception.

What irritated one most about the film was the implication that many lesbian women were either closet heterosexuals or more bisexual than homosexual, as if to render the lesbianism less dangerous. This was also the case with Dominique Sanda and Stefania Sandrelli in Bernardo Bertolucci's *The Conformist*.

One of the greatest films made in 1967 was *Bonnie and Clyde*, much of its merit down to the editorial skills of Dede Allen. Allen worked on many classic films of Hollywood's golden era (*Odds Against Tomorrow, The Hustler, America, America*) as well as many later ones (*Little Big Man, Serpico, Dog Day Afternoon*). She wasn't referred to as an editor when she first went into films in 1943 but rather as a messenger girl. "I came out of a period where you just didn't take a job away from a man," she recalled, "It was a sin. They said, 'Girls will get married and then they'll have children and they won't be able to work.' I had to work as a messenger girl for ten months before I could move up. When I finally pestered my way into the cutting room I swore more than anyone else. That way I proved myself. I felt the men accepted me."[13]

Jack Warner did his best to have her sacked from *Bonnie & Clyde* because of her imaginative cutting techniques but Warren Beatty fought for her to stay, even paying her salary out of his own pocket for a time. Allen was never bitter about her poor treatment by Warner Brothers or by the fact that she was never nominated for an Oscar. "I don't think it's because I'm a woman," she granted. "I think Hollywood and its politics looks down on New York editors."[14]

Doris Day's husband Marty Melcher died in April 1968. It was only after his death that she discovered how much he and his business partner Jerome Rosenthal had swindled away from her. She always felt Melcher was duped by Rosenthal but others weren't so kind to his memory. Her son Terry believed the only thing that saved her from total financial ruin was Melcher's death. He'd been physically violent to Terry for years but what chiefly angered Terry was the way he helped himself to Day's money and then transferred it from her accounts to tax-free ones in Switzerland. Her naiveté allowed such behavior to continue unchecked for years. She threatened to leave him on occasion but he convinced her that if she did so, she'd have bankrupted herself because their business affairs were inextricably linked.

Before Melcher died, he committed Day to a TV series. Called (with some imagination) *The Doris Day Show*, it ran from 1968 to 1973. She hated it but had to do it to pay off all the debts Melcher and Rosenthal ran up in her name.

Jane Fonda was also under a man's thumb at this time: She appeared in Roger Vadim's sci-fi sex spoof *Barbarella* in 1968. She'd been reluctant to take the part but Vadim convinced her it would be good for her, telling her it would do for her what *And God Created Woman* did for Brigitte Bardot. She wasn't quite sure she wanted this but she went along all the same.

Barbarella was trivial, what limited humor it possessed being mostly down to her wide-eyed immersion in the loony plot (or rather lack of plot). Its main achievement was to spiral her out of this kind of movie by default, reminding her of all the sex kitten roles she'd been making in Hollywood. She now saw these in a different light: "Most of the pictures where I was dressed to the teeth and played a cute little *ingenue* were more exploitative than the ones with the nudity because they portrayed women as silly, [and] motivated purely by sex in relation to men."[15] She'd been a victim of emotional pornography for so long, the shedding of her clothes for a more subversive commentary on sexual stereotyping became, by contrast, cathartic.

Robert Aldrich directed Kim Novak in her last major feature later in the year. *The Legend of Lylah Clare* was about a faded Hollywood director trying to create a young woman in the image of his dead wife. She was effective in it but when it didn't endear itself to the public she became part of the collateral damage. It was "another Novak stinker" but if it was a success it would have been a "directorial coup."

It was after this debacle that she first considered "doing a Garbo" and departing the Hollywood stage prematurely. Few could blame her. For most of her later career she'd been unfairly maligned. Her *Of Human Bondage* (1964) had been seen as a laughably bad rerun of the Bette Davis classic, while *Kiss Me, Stupid* was the film that "should have had Marilyn Monroe in it."

Maybe part of her problem was the fact that, though she resisted most of Harry Cohn's efforts to make her into a manufactured product, she wasn't assertive enough to openly rebel against him, or the machinery propelling him. "I think she was a much better actress than the press wanted to give her credit for," said George Sidney, who directed her in *Pal Joey*. "Maybe if she'd gone to the Trocadero every night, they would have been kinder."[16] That was another thing about her: She always refused to suck up to the hatchet men of the press and that increased the amount of negative column inches they threw in her face as revenge.

Aldrich's *The Killing of Sister George* promised to be a more sensitive treatment of lesbianism than *The Fox* but it was a tawdry offering in the end. In one scene Susannah York "proves" her love for Beryl Reid by drinking water that Reid had bathed in. As was often the case when directors with good intentions approached an unfamiliar theme, they felt they had to go over the top with the intensity. This often resulted in melodrama or grossness. Or in the present instance, both. Harold Clurman wrote in *The Nation* that the love affair between the two characters was a failure because we "don't give a hoot" for either of them: "Their psychology becomes falsely pathetic, a pretense of sympathy through frankness." A scene involving York's left breast, for Boze Hadleigh, evoked a special low: "Coral Browne approaches it like an ichthyologist finding something that had drifted up on the beach."[17] A few years later in *X, Y and Zee*, York was again drafted to be the token lesbian. This time she was Elizabeth Taylor's love object, Taylor getting in touch with her inner lesbian simply because Michael Caine has been unfaithful to her. The message from women was clear: "Behave yourselves, boys, or we'll go off with someone else— not necessarily a man."

One person who wasn't behaving himself very well was Frank Sinatra. Ava Gardner still carried a torch for him and one day she received a cable from him from Mexico saying, "I need you. Come at once. You'll know why when you read the headlines in the morning papers."[18] When she did so, she saw that he'd just been divorced from Mia Farrow. She made her way from Europe, where she'd been filming *Mayerling*, to Puerto Vallarta, only to discover that he'd already left. Once again she'd foolishly let her heart rule her head.

At this time Farrow was making *Rosemary's Baby*, the film that launched her career, but she almost had it taken away from her by Sinatra. He wanted her for his more standard issue movie *The Detective* and issued her an ultimatum to that effect on a phone call. She hedged, and the mercurial star set about drawing up divorce papers almost before he set down the receiver. It was an object lesson for Farrow in the quickest way to end a bad marriage with a man old enough to be her father: develop a career.

Sinatra made another forgettable movie straight after *The Detective*: *Lady in Cement*, a jaded sequel to *Tony Rome*, had Raquel Welch in her familiar sex object guise. She was believed to have taken his mind off Farrow, though he didn't seem to have had many feelings for her in the first place. He was rumored to have consorted with a prostitute during the shooting of the movie, and even to have eaten his breakfast off her chest one morning.[19]

Sinatra's sixties work was largely forgettable. How could routine films like *Lady in*

Cement or *The Detective* compete with *Rosemary's Baby*? Audiences were demanding more cutting edge material and he seemed *passé* with his jaded machismo. Crime capers like this suddenly looked almost quaint.

Another dying genre was the western but it received a kiss of life from *Butch Cassidy and the Sundance Kid*, a "buddy" movie featuring Paul Newman and the emerging star Robert Redford. As was the case in *The Graduate*, Katharine Ross had a thankless role. This time she played second fiddle not just to one man but two, Ross' function being to oscillate between Newman and Redford, two anachronistic cowpokes. Director George Roy Hill tried to create a love triangle (Ross wants Redford as a lover and Newman as a friend) but it came across as too convoluted and contrived. If the film was a lament for individualism, Ross was little more than a spectator of events, a signpost to the forthcoming doom of the heroes. Some viewers saw the film as a kind of *Bonnie and Clyde Go West* and in many ways it was, though with the obvious difference that Bonnie was a woman. Maybe *Clyde & Clyde Go West* would have been a more appropriate title.

Shirley MacLaine saw this kind of film as emanating from men's nervousness around feminists. "The women's movement," she said, "has intimidated the writers. So when a writer who's a really nice man—sensitive, intelligent—sits down to his typewriter to write a story for me and Paul Newman, and he knows I don't want to play any more prostitutes, and he doesn't want to make me anybody's housewife, what's he going to do? He doesn't know anybody but prostitutes and housewives. He's afraid his chauvinism will show on the page so he says, 'Screw that, why don't we make this with Robert Redford and Paul Newman? That'll be easier.' And that's what's happened."[20]

Marlon Brando was originally considered for the Cassidy role but instead he made *The Night of the Following Day* with his former lover Rita Moreno. She was married to someone else now but still had feelings for Brando. They rekindled their romance on the set but Brando's feelings didn't run as deep as Moreno's. He was sleeping with other women at the time as well—wasn't he always?—"shipping in his various dusky maidens" in front of her eyes.

During the third week of shooting they had a fight scene together and Moreno found herself lashing out at Brando for real, the frustration of all their years together, and all his false promises, finally erupting inside her. What made it even more crazy was the fact that her husband and child were watching it take place. Brando didn't know what "hit" him, to coin a phrase.[21]

The year 1968 was also notable for the death of the legendary Alice Guy Blaché. She bowed out at the age of 95, a totally forgotten woman despite her huge influence on the birth of film. As already mentioned, she was the first female director in movie history, and also the first director of a narrative film, but her achievements were either trivialized or ignored and her works frequently attributed to her colleagues rather than herself. After her production company folded in 1919 she returned to her native France but found herself unemployable there. She went back to the States in 1927 but visits to the Library of Congress and various film depositories made her agonizingly aware that she'd been airbrushed out of the records.

Judy Garland died the following year, the cause of death given as barbiturate poisoning. She was 47 years old, 47 going on 70 to some people's way of thinking. Bankrupt and battered, this Dorothy had finally gone over the rainbow. Like Elvis Presley she died in a bathroom, and from similar causes, but with her there were more suspicions of suicide because of her previous history. After so many dramatic near-things, so many theatrical walk-outs, so many wrist-slashings and overdoses and diva-like breakdowns, the end, when it came, was very quiet. Ray Bolger reflected on his radio show, "Judy didn't die, she just plain wore out." Dirk Bogarde saw her passing as similar to that of Marilyn Monroe: "Take someone as magical as Marilyn; she was totally and utterly murdered by the studio system. And to a degree, so was Judy. They killed her just as surely as they've killed anybody of any sensitivity."[22]

Her life had been lived in the public gaze almost since she first drew breath. "I never looked through a keyhole," she once lamented, "without finding someone was looking back." She would now have privacy for the first time in her life in movie heaven even if her image and legacy remained public property.

Garland's passing was overshadowed by the much more horrific death of Sharon Tate at the hands of Charles Manson's gang of crazed marauders. Tate was pregnant at the time, which made her brutal slaying even more horrific. She wasn't the only person killed on the night in question but she was the most high-profile one. Her slaughter bore dismal echoes of her husband Roman Polanski's *Rosemary's Baby*.

After Manson's massacre he declared that Tate was just one person on a list of possible victims he could have chosen for his killing spree. He probably chose her residence thinking it would be occupied by its previous owner, Doris Day's son Terry Melcher. Melcher was a record producer who'd rejected Manson's musical compositions some years before when he (Melcher) was living there with his girlfriend Candice Bergen.

Many people felt the sixties ended the day Manson and his gang created their carnage on 10050 Cielo Drive. From now onwards, movies would show a harder edge—not only to women but to everyone.

Leaving the Doll's House

Jane Fonda finally broke away from the constraining influence of Roger Vadim when she took on the role of Gloria, the self-destructive Depression era dancer in Sydney Pollack's grim drama *They Shoot Horses, Don't They?* (1969).

Fonda shed her *Barbarella* mane for a tight 1930s bob.[1] The part took her over and changed the way she felt about motherhood, about domesticity, about life in general. She grew alienated from Vadim as she was making the film and began to see the shallowness of his hedonistic lifestyle. She also succeeded in "feminizing" him somewhat, relegating him to mothering duties with their child as she stayed late at the studio finetuning her performance. She was starting to become politicized at this point and watched the escalation of the Vietnam War with growing concern. Her mother had been unpoliticized and unliberated, she told people, and had died young by her own hand. Jane was determined not to be a similar casualty—and not to be another Gloria either, except on screen.

Her demonstrations against Vietnam resulted in her being placed on the "Enemies of Richard Nixon" list, a fact that gave her much cheer, but she crossed a line when she went to North Vietnam and had herself photographed sitting beside an anti-aircraft gun used to shoot down American planes. For many people, especially veterans, this was the last straw in agitprop attention-grabbing. Fonda herself also regretted it in time but felt it was used too much as a stick to beat her with, thereby deflecting attention from her righteous indignation about the war.

It was regarded as a cheap photo opportunity from a pampered diva. Afterwards the moniker "Hanoi Jane" dogged her wherever she went. Her rebellion against the establishment alienated many fans and also, more notably, her father Henry, who'd always been an old-fashioned middle-of-the-road liberal, and someone who believed that politics was essentially a man's game. In 1970 Jane was arrested at Cleveland airport on suspicion of drug trafficking but upon closer inspection her luggage contained nothing more harmful than vitamin pills. It was a clear indication that she was on a hit list from the powers-that-be and she dined out on the incident to advertise that fact.

Anti-Jane feelings gathered speed in the years to come. Even though public opinion turned more and more against America's military presence in this corner of the globe, there were repeated calls for "Hanoi Jane" to be tried for treason.[2] An article that featured a photograph of her being arrested at an army base carried the caption "Jane, a mouthy twerp." The accompanying slogan went: "Treason Howl Over Fonda Girl's Vietnam Broadcasts." Fonda was 34 at the time and objected as much to being referred to as a "girl" than being "mouthy."[3] Another article tried to trivialize her political *nous* by featuring a nude photograph of her on a beach with the caption, "Jane Fonda in the days when Roger Vadim designed her image." The fact that Vadim had been the Svengali of another sex queen, Brigitte Bardot, went against her. Bardot wasn't yet politicized, though she'd begun to be disenchanted with men, and to have largely replaced them with animals in her affections. It meant it was harder for people to take her causes seriously. Vadim himself complained that life with her was "no fun" since she became a "women's libber": "It was like living with Joan of Arc."[4] God may have created Bardot but Vadim created Fonda. He didn't like what she'd turned into and tried to discredit her "cause kick" by accusing her of having a messianic complex.

One of Fonda's great role models, the "troubled" star Frances Farmer, died in 1970. Her passing raised few murmurs from an industry that had thrown her to the lions. She was buried in a quiet cemetery outside Indianapolis and her coffin carried—significantly—by six female pallbearers. Her obituary only made the back pages of the local Seattle newspaper. It trotted out the usual clichés about the fact that she suffered from schizophrenia (which she didn't) and ended with the blunt, "She had no children and there are no immediate survivors." The cause of death was cancer. She died as she lived, alone. She was 56 years old.

Society made an example of Farmer. In an era of ignorance and intolerance she became a sacrificial lamb, a burnt offering to the tin god of fame. Her star burned all too dimly and for too brief a time. She would have been the first to admit she had self-destructive tendencies but she was purified by suffering and became spiritual in later life. Her tragedy wasn't only that she was mistreated both in her home and in sanitariums but, more importantly, that she wasn't allowed revive her career after she mellowed. If we wish to be frivolous about it, we could say she was locked up for the best part of a decade for no better reason than having had a bad temper.

If she was born a decade before she was, she could have been an iconic figure like Vanessa Redgrave or Jane Fonda, a feared and fearful rebel. But she wasn't. She came into a world that was still smarting from the effects of the Depression, and not too many people wanted to hear talk of lofty socialist ideals. Neither did they fancy being lectured by an actress they saw as a jumped-up brat.

She had the insolence of a Brando but Brando was a man. Women weren't expected to be disenchanted with fame, were they? Neither were they meant to object to cattle calls or studio demands. When a starlet dressed in casual sweaters instead of full evening wear, it sent out the wrong message. She was meant to fawn at her overseers instead of sneering at them.

"I hated everything about Hollywood," she said, "The brassy lingo. The lack of sensitivity and individuality. The grist mill philosophy. The yes-men. The crude and influential giants. The Seventh Avenue intrigue. The cruel caste system. The fakery. I hated everything except the money."[5]

Her story was one of survival, her strength of character the thing that kept her sane when the treatment she got from Hollywood and the medical establishment (if not the judicial one) would have driven most other women out of their minds. What she endured, in fact, was proof of that great sanity. She was also a sweet person and a fine actress, qualities that lay buried under the mound of negative publicity her rebellious personality engendered. The fact that she had a mind which challenged the political and religious mores of the time made her a threat to the establishment. That threat dissipated when her insolence and weakness for alcohol were used to liquidate her. It was left to her biographer William Arnold to give her the eulogy she deserved: "Because she was one of the most glamorous and complicated women of her generation, she became a prize guinea pig for arrogant and ruthless men who were determined to remold her into a more acceptable version of herself. When they couldn't save her by their standards, they destroyed her. She was quite simply—and in the truest sense of the word—a martyr."[6]

A Swedish immigrant who never settled fully in Hollywood, Inger Stevens (above) was a woman more in need of love than career success. She was poorly treated by Bing Crosby, Burt Reynolds and others, her life imploding in a series of emotional traumas that eventually resulted in an early death from suicide.

Inger Stevens, who died in 1970, was tragic in a different way, though she and Farmer shared an overly-sensitive disposition. A native of Sweden, Stevens never settled in the U.S. despite spending so many years there. She was the product of a broken home, her mother deserting her father when she was five. In 1955 she married her agent Anthony Soglio for no better reason than that he was the only person she knew in New York. Her first major role was in *Man on Fire* in 1957 opposite Bing Crosby. Crosby dated her for a year and led her to believe he was going to marry her but instead he married Kathryn Grant. (He'd been seeing Grant at the same time as Stevens, unbeknownst to her.) A romance with the married Anthony Quinn followed but this was equally ill-advised, Quinn having no intention of leaving his wife for her.

She made her first attempt at suicide on New Year's Eve, 1959, swallowing 25 sleeping pills and a half-bottle of ammonia. Amazingly, she survived. She received the greatest injection to her career with the TV series *The Farmer's Daughter*, which ran from 1963 to 1966, but her mind always seemed away from what she was doing. She devoted herself to many causes like helping mentally retarded children and also showed a savvy business sense by investing her money in property and various business ventures but she was always prone to depression. It caught up to her after another aborted romance, her estranged lover this time being Burt Reynolds, her co-star on the TV series *Run, Simon, Run*.

It was only after her death (she overdosed on a lethal cocktail of drink and drugs) that it was discovered she'd been married for nine years to the black athlete Isaac Jones. When Quinn heard she'd died, he gave this *résumé* of her life: "Inger didn't belong here. She should have stayed in Sweden and married a truck driver and had eight kids. She had idealism and purity. The great competitiveness and phony accomplishment we have here can be very destructive."[7]

Perhaps, but did Quinn's mistreatment of her not add to that destructiveness? She once said, "A career can't put its arms around you. The thing I miss most is having someone to share things with. I always used to jump into friendships and give too much. You can't do that. You end up like Grand Central Station with people just coming and going."[8]

She made dinner for Reynolds the night before she died but they argued afterwards and then he punched her and went home. She put a bandage on her chin and then called a friend in the antique business and told him she'd saved $20,000 to buy some furniture. He promised to collect it the next day.

She was discovered by a friend the following morning, the bandage from the Reynolds injury still on her chin. There was a half-empty bottle of asthma medicine beside her body but she didn't have asthma. The $20,000 was missing, leading one to believe that she could have been murdered. Similar suspicions surrounded the death of Dorothy Kilgallen in 1965 and of course Marilyn Monroe three years earlier. The point is that she wasn't depressed on the night of her death, having secured the new TV contract. There was also a half-made sandwich on her kitchen counter. Laurie Jacobson asked: Who stopped in the middle of making a sandwich to kill themselves? "Let's see, a little more tomato, another, bacon strip ... oh, the hell with it, get the pills and liquor."[9]

Two other actresses killed themselves soon after Stevens, Bella Darvi gassing herself because of gambling debts and a failed career and Pier Angeli overdosing on barbiturates as a result of depression over her career and love life. Angeli's tale was the most tragic of all. She promised so much when she started out, her elfin beauty intriguing James Dean, whom she would always claim was the great love of her life.[10] But her mother didn't approve of Dean and steered her away from him. She married the singer Vic Damone instead. Sadly, this marriage was a disaster and they divorced, their split followed by a bitter custody battle regarding their children.

She turned to drink for comfort. When Dean died in 1955, it brought up all her feelings of guilt and frustrated love. A subsequent marriage to the Italian composer Armondo Trovajoli also failed. When Hollywood tired of her "angelic" looks, which gave way to the more blowsy image of 1960s objects of desire, she felt she'd passed her sell-by date. She also felt there was a concerted policy by the *paparazzi* to show her in her worst light. Like Inger Stevens she trusted people too much and suffered the consequences of this when Hollywood went cold on her.

As she aged she became dependent on a dangerous cocktail of pills to help her sleep, or blot out the dark feelings brought on by the fact that she was appearing in fifth-rate movies like the near-pornographic *Love Me, Love My Wife* and the science fiction clunker *Octaman.* The failure of her husbands, and other men she found herself sleeping with, to try and assuage her anxieties increased her frustration. Her motive for sleeping with them was a misguided attempt to become "modern," to reinvent herself in the contemporary mode of promiscuity, but she'd have been better served to stay true to her own lights. After she lost her center, she was like a leaf blowing in the wind, and liable to be picked up by those who would use it for their own nefarious ends.

Shortly before she died she wrote to a friend, "Love is behind me, love died in a Porsche."[11] It was obviously a reference to Dean. Would her life have turned out differently if she married him instead of Damone? One can only surmise. (Damone's second wife Judith Rawlins, another actress, also committed suicide around the same age after *her* marriage to Damone failed.)

With Angeli as with so many others, it was the combination of a failed relationship and a declining career that hastened her date with destiny. This was also the case with Rachel Roberts, who finally became divorced from Rex Harrison in 1971. Joan Collins divorced that year too, her marriage to Anthony Newley going into freefall, but she was made of sterner stuff than the other women and less likely to gush out her emotions as they did. "I never speak of my husbands," she droned, "except under hypnosis."[12]

Jane Fonda won an Oscar for playing a hooker in *Klute* in 1971. Henry thought she gave a brilliant performance in the film but he didn't say this to her face, revealing it only four years later on a TV show in Britain. She wasn't surprised, saying, "Many of us know parents who are wonderful with strangers, especially after a few drinks, but in the living room or the bedroom with their intimates they don't know how to show up. They don't know how to love."[13]

Fonda was interested in playing a hooker because in her own way she knew what selling her body felt like. Sean French saw her character in the movie as symbolic of women in all movies. He wrote about the "debased sexual power exercised by casting directors" which Fonda would have experienced.[14] Fonda viewed her abuse by men in the film as a microcosm of a wider general misogyny. For her, this ran the gamut of everything from politics ("Radical men did the talking and made policy; radical women licked envelopes, cooked and were supposed to be sexually available") to everyday concourse: "Like when a woman starts telling a story, the men interrupt and finish it because they assume no one will really understand or find amusing or interesting the way the woman tells it. So the man has to take over and tell it his way."[15]

Fonda believed there was a two-tiered system of values in Hollywood, one for men and one for women. We always knew that, but sometimes the distinctions were blurred. The battle of the sexes was played out in miniature in a 1971 movie called *Play Misty for Me* which sees Clint Eastwood being stalked by a psychotic woman played by Jessica Walter. In one scene he throws her through a window. Was this Eastwood behaving with unacceptable aggressiveness or was there something deeper afoot? Eastwood defended himself by saying, "It was a simple question of survival. She was trying to put a knife in my forehead."[16]

He defended his Dirty Harry–Man with No Name persona more generally when he proclaimed, "I see my films as first aid to the modern male psyche. Masculinity is becoming obsolete. Most jobs today can be held by women. Men enjoy being taken to a period where masculinity was important to survival." Many women saw this line of thinking as a convenient excuse for misogynistic behavior.

Considering *Play Misty for Me* dealt with a psychotic woman, many people felt that it was written by a man. In fact it wasn't. Jo Heims was the woman behind the pen. She saw it as inverse sexism for anyone to imagine a woman wouldn't be interested in writing a screenplay where the "villain," as it were, was another woman. (Of course Walter had sympathetic qualities too.) In fairness, some of the confusion resulted from the fact that her name was sometimes misspelled as "Joe."

Another female screenwriter, Eleanor Perry, scripted *Diary of a Mad Housewife*. It was directed by her husband, Frank, but they had an acrimonious break-up after it was released. This was ironic considering the plot dealt with an unhappily married character, Tina. Tina finds release from a stale marriage by having an affair with another man. This wasn't an ideal scenario for Perry. After her divorce she revealed, "Today I would write the ending differently. I'd [still] show Tina liberating herself, but not through a man. She'd get a job, or go back to school or whatever."[17] Perry went on to become a spokesperson for the dismal status of women in films. On a discussion panel at the 1971 New York Film Festival she said she was tired of seeing women portrayed as prostitutes and sex objects in films.[18] The following year she led a group of protesters who sprayed paint over a poster of a woman with three breasts which was being used to advertise *Fellini's Roma,* waving a placard with the words "Women Are People, Not Dirty Jokes."

She also campaigned strenuously for women to have greater power in the movie business and to have better movies written for them. As she put it before her premature death from cancer in 1981, "Few of them are about women as human beings. They're about women who get hacked up and raped and knifed and cut, and who make biscuits and stand behind everybody like squaws. Most pictures are male buddy-buddy friendship films or violence pictures. You wouldn't know women were part of the human race from most of [them]."[19]

Ken Russell would have inhabited the "violence" category. Or to be more specific, the "sexual violence" one. This was particularly apparent in *The Devils*, his 1971 feature dealing with witchcraft and religious profanity in 17th-century France. Many people were unimpressed by Russell's near-adolescent shock tactics when it came to cloistered repression. According to one writer, the film played on the "skewed notion that beneath every wimple lies lacy scanties and barely suppressed rampant nymphomania."[20]

Women also got short shrift in *The Last Picture Show*. This was a finely-made film but it seemed to see women as little more than "rite of passage" creatures for hormonally-charged young males on the cusp of manhood. Cybill Shepherd fulfilled the "eye candy" function whereas Cloris Leachman essayed the "older woman past her prime" one. The fact that both parts were played brilliantly didn't take away from the fact that they were stock figures. Once again, the May-December relationship between a man and a woman would hardly have been noticed if the "May" role was played by the woman but here Leachman is older than her lover Timothy Bottoms so age became the focal point of the relationship, intensifying Leachman's poignant hopelessness.

Shepherd had an uneven career after the film and an equally uneven set of personal relationships, capping them with the observation: "When you finally catch on to the fact that most men aren't interested in what you have to say and are only looking at you because you're pretty, it's a big shock."

Stanley Kubrick angered women with a depiction of rape in *A Clockwork Orange* that seemed to condone, nay celebrate, the act. Similar charges had been laid at Sam Peckinpah's door for *Straw Dogs*. Both men argued (legitimately) that to depict something wasn't to endorse it. If it was, every murder that had ever been shown on screen would have been an endorsement of killing. It was a fair point, but the increasing brutality of sexual crimes against women engineered on screen by the likes of Kubrick and Peckinpah seemed to normalize this behavior, or to be attempting to render audiences increasingly immune to it. Women complained that they were hoarse from campaigning against such scenes, largely in the dark, and that their prevalence caused an increasing danger of scandal fatigue.

Straw Dogs was a powerful film, but powerful in an exploitative manner. When Peckinpah had Susan George baring her breasts to the hotblooded males of the small Welsh village in which the film was set, he seemed to be giving them some kind of a license to abuse her. The film could have been a feminist parable but instead it opted for sensationalism. This was apparent especially towards the end, and in the scene where George is raped. She wanted to use a body double but Peckinpah threatened to sue her if she didn't do it herself. This caused a *rapprochement* between director and star and George had to give in. She had so little respect for Peckinpah she even feared the rape would take place for real in the scene.[21]

Kubrick was the target of more outrage from women than Peckinpah, especially for his depictions of sex, which often seemed perverse. His biographer John Baxter wrote, "Sex in Kubrick's films is never between loving couples. Instead he explores, as did Mickey Spillane, the furtive and violent side alleys of the sexual experience: voyeurism, domination, bondage and rape."

To buttress his argument Baxter name-checked virtually every other film Kubrick made: "The fate of the peasant girl in *Fear and Desire* and Gloria in *Killer's Kiss,* both bound and terrorized by groups of men; Davy watching Gloria through her window in

Killer's Kiss and fondling her underwear; the post-coital tearfulness of Fay in *The Killing* and Sherry's death on the bed in the same film; Varina and Spartacus spied on in their cell; Tracy Reed in bikini and high heels on Buck Turgidson's bed in *Dr. Strangelove*; group sex and rape in *Barry Lyndon* and Barry consorting with a gaggle of whores; the ghostly bathroom embrace of Jack and the nude phantom in *The Shining*."[22] There seemed to be a conscious search for deviation in all his *oeuvre* for Baxter, reaching its nadir in *Eyes Wide Shut*.

Neither were Peckinpah and Kubrick the only practitioners of perversity in the early seventies. Films like Mike Nichols' *Carnal Knowledge* (1971) made one more than aware of this. The film presented us with a skirt-chasing Jack Nicholson which seemed to lay down a marker for the party animal Nicholson parlayed off screen as well. Tapping into most of the clichéd images of women as sex objects and men as rampaging beasts of testosterone, much of it seemed the emanation of notches-on-the-bedpost bravado. But in the end we saw the vapidity of this kind of life, which made it into a possible feminist tract. Nicholson was brilliant in his solipsistic bubble, conjuring up the kind of conviction that would be more evident in the later roles, but for now this was enough to be going on with. Ann-Margret also showed what she could do when presented with an all-too-rare decent part. For the first half we think we're watching a film that wants to make us hate women but it ends up ridiculing men: an interesting style shift.

Later that year Nicholson became the next door neighbor of Marlon Brando on Mulholland Drive. For the first time the two playboys were living side by side. They didn't only share a driveway; they shared women as well. In that one house move, the testosterone level of the drive seemed to go through the ceiling. It was time for nervous mothers to lock up their daughters.

Brando had had his *Godfather* renaissance by now and built on it with another powerhouse movie, *Last Tango in Paris* directed by Bernardo Bertolucci and co-starring Maria Schneider as Brando's lover and, ultimately, his killer. On one level this looked to be a serious attempt to deal with subjects like male menopause as experienced by a grief-stricken widower but on another it seemed more like an attempt to make pornography respectable. Somewhere in the middle of these two extremes was Schneider with a "deer in the headlights" expression. Bertolucci didn't seem to know what to do with her after she was finished with the sex scenes. Was her murder of Brando a kind of ersatz castration? All sorts of theories flew about as the film was analyzed out of all proportion.

Schneider became defined by the role, which impacted negatively on the rest of her career, or rather non-career. Because she did little else of note, in the eyes of the public she became like a glorified porn star, the *tabula rasa* upon which other equally angst-ridden men could write their instructions. "Bertolucci is more of a gangster than a movie director," she said afterwards. "He's one of my enemies."[23] Schneider was only twenty when she made the movie and couldn't have conceived of the impact it would have. By the time it was over, she felt "manipulated" both by Bertolucci and Brando. "People were insulting me in the streets," she recalled, and—in a reference to the anal sex scene in the movie— "in restaurants waiters would bring me butter with a funny smile."

Another film of this time that exploited women sexually was *Deep Throat*. This played into men's delusion that women enjoyed oral sex as much as they did, a fantasy achieved by a plot device that located Linda Lovelace's clitoris in her throat. One viewer wrote, "Her vagina is desensitized, unimportant; the only juices of hers that flow are saliva. Fellatio can now satisfy both her partner and, by some lazy masculine relocation, her too."[24]

One wondered why Lovelace did it in the same way as one wondered why Schneider did *Last Tango*. "I was naïve," she explained. "Linda Lovelace was a robot who did what she had to do in order to survive. We all had to start somewhere. Marilyn Monroe did it with that calendar, Lana Turner with a sweater. I had to go a little better."[25]

The film was financed by Mafia member Louis Peraino. Lovelace's then boyfriend Chuck Traynor forced her to have oral sex with Peraino to ensure the film got made. This was performed with a gun to her head. Said Lovelace chillingly, "When you see the movie you're watching me being raped."[26] She claimed her life was defined (if not quite destroyed) by it. In later years the kind of comments made to her by casting directors were along the lines of, "All you have to do is throw in one little deep throat scene and the producer will kick in an extra $40,000."[27]

Marlon Brando's (nameless) concubine in *Last Tango in Paris* was played by Maria Schneider. The role came to define her for all the wrong reasons and prevented her from appearing in anything else of note. She always felt betrayed both by Brando and Bernardo Bertolucci, the director of the movie, for its (s)exploitative nature.

How would the film community have reacted if it had been a man who was in Lovelace's shoes? It's interesting to look at John Boorman's *Deliverance* from this point of view. In one scene Ned Beatty is anally raped by a sniveling backwoods man. Audiences were universally shocked at what they saw, much more shocked than they had been at *Deep Throat*. Admittedly the circumstances were markedly different but there seemed to be a double standard at play. Women weren't allowed to be humiliated. They weren't allowed to be victims.

Undoubtedly there are a huge number of men in Hollywood who love and respect women, but there are also many who seem not to, either in their lives or their work or both. They may give lip service to liking them but often it doesn't seem to be evident in what they do or say. Sometimes they censor their comments and it comes out in coded language, or in a Freudian slip. As far as women are concerned, they seem to have card-carrying licenses to misbehave because they're not answerable to them in any great degree.

One of the most rabid chauvinists was the late-lamented Steve McQueen. McQueen treated women as sex objects throughout most of his short life and often seemed proud or at least unrepentant of this fact. He fell in love with Ali MacGraw when they starred in *The Getaway* (1972) and she left her husband, Robert Evans, for him. The marriage was tempestuous. He admired her ladylike qualities but still asked her to cook junk food for him before he took off on his motorbike or flopped down in front of the TV. If her friends called, he made himself scarce. Sometimes he hit her during their arguments, on one occasion tearing the skin beside her eyebrow open as he backhanded her on the forehead.

MacGraw occasionally threw crockery at him in retaliation. Like most bullies, he couldn't take it when she fought back. "One thing about Steve," she blasted, "he didn't like the women in his life to have balls."[28] But he still seemed to attract women like moths to a flame. Was it the whiff of cordite they liked? The author James Bacon said MacGraw started seeing a psychiatrist after marrying McQueen, but added, "Of course for an actress in Beverly Hills to see a psychiatrist is like belonging to a Book of the Month Club."[29]

One night McQueen slept with not one other woman but two. He was making love to them in an apartment next door to their own one and MacGraw heard them. The next morning he even had the audacity to ask her to make breakfast for him. Worse again, she did.[30]

MacGraw broke up his marriage to Neile Adams. He'd been married to her since 1956 but slept with almost any woman who had a pulse during the marriage. It lasted mainly because Adams turned a blind eye to her husband's voracious sexual appetite. Sometimes it didn't matter if she did or not. When he slept with Lee Remick on the set of *Baby, the Rain Must Fall* (1965) he told Adams about it even though he didn't have to: "There was no reason for me to find out except for his compulsion to tell me. Not to hurt me—just to make it all right. For him."[31] She threw him out of the house a few times but always took him back. Eventually she had an affair herself, with Maximilian Schell. McQueen took this so badly he "drunkenly yet seriously" considered hiring a hit man to "ice" her—conveniently forgetting that she was merely getting back at him for his own duplicity.[32]

One night under the influence of cocaine he kicked and struck her repeatedly for sleeping with "the kraut." He screamed, "Why, why, you whore?" Adams replied, "I'm going to have to leave you because if I don't, some day you'll kill me." According to his daughter, "My dad hated all women but me."[33] McQueen died in 1980 at the age of fifty, unreformed but raging against the dying of the light. Maybe the greatest love of his life was cars. Women (and even movies) seemed to come a poor second to anything he did on the track.

George Sanders, who committed suicide in 1972, shared McQueen's poor view of women. "Men have proven themselves supreme in all the arts and crafts," he maintained. "I see no reason why women should presume equality with us." He went on to say, "They often advance the specious argument that they're the power behind the throne. What they mean is that great men wouldn't have been so great had they not had brilliant and enterprising women behind them. Granted. But the women in back of them were just that—in back of them. Where they belong."[34] Such arrogance wasn't unusual for this man. Zsa Zsa Gabor, who had the misfortune to be married to him for a time, put it well: "We were both in love with George Sanders."

Gia Scala also killed herself that year. It was a tragic end to an unfulfilled career. She once revealed that all she ever wanted was to get married and have babies but her marriage was both unhappy and childless. Depressed over such events, she took to drink and some wild behavior that resulted in her husband seeking a restraining order against her. Afterwards she was arrested for drunk driving and placed under psychiatric observation. "I feel sorry for those who try to get by on beauty," she said, "because when the beauty is gone, what will they have left to build a career upon?"[35] Ironically, she herself succumbed to that syndrome. She cut a sorry figure after her career went downhill in the late 1960s, her mood swings accelerated by the onset of a condition called arteriosclerosis which deprived her brain of oxygen.

One woman who wasn't going to end up self-destructing was Jane Fonda. Fonda was as fiery as ever at this point and now starred in Joseph Losey's adaptation of Ibsen's *A Doll's House*. It was a part that had been waiting for her for ages; the surprise was that it took her so long to get around to doing it. She had, after all, crawled out of her own doll's house after jettisoning the worlds represented by everyone from her father to Roger Vadim.

The film, unfortunately, wasn't everything it might have been. This was partly due to the fact that the production team was comprised entirely of men, which was ironic considering the theme of the film. Fonda found them hostile. Neither did she get on with Losey. She felt she was expected to play the role of a "little girl" for him on the set to put him in a good mood. "I found I had to become Nora with him," she chastised. This meant batting her eyelashes at him and even pretending any ideas she had for developing her character were his rather than her own.[36]

Veronica Lake died that year at the age of just 53. Her beauty had long since gone and she was now bathed in a haze of alcohol as she contemplated past marriages, past glories, past betrayals. Her son Mike, who'd been estranged from her for some years, heard the news over the radio and borrowed $500 to fly to Vermont for the funeral. Only thirty people showed up to wave a final goodbye, causing him to deride all the so-called friends who fluttered around her when she was a star. "None of them turned up at the funeral," he fumed. "None of them sent any flowers. Her four husbands, her two daughters, none of them came. She died a lonely and forgotten woman."[37]

"If I stayed in Hollywood," Lake had ruminated in the sixties, "I'd have ended up like Alan Ladd or Gail Russell, dead and buried by now."[38] "When I look back," she said, "I see Veronica Lake as someone quite separate from me, something that was invented by Hollywood and that ceased to exist when [Hollywood] had no further use for it."

There was another movie exit in 1973, though not in a coffin. Brigitte Bardot decided, like Garbo, to walk away from films. Her swan song was Roger Vadim's *Don Juan*. Here she realized a long-held ambition to play a character who used men as men had traditionally used women. One of her lines was, "Men are the real beasts, not animals." It was a sentiment she took to her heart and went on to repeat many times in the future. After leaving movies she devoted herself to numerous animal causes like the preservation of seals. "Unlike men," she liked to say, "animals don't bite you when you pat them."

Bardot got out before becoming a Gail Russell or a Gia Scala. She knew the trip wires. Soon the offers would probably have dried up anyway now that she was losing her beauty and beginning, as she put it, "to look like a map of France." It was time to grow up and try to make the world a better place.

Other women believed they could still make a difference working from *inside* the business. To this end Eleanor Perry wrote the screenplay for *The Man Who Loved Cat Dancing*, describing it as the first women's lib western. It had Sarah Miles as a feisty woman who runs away from her husband (George Hamilton) and then has a relationship with Burt Reynolds. Perry was promised equal control over the material with producer Martin Poll but when she arrived on the Metro-Goldwyn Mayer lot she found Poll's office had rugs, leather furniture, leaded glass windows and a secretary, whereas hers (situated down a hall beside a grubby toilet) was "full of cracks, with a broken air conditioner and a tiny desk." She wasn't consulted about casting and Poll informed her that Reynolds didn't want to work with her because she was a woman and "only jocks" could write westerns.[39]

Reynolds denied saying this but as time went on she found her script was changed. The Miles character was softened and a crude rape scene was inserted because, as Poll put it, such scenes "turned men on."[40] Perry hated the final cut and made her disapproval manifest but it did no good. The film wasn't a success and she didn't get other offers afterwards. Frustrated at the demise of her writing career, she tried to make things better for other women by campaigning for equality for women in films. In 1977 she interviewed Grace Kelly on the subject but was disillusioned to discover that Kelly's ideas on the subject were still "stuck in the fifties."[41]

In the absence of anyone lighting a bomb under the people who ran movies, things looked unlikely to change much on the frontline. Raquel Welch was asked to do a sex film, *The Fan Club*, in 1973. She would have been the first to admit that she used her body to get ahead but she never became salacious. The *Fan Club* script insulted her so much she sent it back to her agent but it kept getting re-sent to her. Each time she refused, the salary she was being offered went up. They reduced the number of rapes in the film from ten to a "mere" (!) six to placate her but she still refused. She was then branded "trouble" by the director, who barked, "Do you know what the life span of a sex symbol is in this business? It's short, very short. So you should cash in on your image before it's too late."[42] Welch was a ripe old 34 at the time.

Other injustices against women came from freakish circumstances rather than conscious bigotry, as in the case of Florence Marly, who made her last film, Eddie Saeta's B-grade shocker *Dr. Death, Seeker of Souls* in 1973. The career of this fine actress was ruined when, years before, she was mistaken by the U.S. Consulate for the left wing nightclub singer Anna Marley. This caused her to be blacklisted by the House UnAmerican Activities Committee. What little work she got during the 1940s was mainly in Europe. The truth was eventually discovered but it didn't seem to make much difference: "Even after I'd been cleared and my story had been in the papers and on television, I was at a party one night and a friend started to introduce me to Jack Warner but he turned his back on me."[43] Unable to secure work in films, she turned to theater but her Czech accent made her difficult to cast. It was a sad reflection on Hollywood that all she was offered was schlock like *Dr. Death* and the gimmicky space opera *Queen of Blood*. Marly died shortly after making *Dr. Death*, aged only 58.

Other actresses suffered simply because they didn't like the people they were working with, or were disapproved of by them. Roman Polanski directed *Chinatown* in 1974 but didn't get on with Faye Dunaway, seeing her as a diva. When she asked him about her character's motivation for a particular scene he retorted with the familiarly sarcastic, "All the money you're being paid to do it." When he was lining up a shot and a rogue hair protruding from her head was disturbing it, he pulled it out without asking her. Dunaway exploded, retreating to her dressing-room and demanding that he be replaced with a "more professional" director. Polanski kept his place by apologizing to her but relations were so strained between them afterwards that for much of the time they communicated through a third party. After the film was released, Dunaway huffed, "What he did to me throughout the film bordered on sexual harassment."[44] Polanski countered by saying that Dunaway was "a gigantic pain in the ass" and someone who demonstrated "certifiable proof of insanity." (Was this, one wondered, because she didn't appreciate strands of her hair being pulled out?)

There seemed to be a presumption with many men that they could do what they liked with women. Male chauvinism reached its nadir with Oliver Reed, who announced, "I like women in their place. I like them on their knees in the kitchen, doing the dusting or whatever. In return I feed them, wine them, make them laugh, and give them a punch on the nose and a good kicking when they need it. A woman should behave like a lady— a nun by day in the kitchen and a whore in bed at night."[45]

Telly Savalas was another man who seemed to regard it as his right to be physically abusive to women. Savalas divorced Marilyn Gardner in 1974. Like Oliver Reed and Sean Connery he made statements throughout his life which appeared to endorse his right to strike a woman physically if she "deserved" it. "I adore women," he claimed, "I am their total slave up to a certain point. I pamper them and cater to them but, when necessary, you have to bop 'em."[46] It's almost as if the "love" condoned the violence, or at least softened it in his eyes. Maybe the "pampering" was the flip side of it. Such terms harken back to an era where women were the cute things on the side, appendages to hang off one's arm, to flatter, applaud ... and hit when "necessary."

Interviewed in *Playboy*, Sean Connery was asked how he felt about "roughing up" a woman. He replied, "I don't think there's anything wrong about [it] although I don't recommend doing it in the same way that you'd hit a man. An open-handed slap is justified if all other alternatives fail. And there has to be plenty of warning. If a woman is a bitch, or hysterical, or bloody-minded continually, then I'd do it."[47] The question referred to screen violence by his Bond character but one felt he was speaking about real life too. By now he was "out of Bondage," Roger Moore having taken over the 007 mantle. Britt Ekland was a Bond Girl in *The Man with the Golden Gun* (1974). Feminists thought it was trash "but I was a single mother with two kids to support. In order for there to be a Jane Fonda or a Vanessa Redgrave there have to be people like me."[48]

Some women were strong enough to break free of the shackles that held actresses like Ekland back. The screenwriter Joan Tewkesbury epitomized this. She'd walked out on her husband and two children to become a fulltime screenwriter, which to some people sniffed of self-indulgence. (For a man it might have been seen as "obsessive dedication to the craft.") She feared she'd have a breakdown if she continued to live the life of plenty in suburbia with all her creature comforts—she was married to a financier—so opted for a one-room apartment instead. She then suffered the brickbats of those who tarred her with the "desertion" brush.

One of the people who paved the way for women like Tewkesbury was Ida Lupino. Lupino was in semi-retirement by now. When an interviewer asked her if she'd like to direct again, she gave an interesting answer. "I've had offers but they would have taken me out of the country, which would have meant leaving my home, my daughter, and being away [for] months on end. That's where being a man makes a great deal of difference. I don't suppose men particularly care about leaving their wives and children. During the vacation period the wife can always fly over and be with him. It's [more] difficult for a wife to say to her husband, 'Come sit on the set and watch.'"[49]

Fay Kanin wrote the screenplay for the TV hit *Tell Me Where It Hurts* in 1974. She put the success of the movie down to the fact that it didn't wear its message (the importance of self-awareness for women) on its sleeve: "You didn't say the word 'consciousness-raising.' That [would have been] the kiss of death. It was about women who didn't even know what consciousness-raising was all about." They were housewives in a blue-collar neighborhood just starting to talk to one another and take baby steps towards self-realization. Kanin's winning ticket was her refusal to bow to genre stereotypes. "I don't believe there's such a thing as a woman's story," she reflected. "I resent it when men say emotions are the precinct of women. The men I like best are the ones who show their emotions. Both sexes lose out when we're categorized this way."[50]

Another hit with women that year was the documentary *Self-Health*. This was a medical movie that returned women's bodies to themselves. It gave advice on matters we often take for granted today, like how to check for lumps that may be malignant. Julia Lesage wrote, "A doctor can spot such phenomena from having had the opportunity to feel many women's breasts. Why should such knowledge not be made available to women themselves?" Lesage believed the mass media's use of breasts (etc.) to sell consumer goods robbed women of ownership of them. The side effect of this was that many women had little sense of what sexuality on their own terms might mean. *Self-Health*, hopefully, did something to put that to rights.[51]

Another positive sign for women was the fact that in September 1974 Doris Day was awarded $22 million by a court for being defrauded on a consistent basis in the preceding decade by her aforementioned manager Jerome Rosenthal. He'd invested her money in non-existent oil wells and suspect hotel developments. He'd also charged exorbitant fees to her for routine duties and in general did everything he could to conceal his double-dealing from her. Rosenthal contested the judgment and hauled Day back into court on multiple occasions before finally being disbarred in 1988. By then it was far too late for Day to get her rightful due from him, extracting only a fraction of the 1974 sum in subsequent hearings. Rosenthal had also duped other stars like Dorothy Dandridge, his mismanaging of her affairs almost certainly contributing to her depression and early death. It was estimated that in the end, Day only recouped about $3 million from him.

The most talked-about "woman's film" made that year was Martin Scorsese's *Alice Doesn't Live Here Anymore*. It would have been even more talked-about if it was helmed by a woman, as it should have been, but it had a brilliant leading role for Ellen Burstyn. She played a woman trying to get herself together after the death of her husband, getting solid support from Kris Kristofferson as the new man who enters her life.

Burstyn clashed with Scorsese on the set. When he discovered she was helping Kristofferson (who had virtually no experience as an actor) with his performance, he freaked out. When she advised Kristofferson about a scene behind Scorsese's back, the director lashed out at her with this tirade: "I didn't know you were giving him directions between shots. We're gonna reshoot that whole scene."[52] Would he have huffed quite as much if Burstyn was a man? It's unlikely.

There were problems about the end of the film as well. How could a would-be feminist parable end with Burstyn riding into the sunset with Kristofferson? Scorsese didn't want this but production head John Calley was insistent that "she has to end up with a man." Scorsese felt his artistic credentials were on the line. Would he sell out to commercialism or follow his artistic light? In the end he compromised. The ending wasn't schmaltzy but neither was it as woman-friendly as Burstyn would have wished. When she saw the final cut, she laid into Scorsese, so much so that he warned, "I will never allow an actor in my editing room again."[53] His use of the word "actor" was significant. One felt he might allow an actor in, but not an actress.

There was a similar compromise in Sidney J. Furie's *Sheila Levine Is Dead and Living in New York* (1975). This tale of a pampered girl contemplating suicide after her boyfriend jilts her betrayed the best-selling novel on which it was based. It had Levine opting for marriage to a doctor in the final reel, an ending that infuriated women. Once again a movie chose a cheesy finale that was totally out of character.

Maybe the year wouldn't have been complete without a tragedy. In fact, it had two. Mary Ure died from a lethal combination of alcohol and pills, having abused both for most of her short life. Her talent was never given the proper opportunity to shine, largely due to the fact that her two husbands—John Osborne and Robert Shaw—were manipulative men subject to violent rages. In the course of these they tended to demean her and everything she represented. She fell prey to the bottle to drown her sorrows and eventually it caught up on her. With Osborne she also had to contend with infidelity. Shaw she accused of destroying her career and turning her into a housekeeper.[54] The night before she died, she had a violent row with him and afterwards fell asleep in the living-room. She never woke up, choking on her own vomit. Shaw passed through the room the next morning but didn't even check to see how she was, going off to a studio to shoot a film. When he returned a few hours later, she was dead.[55]

Another tragic star, Margaux Hemingway, appeared in *Lipstick*, playing a model who's raped and who then makes an effort to exact justice. The abysmal film featured her sister Mariel in a smaller role. Mariel would go on to become a successful actress while Margaux, an epileptic, languished in a fog of alcohol and junk food after a promised modeling career failed to materialize. "I loved to dance," she revealed, "and went to Studio 54 at least twice a week but I always felt nervous around the people there. To me they were the real celebrities and I was just a girl from Idaho." She drank to relax but it only made her tensions worse: "In my grandfather's time it was a virtue to be able to drink a lot and never show it."[56] She was referring to Ernest Hemingway, the famous writer who killed himself on July 2, 1961. Margaux committed suicide on July 2, 1996, the 35th anniversary of Ernest's death. Perhaps she was making some kind of statement about the price of fame, or even its transience.

Why did Mariel make it and not Margaux? We may as well ask why the sky is blue or why grass is green. Maybe she was too pure to succeed in the Hollywood jungle. Whatever the reason, few people remember her today. Her career didn't so much stop as fail to start. Another delicate flower born to blush unseen, she was catapulted prematurely to "Hollywood heaven."

Before she died, she made a cryptic comment about the difference between the sexes which may have been significant: "Men are six feet," she said, "but women are five feet twelve."

The Beginnings of Cynicism

Veteran director Dorothy Arzner railed against male supremacy in the cinema in a 1976 interview: "Today, of course, even the stars are all men. When [they] put women in pictures, they make them so darned sappy, weeping all over the place, that it's disgusting."[1]

She might have been speaking of Jessica Lange, who came into prominence that year with John Guillerman's remake of *King Kong*. Lange played the Fay Wray role and feared she would become identified with it, as was Wray's fate. The remake was much more sophisticated than the 1933 original, but Lange felt she was little more than another special effect. She imagined that after the film was released, audiences would think she was "phenomenally stupid" like her character in it.[2] In this Beauty and the Beast fable, she felt her own beauty could be a career-threatening "beast" for future performances. Her biographer J.T. Jeffries took up the point:

> Beauty is not an easy thing to survive. It is the most forgettable, the most fleeting of powers. Automatically painted on by every man or woman who sees her, the beautiful woman's very presence is freighted with assumptions and expectations that go back to the farthest reaches of fables. The beautiful woman is a walking myth, the only woman in every movie. For such people, life and legend are the same. The dumb blond and the doomed blond, they're the same people played in succession. Destruction is inherent in the part. Lana Turner the Sweater Girl becomes Lana Turner pleading for her daughter's life in the murder trial of her gangster lover. Marilyn Monroe is inseparable from her suicide. The two legends unite: The blond American sex goddess is created to be destroyed, like some virgin chosen to be sacrificed to appease the Gods.[3]

Judith Crist outlined the plot of the film succinctly in *The Saturday Review*: "A dumb blond falls for a plastic finger."[4] "It was a joke," Lange added, "and because I was the central character, I was sort of a joke [too]." She didn't find it too funny, however, when its producer, Dino de Laurentiis, referred to her as the next Marilyn Monroe. "That really upset me," she told *Time* magazine. She didn't want to be compared to a tragic figure who "wasn't taken as the serious artist she was."

What made the film even more demeaning for her was the fact that she spent the first three months on the set running around in a bikini top and a grass skirt, delivering her lines to a non-existent character. "I never saw another actor," she stated, "There was no real Kong to react to. I had to play to the ceiling; or to the wall, or to the floor."[5]

Lange escaped victim status by carving out a productive career after this poor start but others weren't so lucky. Some had an early hit and then disappeared; others took the dollar and ground themselves into "samey" roles for the better (or rather worse) part of their careers; others never got off the ground in the first place.

Sondra Locke was a young woman who could have fallen into any of these categories and in the end seemed to inhabit them all in different ways. She first came to attention in 1968 in Robert Ellis Miller's fine adaptation of the Carson McCullers novel *The Heart Is a Lonely Hunter* but is better known today for her frequent collaborations with Clint Eastwood. She began a love affair with Eastwood during the shooting of his western *The Outlaw Josey Wales* (1976), a film in which she co-starred. She was only 15 at the time and Eastwood was married. She appeared with Eastwood the following year in *The Gauntlet*.

Other Eastwood pairings followed. Then she got married, but continued to live on and off with Eastwood. She was one of a string of mistresses he bedded during his marriage, many of them resulting in out-of-wedlock children. Locke also became pregnant by him but he prevailed upon her to have abortions whenever she did.

Seen here in *The Deep* (1977), Jacqueline Bisset was well aware how alluring she could look in a wet T-shirt but she was determined to make more of her career than this kind of sensuous posturing—even though she used such posturing to good effect in her early years to get where she wanted to be.

Locke's husband was gay so her interest in Eastwood was understandable. Eastwood gave her to believe his marriage was unhappy and that he was considering leaving his wife Maggie for her. But this wasn't the case. He believed in having an "open" marriage—at least on his side. "The sophisticated woman," he believed, "accepts the chances are that a guy's not being 100 percent faithful."[6] Such "logic" was tantamount to a license to cheat.

Maybe we can blame Locke for getting herself into a pickle of her own making, even if she couldn't be expected to see the long-term consequences of it. Hollywood women knew they had to make compromises but sometimes the extent of these increased exponentially as the years went on, and these they shouldn't be blamed for.

Another actress who made "limited" compromises was Jacqueline Bisset. The fact that she didn't find herself in the position of someone like Locke was due to a more clear-headed overview of where she was going and what she represented. Bisset appeared in *The Deep* (1977), a film directed by Peter Yates and based on a Peter Benchley novel. *Jaws* it wasn't. Yates used Bisset's body to sell the film just as he had in *Bullitt* to a lesser extent a decade before. On that occasion she showed enough of her thighs to set male pulses soaring; here the emphasis was on a wet T-shirt and no bra underneath it. One was reminded of a comment on Esther Williams, "Wet she's a star; dry she ain't."[7] Bisset was aware of the problem, complaining, "If you work long enough [in films] you get some sort of physical image and people think of you in that light. That upsets 'me.'"

Bisset felt that directors tried to exploit not only her body but also her mind: "Everything in movies is exploitation. They ask you for something extra in each scene, hoping to capture some part of you. That's stealing. Directors try to steal emotions from you."[8] Elsewhere she added, "I'm either offered window dressing parts in large movies or little art films no one ever sees. People think the movies I end up doing are my real choices but they're not. I do the best things I'm offered."[9]

Bisset was never under any illusions about the perch she occupied and how she came to be there: "The male computer says short skirt, nice high heels, good legs because that's the way he's been brought up to react."[10] She played the game up to a point, realizing she was getting many of her parts because of the way she looked but using her sexuality as a platform rather than a destination. It was her bargaining chip, a foot in the door that might lead to better things. Perhaps she never gave what might be termed a classic performance but she had longevity, unlike many beauties whose careers faded with their looks.

Her point about directors exploiting women for their bodies took on a darker aspect that year when Roman Polanski hit the world's headlines for all the wrong reasons. At the beginning of the year Polanski persuaded the mother of 13-year-old Samantha Gailey to allow the young girl to be photographed by him at her home with a view to putting her in films. The following month he took her to Jack Nicholson's house where he promised to introduce her to the star. Nicholson wasn't home as it happened so Polanski took the opportunity to do his own thing with Gailey. He plied her with champagne and then asked her to take off her clothes and step into a bath, where he planned to film her. She was feeling sick from the champagne so he gave her some tablets to, as he put it, make her "feel better." But instead they made her drowsy. Polanski then stepped into the bath with her and had various forms of sex with her against her will.

Anjelica Huston, who was living with Nicholson at the time, returned to the house and, sensing what had happened, told Polanski to leave. Polanski brought Gailey out with him and drove her home. When she went inside her house, she phoned her boyfriend and told him what had happened. Her sister overheard the call and told their mother, who phoned the police. Soon afterwards Polanski was arrested. After being questioned he was charged with oral sex, sodomy and furnishing Quaaludes to a minor. His attorney managed to get the charges reduced to one of unlawful sexual intercourse if he pleaded guilty. He did that, and served some time in prison awaiting trial. His lawyer also put plans for a plea bargain in place, and the prosecution's legal team seemed agreeable to this. But then the judge announced his intention of "throwing the book" at Polanski. When Polanski heard this, he fled to Europe for sanctuary.

Technically speaking Polanski has been a fugitive from justice ever since. There have been various calls for him to be extradited or pardoned, the former imprecations coming mainly from outraged members of the public and the latter from Polanski's friends and colleagues within the film industry.

Gailey herself, who became Samantha Geimer after she married, forgave him and said she didn't want to see him imprisoned. Polanski made great films in Europe in the ensuing years but many people still feel he should be put back in jail for a considerable period of time. Polanski says he feels victimized by the whole affair, claiming it was wrongly reported by the media, who'd had it in for him ever since he had the "bad taste to have a wife who was murdered."[11] That, of course, was Sharon Tate. It seems a lame excuse and a largely irrelevant harking back to something that happened so long ago.

Away from all the hullabaloo about Polanski, a member of "Old" Hollywood breathed her last. Joan Crawford died in May 1977, having faded almost totally from the public eye. Her last public appearance was with Rosalind Russell at a book launch. The following morning she opened a newspaper and was stunned to see a photograph of herself looking bloated from antibiotics she was taking for arthritis. "If that's how I look," she snorted, "they won't see me again."[12] She was true to her word, living a Garboesque existence for her remaining months.

After she left films, Crawford continued to have an executive profile because of her marriage to Alfred Steele, the president of Pepsi-Cola. Her standing diminished there after he died, and when she reached 65 she was elbowed out. She lost her salary, her expense account, her limousine service, her secretary and even her hairdresser. Pepsi wanted her to be guest of honor at their San Francisco convention the following year to commemorate her achievements with the company but she was too devastated to agree. "I worked my ass off for that company for almost twenty years," she snarled, "and now they've washed me up. Well, screw 'em."[13]

She spent much of her retirement watching her old movies on TV like a latter-day Norma Desmond, a prisoner of her legend. "A pillow is a lousy substitute for someone who really cares," she proclaimed. "And when it comes right down to it, aside from Alfred and the twins, I don't think I came across anyone who really cared."[14] When the twins castigated her as the Mother from Hell in later years, her undoing seemed to be complete.

A new type of woman was coming into films at this time, harder and more flinty than her predecessors, but running into the same "caveman" attitudes from men who had been so prominent in the Crawford era. Sherry Lansing became senior vice-president of production at Columbia in 1977. She'd been an actress but left that to do script reading and then rose through the corporate ranks speedily to become one of Hollywood's first female executives. She ran into Michael Douglas at a studio meeting for *The China Syndrome* and his first thought was, "Who did she sleep with to get into this room?" Even after he learned how adept she was at her job, he still insisted on trying to keep her in her place.[15] Lansing promised to try and eradicate this type of chauvinism from films, and actors, and also to "reform" the film industry itself by making strong films for women. These were ambitions she only partly fulfilled in the years ahead.

Why didn't she look for a project like *An Unmarried Woman*, which was made by Paul Mazursky in 1978? This was an important film for women. It started by showing us an ostensibly happy marriage between Michael Murphy and Jill Clayburgh, but then one day out of the blue Murphy tells Clayburgh he's been seeing another woman behind her back and has fallen in love with her. Clayburgh is distraught when he tells her he doesn't love her any more and is leaving her for the other woman. Clayburgh throws up in horror. Afterwards she visits a therapist and tries to get her life together. She has a fling with a friend and then meets an artist (Alan Bates) whose eccentricity amuses her after the relatively staid life she's lived with Murphy. Towards the end of the film Murphy tells her his new "love" has left him and that he wants Clayburgh to take him back. He asks her to think of him as a man who was suffering from an illness and is now healthy. A 1930s screen heroine would have taken him back. So would one from the forties and fifties, and maybe even the sixties. But she rejects him with a flat "No."

This wasn't a film about infidelity but rather about how a woman who's been betrayed moves on with her life. The fact that it was written by Mazursky as well as directed by him is interesting as this is most definitely a "woman's film." Murphy comes across as pathetic and childish, blubbering as he leaves Clayburgh and smiling ruefully as he tries to get her to take him back. Clayburgh displays the kind of resilience one saw in past screen women but here it's more aggressive than that of her forbears. The "modern" woman has arrived. She's not willing to accept her husband's dumping of her as a temporary aberration. Having had her trust in him betrayed, she now refuses to re-align that trust. From now on, her life will be her own. At the beginning of the film, one of her friends tells her she's taken a lover many years younger than her, a teenager in fact. Clayburgh also rediscovers her youth with Bates, a fact brought home to us in the film's last scene where he makes her carry a huge painting of his through crowded streets. It's a ditzy moment for her in a hitherto un-ditzy life. Murphy has, in a sense, done her a favor by leaving her. He's unfettered her, giving her her new self.

"Real" life was much more messy than Paul Mazursky's film that year in terms of marital break-ups. Ryan O'Neal divorced Leigh Taylor-Young to move in with Farrah Fawcett-Majors, parting from her with the kind of trite remark that seemed to allude to his own shallowness: "Marriage is the best magician there is. In front of your eyes it can change a cute little dish into a boring dishwasher." The most publicized split, however, wasn't from a married couple at all. In January 1979 Michelle Triola took her estranged lover Lee Marvin to court in a palimony case, which changed the face of live-in relationships in Hollywood forever.

Triola's claim for financial compensation from Marvin—what came to be called "galimoney"—was fortified by the fact that he'd made her have two abortions after becoming pregnant by him, and by the fact that she'd changed her name to Triola-Marvin (though she wasn't married to him) and even had that name on her passport and apartment bell.

The pair also had an oral agreement to "share equally any and all property accumulated" by them during their time together. Despite the fact that they didn't have a "three dollar marriage license," Triola would go on to become "the most expensive mistress in the world."[16] Marvin ended up paying her the then-phenomenal sum of $104,000, despite his original claim that "about one dollar" would be all she'd get from him. When Triola charged that she'd given him the best years of her life, he snarled back, "I also gave *her* the best years of her life."[17]

The final judgment caused ripples of apprehension to spread across the Hollywood board, making every man who lived with a woman for any considerable length of time nervous about his finances whether he took her up the aisle or not. For Triola it was an endorsement of her validity as a woman because she'd given up her career for him and often endured his hellacious behavior under the influence of drink. She also had to listen to him describe his feelings for her as being "like looking at the petrol gauge in your car. You can be empty, half-full or full."[18]

On a more ominous note, Jean Seberg committed suicide in 1979, a victim not only of Hollywood's casual cruelties but also the racial intolerance of the day. A woman with a big heart, her generous financial contributions to organizations like the Black Panthers and the Malcolm X Foundation led to J. Edgar Hoover forming a plan to "get" her any way he could.[19] She was married to the novelist Romain Gary and when she became pregnant with his child, a rumor circulated that it wasn't Gary's but rather that of a member of the Panthers.

Hoover allegedly gave this information to Joyce Haber, a *Los Angeles Times* columnist who published the story in that newspaper on May 19, 1970. It was then picked up by *Newsweek*. Seberg was in Majorca at the time. When she read it she became so upset she tried to kill herself by taking an overdose of pills. She recovered, but went into labor two months prematurely and the baby was stillborn. This prompted another suicide attempt. Afterwards, according to Gary, she tried to kill herself every year on the anniversary of its birth, August 28. It was born white, as she knew it would be, and at the funeral she insisted the casket be kept open so everyone could be a witness to that.[20]

Seberg went on to sue the publications that ran the Black Panther story. She received generous settlements but the money was cold comfort to her. Then Hakam Jamal, a cousin of Malcolm X, was murdered. This sent her into a further depression and she underwent treatment for it in 1972. In the same year she married the blacklisted director John Berry, having divorced Gary, but this marriage also failed. By now she'd developed a serious alcohol problem to add to all her other ones.

In her last years she was grossly overweight and plagued with guilt over everything from how her career went wrong to her voracious sexual appetite. To punish herself she burned herself with the stubs of cigarettes and then tried to ease the pain with pills and booze. Twelve days before she died she tried to throw herself into the path of an oncoming train. Her actual suicide took place on September 8, 1979. In her suicide note she wrote, "I can't live any longer. I can't deal with a world that beats the weak, puts down the blacks and women and massacres infants."[21] Her death shocked the world, and more particularly

Gary, who never got over her. The following year he shot himself, unable to deal with her absence.

Jane Fonda's reaction to her death was, "If I hadn't taken up a cause, today I'd be a dyed blond, a numb and dumb pill-popping star. And I could very well be dead." The point was that Seberg *did* have a cause, or rather many causes, and they contributed to her death. Fonda co-starred with Robert Redford in Sydney Pollack's *The Electric Horseman* the same year. It was the first time Redford had appeared opposite an actress of his own age since he made *Barefoot in the Park* with her twelve years previously. The grim statistic wasn't lost on Fonda, who railed, "What I really hate is watching Robert get younger and younger leading ladies. We're living in a society that makes it more difficult for women to get older than men. Men get lines of distinction; women get crow's feet."[22] (Redford's next two co-stars, Demi Moore and Michelle Pfeiffer, would be 25 and 20 years younger than him respectively.)

Fonda began her fixation with workout regimes at this time, setting up studios in a wide range of locations and preaching her new gospel of keeping fit to fill the place in her heart once occupied by antiwar campaigning and pleas for sexual liberation. Some people were cynical about it, seeing it more as a smart business investment rather than a range of activities designed to make women feel proud of their bodies. Joan Rivers quipped, "Jane didn't get those muscles from lifting weight; she got it from counting all her money."

Fonda followed *The Electric Horseman* with *The China Syndrome,* another of her "social issue" films, this one focusing on a nuclear leak. She received an Oscar nomination but was beaten by Sally Field for *Norma Rae.* Meryl Streep won Best Supporting Actress for *Kramer vs. Kramer,* a film that seemed to be about to say something profound about the new, liberated mother before it descended into sentimental mush.

Norma Rae was scripted by the husband-and-wife team Harriet Frank Jr and Irving Ravetch. It was labeled a "woman's picture" but Frank disputed this, saying it was simply a film about somebody who had to make do for herself under considerable pressure. She prided herself on the fact that it featured a male-female relationship that didn't result in sex. This, she felt, was unusual for the time—or any time.

Joan Tewkesbury directed her first full feature in 1979, having been given her wings by Robert Altman, with whom she'd collaborated on *Thieves Like Us* and *Nashville.* She said that, on her first day on the set, "I actually waited around a few moments for Altman to say 'Action!' before I realized that was my job now."[23] The film was called *Old Boyfriends.* It had Talia Shire going in search of her former lovers to try and understand herself better. It didn't do any business at the box office and Tewkesbury was afterwards shunted into television work, the penalty for failure being more stringent for women directors than men. (They usually only got one chance.)

As the seventies drew to a close, the demise of the star system which was threatened at the end of the previous decade was now a *fait accompli.* Stars ran for cover, searching anywhere they could for work that was once automatic. Some of them gravitated towards television and became mini-icons there. People spoke of the Joan Collins of *Dynasty* or the Linda Gray of *Dallas* in the same breathy tones they once reserved for Garbo and Crawford. The dethroning of past goddesses seemed complete with the new plasticization of glamour on the small screen. Many of these shows were suffused with a tackiness that mocked their own excesses.

Other actresses ran to the theater for sustenance. Had the cinema turned its back on women forever? Looked at from a bird's eye view, it certainly seemed that way. Most of the seminal blockbuster movies of the sixties had male themes, male actors, male slants: *The Alamo, The Guns of Navarone, Judgment at Nuremberg, Lawrence of Arabia, The Longest Day, Tom Jones, Dr. Strangelove, Alfie, In the Heat of the Night, Butch Cassidy and the Sundance Kid* and *Midnight Cowboy*. When women were featured, as (say) in *The Graduate*, it was often as an adjunct to the main theme.

Such a pattern continued in the seventies with features like *M*A*S*H, Patton: Lust for Glory, The French Connection, A Clockwork Orange, Deliverance, The Godfather, Dog Day Afternoon, Rocky, Taxi Driver, The Deer Hunter* and *Apocalypse Now*. When women had quality roles, it was often as unsavory characters (Faye Dunaway in *Network*, Louise Fletcher in *One Flew Over the Cuckoo's Nest*, etc.) We had *All the President's Men* but not *All the President's Women*. (If we had, they'd probably have been call girls.)

There were exceptions, of course, even if the material was lightweight, as in *Mary Poppins, My Fair Lady* and other family-friendly programmers. But even here, there was a certain amount of patronization of women. The same could be said of *The Graduate* where both women ("good" girl Katharine Ross and "bad" woman Anne Bancroft) seemed like throwbacks to a simpler era. In *Last Tango in Paris*, as already mentioned, we were presented with Maria Schneider first as an object of humiliation and then as a murderess.

When directors like Steven Spielberg and George Lucas arrived, the "human interest" story, which had vouchsafed women some interesting roles in the past, became virtually non-existent. Instead we had special effects, computers and intergalactic extravaganzas.

Was there anything for women in *Jaws* except being allowed to scream? Was there anything for them at all in *Apocalypse Now*? Did Princess Leia "rescue" *Star Wars* for them? In many ways they seemed to have regressed back to the cloisters of the Hays Code days.

In 1977 Richard Dreyfuss won an Oscar for *The Goodbye Girl*. Marsha Mason was nominated for Best Actress but didn't win, Diane Keaton beating her for *Annie Hall*. The title of the film seemed an appropriate one to sum up the inequities of the century up to this point. Goodbye girl, hello man—once again.

Fatal Attractions

Anne Bancroft directed the offbeat comedy *Fatso* (1979), employing another woman, Brianne Murphy, as her director of photography. Her reason for doing this was unusual: Bancroft felt uncomfortable giving orders to men. Murphy also had writing and directing credits, but photography was her main talent. She'd worked on many substandard films in previous years, mainly due to the fact that she wasn't "union," the boss at the International Alliance of Theatrical Stage Employees (IATSE), the union for film technicians, informing her in no uncertain terms, "My wife don't drive a car, you ain't gonna operate a camera." He told her she'd only get into the union over his dead body, which was ironically prophetic as he died soon afterwards. "Right after his funeral," Murphy crowed, "I got in." She could have made an issue out of his boorishness but chose not to: "A lot of people expect me to be a leader. They think I should be out making speeches telling other women how to get jobs. [But] I'm not the type to lead movements. I just wanted to make movies badly enough to pay the price [of being] kicked around."[1]

Fatso was no masterpiece but at least it had two women at the helm. The following year a survey conducted by the Directors Guild of America revealed that only 14 of the 7332 features made in Hollywood in the previous thirty years were directed by women. There were signs that trend might change when Sherry Lansing was made president of Twentieth Century–Fox. Was she going to do something about this worrying statistic? "You betcha."

Lansing's good intentions were only fitfully successful in the following years. There were thought-provoking films made for and by women but they always seemed to be undercut by an acceptance of the *status quo*, even if this wasn't immediately apparent.

In *Nine to Five,* for example, three women conspire to subvert workplace chauvinism by kidnapping their boss. Jane Fonda, Dolly Parton and Lily Tomlin played characters who try to change the system from within but the concept was trite. The film became little more than an escapist fairy tale, a would-be role-reversal polemic in which the kidnapped boss is forced to see life from the female side, sitting at home like a couch potato with only his television for company.

How near was this to real life? Even if it *was* real, what could it achieve? Far from being a feminist statement, it came across more as a jejune cry in the wilderness for a Better

World. In some ways we were better off with the Fonda of *Barbarella*. At least there was some genuine satire rather than a self-congratulatory nod towards social reform. On the credit side, it was good to see Dolly Parton stepping away from her country and western image as a dumb blond. Though as she often claimed, "I'm not dumb and I'm not blond."[2]

Goldie Hawn was in a similar quandary. In 1978 she appeared in yet another wacky comedy, *Foul Play*, and wondered where she might turn to next. She felt she'd exhausted her comedic side but Hollywood wasn't ready to accept her any other way. The question she had to face was, "How old can you be and [still] play a dizzy blond?"[3] The answer came with *Private Benjamin* (1980). Hawn shed her "bubblehead" image in this movie, at least temporarily. A career changer for her, it had her playing a woman whose husband dies on their wedding night, forcing her to rethink her direction in life, eventually plumping for an army career that changes her outlook so much that by the film's last scene she's able to run away from the altar instead of marrying a bully.

Raquel Welch was also regarded as a bubblehead by many directors. She was contracted to appear in *Cannery Row*, based on two novels by John Steinbeck, but was sacked before shooting began because she was regarded as too old for the part. (She was an ancient forty at the time.) She sued MGM for "wrongful termination" of her contract when Debra Winger was chosen to replace her. She knew it was a dangerous move to "buck the male-dominated system" but she had to do it. As the trial progressed she learned that her dismissal was premeditated. She was awarded $25 million (the amount was later reduced to $11 million) but it spelled the end of her film career. Her phone didn't ring for a year, after which time she went to Broadway to pick up the pieces.[4]

Welch's case proved that where women were concerned, appearance was everything. Not so for men. Robert De Niro won an Oscar for *Raging Bull*, the role requiring him to put on a record 60 pounds to play the self-destructive boxer Jake La Motta. The weight gain commanded almost as many column inches as the performance as people went into ecstasies about his commitment to the part. Brenda Fricker sniped, "When a man gains weight for a part it's called artistic dedication but when a woman does it it's called 'Letting herself go.'"

In some ways the film was like a sequel to *On the Waterfront*. De Niro's hero was Marlon Brando and he indexed Brando's "Brother Charley" speech from *Waterfront* in the last scene. By now Brando had long lost the finely-tuned body he had in that movie, turning from Terry Malloy to Jake La Motta in his ever-expanding girth. He had also more or less retired, though for a few minutes in *Superman* he made more money than most actors (and certainly most actresses) made in a lifetime.

Margot Kidder played Lois Lane in *Superman*. She looked set for a productive career but, like her life, it went off the rails afterwards. Nobody is quite sure why she went for "a walk on the wild side" but at one point there were newspaper reports that she was living as a hobo. Was it due to something as simple as the fear of getting old? Hollywood was very much a man's town, she declared after she hit thirty: "When you reach my age you're supposed to disappear or get six facelifts or eye jobs or tit jobs or whatever which I'm not going to do, and come back when you're a respectable grandmother at sixty."[5]

The most shocking story of the year involved Dorothy Stratten, one of Hugh

Hefner's "playmates," who was shot to death by her estranged husband-agent, Paul Snider. Snider was a major factor in Stratten's rise to prominence but he couldn't take it when she became romantically involved with Peter Bogdanovich. Bogdanovich believed Stratten was a victim of "the *Playboy* machine," which shredded women of their dignity and made them into so many Barbie Dolls for men's pleasure. He outlined these views in many interviews and in a book devoted to Stratten, *Death of a Unicorn*.

Bogdanovich fell head over heels in love with Stratten the moment he saw her. He knew she was married but also that she was unhappy with Snider. He became a kind of father figure to her, a confidante. He told her he'd made a star of Cybill Shepherd with *The Last Picture Show* and promised to do the same for her with the film he was about to shoot, *They All Laughed*. He wrote a part for her into it.

After she moved in with Bogdanovich, Stratten told Snider she wanted a divorce. Snider went ballistic. He bought a shotgun and started to stalk both Stratten and Bogdanovich. One day when she visited him, ostensibly to give him some money (because he'd allegedly "made" her with the *Playboy* shoot) he shot her dead, had sex with her lifeless corpse, and then shot himself. It was almost like a rerun of the Sharon Tate horror. In an ironic footnote, *They All Laughed* was a failure at the box office. Bogdanovich went on to marry Stratten's younger sister Louise. He was accused of everything from pedophilia to a perverse desire to recreate Dorothy in her sister. They were similar in appearance and were both twenty when he met them. "My excuse is, my mother was twenty when she had me," he stated, "so I guess it's [an] *idée fixe* of some sort."[6]

Bogdanovich blamed Hefner for Stratten's death. He felt she was typical of the type of woman he groomed for exposure, pushing her in directions in which she didn't necessarily want to go for his own gratification. He thought Stratten married Snider to escape Hefner after he made sexual demands on her. After his book came out, he went on television to advance its arguments and to further castigate Hefner for being an accessory in her demise. Hefner countered by accusing Bogdanovich of having intimate sexual relations with Louise when she was only thirteen. Everything became very ugly as legal depositions were served on both sides. Both men were tarnished by it. Bogdanovich's career suffered and Hefner got a stroke. Suddenly, it seemed, the carefree life of the *Playboy* stud didn't seem very carefree at all.

It's all too easy to cast Snider as the villain of the piece, and Bogdanovich also, but as one writer pointed out,

> Snider seems to have taken Hollywood by surprise. Being an outsider he obviously didn't understand the rules. Hollywood accused him of trying to cash in on Dorothy's fame, overlooking the inconvenient fact that that was exactly what they were trying to do. Snider's crime, apparently, was that he found Dorothy working behind a shop counter and promoted her modeling career to the ultimate in a model's dream, Playmate of the Year. At this point, and given Bogdanovich's interest, it seemed to Hollywood only natural that he should fade quietly away and leave it to the "professionals," i.e., those who'd exploited more than one girl before.[7]

Another gruesome death occurred towards the end of the year when Rachel Roberts finally made good on her decade-long threat to kill herself, still unable to deal with the absence of Rex Harrison from her life. The date she chose was November 25, the same day that Harrison was interviewed in the *Los Angeles Times*. He was now 72 and with yet another wife. The interviewer found him in ebullient form. His latest spouse, Elizabeth, Harrison described as the "Catherine Howard" one. It was as if he was playing a numbers game like Henry VIII. He may not have had his exes beheaded but he displayed a terrible coldness to them. He once declared, "Nobody is as interesting to spend an evening with as a really good part." Some people believed the only enduring relationship he ever had was with his basset hound, Homer.

He was less than a mile away from Roberts when she died. Carole Landis killed herself over him in 1948 and now a tragic slice of history was repeating itself. Two days after her death, Harrison took to the stage to reprise his most famous role, Henry Higgins, in a San Francisco production of *My Fair Lady*. Roberts lay in her grave while the ever-resilient Rex trod the boards: "The show had to go on."[8] Roberts' friend Pamela Mason explained her death like this: "What Rachel couldn't endure was the apparently effortless success Rex was enjoying without her."[9] The fact that she took her life almost on the eve of his opening night in *My Fair Lady* wasn't coincidental.

Other stars died in equally distressing circumstances at this time. Natalie Wood was drowned in 1981 after an argument broke out between her husband Robert Wagner and Christopher Walken, who co-starred with her in her last movie, *Brainstorm*, and with whom he was allegedly having an affair. It was the end of a life that was lived intensely ever since her first exposure to a camera when she was hardly out of the cradle. Was either man to blame for what happened? Tongues even wagged about the possibility that one of them pushed her off the cruiser after she spent her last evening drinking with them off Catalina Island.

How did she die? Why did she die? Nobody knows for sure. All we can say for certain is that a beautiful woman was cut off in her prime, the victim of her own fragile emotional state, and two men who fought over her didn't take care of her as she walked uncertainly towards her death. As one writer put it, "We'd been looking at Natalie Wood for 35 years and suddenly, when it counted, no one was watching"[10] That's what Messrs. Wagner and Walken should have on their consciences, not the weird conspiracy theories about murder that have fueled the gossip mills since 1982.

Romy Schneider, just 43 years old, was another siren who died in 1982. Some people speculated that it might have been suicide. She was found with a cigarette in her hand and an unfinished letter to a magazine (cancelling an interview she'd arranged) in front of her. There was also an empty bottle of red wine beside her. She'd been depressed over the break-up of her marriage to Daniel Paisini, her second husband, the first having killed himself. "I'm through with married life," she warned not long before, "I spent my life investing all my money on men but it proved useless."[11] An even greater source of her grief was the death the previous year of her teenage son, David. He was returning home to his grandparents' house and, finding the gate locked, tried to climb it. When he was halfway over he slipped and was impaled on a spike which entered his stomach. Schneider never recovered from his death and took to drink and pills in her bereavement, much as she'd done when Alain Delon left her in the sixties. Delon said piquantly after he heard what happened, "Her death began with David's death."[12]

Grace Kelly also died that year, in a car accident. Afterwards rumors flew about marital discord and arguments with her children. It was ironic that the location of the crash was the same place she'd filmed a scene for *To Catch a Thief* in 1955. Her co-star on that occasion was Cary Grant, a former lover and lifelong friend.

So ended the life of the princess of privilege. She was a victim not only of Hollywood's failure to fight harder to retain her, or draw her back, but also of a short-sightedness in herself that imagined a woman as passionate as she could forego all she had for a lifestyle that had all the trappings of grandeur but all the traps too.

Kelly had wanted to make a screen comeback in *The Turning Point* in 1977 but Prince Rainier forbade it just as he pooh-poohed Alfred Hitchcock's repeated imprecations for her to make one last movie for him because it didn't befit her royal status. She once confessed, "I hated Hollywood. It's a town without pity. I know of no other place in the world where so many people suffer from nervous breakdowns, where there are so many alcoholics, neurotics and so much unhappiness."[13] Perhaps, but when she went to Monaco it was like going from the frying pan into the fire.

Barbara Stanwyck was given an honorary Oscar by the Academy of Motion Picture Arts and Sciences in March 1982, its traditional method of apologizing to those it had neglected in the past for "actual" Oscars, and usually when they were on their deathbed. Stanwyck wasn't quite that. She accepted the award graciously even though it spared the blushes of an organization that had passed her by for so many great performances, especially in *Double Indemnity, Stella Dallas* and *Ball of Fire.*

Jessica Lange was nominated for an Oscar for playing Frances Farmer in *Frances*. She deserved the nomination but the film had problems. It was lead-footed in pace and also played around with the facts of Farmer's life. Kim Stanley played Lange's mother but her part was bowdlerized like that of her daughter. "I'm damn mad at a studio," she hissed, "that thinks the American public can sit still for five hours of football but [not] for an emotional study of a grown woman." The editing of the film she described as "constant *coitus interruptus.*"[14]

Lange had problems with this too: "One day I'd be doing a breakdown scene and a month later I'd have to do the scene leading up to it."[15] She pleaded for it to be shot in sequence but no one listened, mainly because the film's budget didn't permit such "luxuries." Another problem she had concerned the scene where policemen broke into a hotel to arrest her and she ran from them into a bathroom, frightened out of her wits in her semi-naked state. The door to the bathroom kept sticking and it took four takes to free it. The scene only lasted three minutes but it took four days to shoot. As a result of all these glitches, Lange started to feel "as used, abused and manipulated" as Farmer had been in real life.[16]

As well as receiving an Oscar nomination for *Frances*, Lange also got one for Sydney Pollack's cross-dressing comedy *Tootsie*, in the Best Supporting Actress category. Dustin Hoffman was nominated for Best Actor. He was bossy on the set, as another co-star, Teri Garr, discovered. He was insistent about doing scenes his way and didn't brook any resistance from her. Even when she gave in to him, he was unhappy. "I don't want to do it my way until you *like* doing it my way," he told her.[17]

Robert Towne made his directorial debut with *Personal Best* in 1982. The film explored a lesbian relationship between Mariel Hemingway and Patrice Donnelly but as with *The Fox* and some other films we've seen, it had the leading star going "straight" at the end. Towne was trying to placate both lesbian and heterosexual audiences with this ploy but in effect he probably lost both. He seemed to lose interest in Donnelly after Hemingway grows away from her, leading one to believe Hollywood hadn't totally given up on its old policy of punishing homosexuals. This time, though, instead of death or suicide, the punishment was simply "narrative banishment."[18] At least Donnelly didn't throw herself off a cliff, as one viewer observed. (She would have done so a decade earlier).

Another problem with the film was the unnecessary amount of closeups of women's bodies, leading viewers to think of it as covertly exploitative.[19] One scene had Hemingway and Donnelly wrestling. Towne insisted it be shot with them naked from the waist down. This seemed unnecessary and gratuitous, a viewpoint shared by the film's editor, Bud Smith.[20] It made it all fetishistic. Would a male-male relationship have been filmed like this? Hardly. One writer put it in a nutshell: "Women making love is a male fantasy; men making love is not—and men still run the industry."[21]

Other films of this time were blighted by bad chemistry between the stars in them. Debra Winger felt Richard Gere was cruel to her during the filming of *An Officer and a Gentleman*. "I liked him before we started," Winger remarked, "but that's the last time I can remember talking to him."[22] Bette Midler appeared in Don Siegel's black comedy *Jinxed!* but she also had a bad time making the movie. Midler's abrasive personality clashed with the quieter one of her co-star Ken Wahl and Wahl became sarcastic with her as a result. Prior to shooting a scene in which he was called upon to hit her, he remarked: "I thought we could save some money on sound effects here."[23] Siegel also argued with her, chiefly about her wish to have more singing in the movie. One day Midler became so incensed about her songs being axed she climbed on Siegel's back in anger. Siegel's wife ended up "slugging" Midler in the *melée*.[24]

Midler thought Siegel was directing the film sloppily. When she said she'd prefer a more professional approach, she was castigated for being a diva. "A man can yell on the set," she believed. "But let a woman yell...." Both men turned on her as the shooting progressed, Wahl at one point remarking that the only way he could talk himself into kissing her for a romantic scene was to pretend he was kissing his dog.[25] The film disappeared without a trace after it was released and Midler had a nervous breakdown as a result. She didn't make another film for two years. "Directors didn't want me," she complained. "I was given the favourite old label of being difficult."

She couldn't understand what was happening as she'd had great relationships with men on previous films; she'd always been "one of the boys." The appropriately titled *Jinxed!* changed her attitude to the general plight of being female: "A lot of times during the women's movement I'd think, What's all the fuss about? If you're smart, you go in and say what you want and that's that." What *Jinxed!* taught her was: That *wasn't* that. "The picture opened my eyes to the world. I said to myself, I'm not the only woman who has gone through this." To protect herself from future humiliations, she formed her own production company, All Girls, and found herself free from male interference there. But Siegel didn't let go of his anger. His parting shot to her was, "I'd let my wife, children and animals starve before I'd subject myself to working with her again."[26]

One of the most interesting films of the year was Mike Nichols' *Silkwood*. It sailed close to the nuclear wind but still stopped somewhere short of being totally true to the life of its subject. In real life Karen Silkwood was bisexual but the decision was made to edit this element out of the film for fear of reducing sympathy for her social crusading.[27] Cher played a lesbian in a supporting role to, as it were, cover this base. She loses her lover, Diana Scarwid, who goes back to her husband in a scenario all too common for us by now. So we still, as Vito Russo joked, don't have a lesbian couple who make it through to the last reel in a mainstream movie.[28] Even so, Cher still felt it broke down sexual stereotyping.[29]

Silkwood scripter Nora Ephron chose to place her emphasis on personality rather than politics because of the human interest angle. "Even heroes have to put their socks on," she believed. This aspect of the film annoyed the critic John Gill, whose view was that it was "rather akin to making a film about Joan of Arc and concentrating on her period pains." This was unfair. If Ephron had championed her too much, critics like Gill would no doubt have spent their time bleating about her God complex. Silkwood's blue collar "ordinariness" made her taking on of the system much more exceptional than it might otherwise have been.[30]

Silkwood was an important film for women but it was surrounded by a lot of dross. Jill Ireland made *Death Wish II* with her husband Charles Bronson, reputedly because no other actress would work with him.[31] Dolly Parton appeared in *The Best Little Whorehouse in Texas*, the title alone enough to advise us of where its sexual politics lay. Goldie Hawn made the forgettable *Swing Shift*, meeting her future life-partner Kurt Russell on the set. By now she had two failed marriages behind her, one to a choreographer, Gus Trikonis, whom she supported financially, the other to actor-musician Bill Hudson, who was jealous of her fame and sued her for alimony after they split. "I never understood my husbands' problems," she said. "They couldn't deal with the fact that I was a big star and making more money than they were."[32] Russell and Hawn made a decision not to marry, which was probably wise. It meant that whatever friction they had in their relationship didn't end up in the divorce courts.

Hawn's career moved in fits and starts in the following years. In *Protocol* (1984) she played a kind of "Mrs. Smith Goes to Washington" type diplomat but the film was too fluffy. In the original script she was a serious thinker but Hollywood felt this wouldn't wash with audiences so her character was changed into the giggly klutz of *Rowan & Martin's Laugh-In* fame. The studio may have been right in this but what they should have done was change the actress rather than the script. As things stood, Reaganomics held sway and the film ended up as a harmless (but financially profitable) comedy. Three years later Hawn was again hijacked by the money men in *Overboard*, a film in which her stout defiance of motherhood is steadily whittled away by a screwball script that turns her from stubborn heiress into a menial homebody at the beck and call of (who else) Kurt Russell and his ready-made family of amiable urchins.

Star 80, a biopic of Dorothy Stratten, was another big budget 1983 release. Directed by Bob Fosse, it earned critical kudos, though Peter Rainer thought Fosse's style of direction made him become more like the alter ego of her killer Paul Snider. "Fosse doesn't seem much interested in Dorothy as a character," he wrote. "*Star 80* isn't her movie. It's Snider's in the same way that *Taxi Driver* belonged to De Niro's Travis Bickle. It's a portrait not of the destroyed but the destroyer."

Rainer pointed out that Mariel Hemingway was exploited in the movie just as Stratten was in real life, having had her breasts surgically enhanced for a role that wasn't so much an empathetic biopic as an excuse for Fosse to present another sex-and-sleaze extravaganza.[33] Neither was it Hemingway's first time to be exploited. She had, after all, been sexually abused by a Snider type in *Lipstick*, and made into a kind of part-time designer lesbian in *Personal Best*. The film purported to be a critique of the *Playboy* empire but in many ways it came across as a celebration of it.

Joan Collins posed nude for *Playboy* in 1983 at the age of fifty and the magazine sold out. Did Collins? Opinions differed on her decision to do the shoot. In one sense it was a victory for "the older woman"; in another it seemed like an undignified action. She said, "One of the first things that stuck in my mind when I was put under studio contract was that at 17 you had to do well as a woman because at 25 you were all washed up." She gave the lie to that dictum but was the price worth it? Maybe not, especially when she went on to make junk like *The Bitch* and *The Stud,* which carried taglines like "Give Your Dad or Your Boyfriend Joan Collins for Christmas!"

Collins had become a kind of elder stateswoman by now. The cheeky upstart of yore was now a middle-aged lady to be contended with. She railed about men in interviews like a British Zsa Zsa Gabor, and also seemed to have Gabor's way with one-liners. When people complained about the number of expletives in *Scarface*, that year's gangster hit, she deadpanned, "I hear there are 183 'fucks' in the movie. That's more than most people get in a lifetime!"[34]

Scarface starred Al Pacino in the title role and Michelle Pfeiffer as his cocaine-sniffing lover but he seemed to have more devotion to his "leetle friend"—a grenade launcher. Neither was he very pleasant to her offscreen. She recalled of an early reading of the script, "We'd sit in a room and it was like pulling teeth to try and find any words at all." It was an unashamed man's movie. Mary Elizabeth Mastrantonio, who played Pacino's sister, summed up the atmosphere: "It was a man's world and [there were] all these people with greasy hair and big guns. We girls didn't know why we were there."[35]

Barbra Streisand also explored a man's world in one of her most talked-about films, *Yentl.* This was a turn-of-the-century tale of a young woman in Eastern Europe who disguises herself as a boy in hopes of receiving a better education. Streisand adapted it from a short story by Isaac Bashevis Singer and produced and co-wrote it as well as directing.

She also put it to music. It was a big hit with Streisand fans and she expected to be nominated for Best Director and Best Picture but all it got was a Best Supporting Actress nomination for Amy Irving. (She didn't win.)

Streisand blamed her failure to be nominated on Hollywood's "rampant sexism."[36] Simone Sheffield remarked, "If Norman Jewison directed it, *Yentl* would be up for Best Picture. He'd be up for Best Director and she'd be up for Best Actress." Her view had many adherents. A poster at the ceremonies pleaded, "An Oscar for *Yentl*—The Lost Cause," citing the statistic "Best Director Nominees from 1927 to the Present: Men 273, Women 1."[37] It was unfair to blame her for putting the project to music as that decision was made for her by the producers. So was the decision to have her appear in the movie as a teenage girl even though she was nearing forty.[38]

Shirley MacLaine won the Oscar Streisand believed should have been hers for *Terms of Endearment*. This swept the boards in 1983. The following year Sally Field won for

One of the more vocal campaigners for women's rights in her lengthy career, Barbra Streisand is here pictured opposite Mandy Patinkin in *Yentl* (1983), a film she imagined would open people's eyes to the sad plight of women in times past. Instead she became largely a figure of fun as a result of it. She didn't win the Oscar she expected for directing it and was castigated for adapting the project to suit her own ends.

Places in the Heart, playing the same type of plucky heroine as she had in *Norma Rae* five years previously. An actress once dismissed as the sexual plaything of Burt Reynolds, she left him and reinvented herself as a spokesperson for women's rights. "My country is still so repressed," she reflected. "Our idea of what's sexual is blond hair, long legs, 22 years old. It has nothing to do with humor, intelligence, warmth, everything to do with teeth and cleavage."[39]

John Sayles made *Lianna*, a film about a young woman who "turns lesbian" to escape a bad husband. Maybe too bad. "Lianna's husband is such a bastard," Vito Russo observed, "the film gives the viewer the idea that if men weren't so odious women wouldn't turn to each other."[40]

No matter where you turned, there seemed to be anti-female agendas, either overt or covert. It was so ingrained into the Hollywood DNA, maybe the perpetrators weren't even aware they were doing it any more. Sex, money and age were the three biggest sticking points. They always had been and maybe they always would be, no matter what little wars were fought and won on the three fronts by individual filmmakers.

Brian De Palma was accused of belittling women on all three counts during various phases of his career but in 1984 he reached a new low. Whatever grudging respect this director may have garnered from critics and/or the public in the past was whittled away by his trashy *Body Double*. Joan Smith felt that, in de Palma's eyes, a woman who's raped and killed in the film seemed to provoke her murder for de Palma by "a sexual exhibitionism which takes the form of deliberately undressing in front of a lighted window every night." Smith saw similar anti-women elements in de Palma's earlier slasher movie *Dressed to Kill* (1980) where Angie Dickinson's character is portrayed as "actually desiring sexual violence" and thereby in some way deserving it. The fact that it's perpetrated by a cross-dressing man (Michael Caine) further exculpates the male, because it's Caine's "feminine" side that slashes Dickinson to ribbons. From this point of view, *Dressed to Kill* makes itself into "a crude response to male fears aroused by the new model of sexuality claimed for women by feminism."[41] It may give us an extra reason to be perversely intrigued by these two movies when we realize that Nancy Allen, De Palma's real life wife, was terrorized by maniacs in both of them. Was this masochism on her part and/or sadism on his? Or his nepotistic protection of himself from female contumely by having the object of such brutal treatment coming from his own house?

Some actresses managed to beat the kind of stereotyping Allen seemed to welcome at her husband's hands. The actress-cum-screenwriter Ruth Gordon appeared in *Maxie* (1985) at the age of 87, even managing to ride a motorcycle and doing her own stunts. Gordon fought sexism right through her career. She was plain in appearance and also short in stature. When someone said, "You're not pretty, you're no good," she advised, "Think of me and don't give up." Her prolific output (which was capped by an Oscar win for *Rosemary's Baby* in 1968) was a ringing endorsement for such an attitude. Another colorful precept by which she held great store was, "Never face facts."[42]

The fact that Gordon was able to secure film roles into her eighties was an eye-opener to all the actresses who felt they were over the hill at thirty. Jane Fonda in particular was shocked at the way woman of a certain age were summarily shunted out of the limelight in films, playing mothers and even grandmothers while their similarly-aged male peers cavorted with nubile teenagers as the genial father figure-cum-lover.

Many of them, as we've seen, retreated to character roles to stay afloat while others opted for the surgeon's knife to stem the aging process. Fonda, meanwhile, held fast to the "Stay natural" ethos she'd been plugging in her aerobics programs since the beginning of the decade. "We've got to make friends with those wrinkles and sags and gray hairs," she insisted. "We see women who've been nipped and tucked and injected and peeled to within an inch of their shiny, taut lives. Are they beautiful? No. Where is the personality, the life experience? It's gone. Besides, you can see an inflated breast a mile away."[43] (The mania for augmentation was entertainingly captured in a sign placed on the door of a Los Angeles restaurant: "Jackets Not Required; Breast Implants Preferred.")

Fonda clawed back on these pronouncements in the following years, having cosmetic surgery to remove fat from her upper and lower eyelids in 1986 and a breast implant the year after that. For her critics this was yet another example of her intellectual wooliness, but one always got the impression that she believed passionately in what she said when she was saying it even if she changed like the wind afterwards.

Hollywood hypnotherapist Wanita Holmes tried to help those who regretted having had augmentation, mainly because they'd had the procedures for the gratification of the men in their lives rather than themselves. She put it down to the shallow mindset of L.A., aka Silicon Valley: "Growing up here is very difficult," she allowed. "You're in a kind of beauty contest from the day you drop from your mother's womb."[44]

So far the eighties looked like bad news for women, but two films made by female directors in 1985 gave them some solace. The first, Susan Seidelman's *Desperately Seeking Susan,* the film that launched Madonna's movie career, was a charmingly kooky comedy that blurred the distinctions between mainstream and underground independent. Seidelman became a director almost by default, applying to the New York Film School mainly because she couldn't think of any other career to pursue after graduating from college. "I just assumed I could be a director," she declared. "I never questioned that I couldn't and as a result I was kind of ignorant. But I also think that ignorance is bliss. I wasn't aware how bad the statistics really were for women."[45]

The second woman-friendly film of 1985, Donna Deitch's *Desert Hearts* was one of the first to deal with a lesbian theme without resorting to melodrama. All too often in the past it was men who made such films. Recent works like John Sayles' *Lianna* and Robert Towne's *Personal Best* had disappointed, partly for this reason. Deitch had a woman's touch and directed the film, in particular the love scenes, with the kind of empathy that was entirely free from male voyeurism.

Desert Hearts became a cult hit. One of the reasons for this, in Annette Kuhn's view, was that the lovers were attractive and their relationship liberating and joyful, unlike screen lesbians of yesteryear who tended to be a depressing lot.[46] *Desert Hearts* was also the first mainstream film about a lesbian relationship in which neither woman is killed, commits suicide or runs off with another man.[47]

178

Seidelman and Deitch led the way for women directors. Others tried to join their ranks but weren't successful, like Sondra Locke. Locke was still involved romantically and professionally with Clint Eastwood and had started working on a Warner Bros. script called *Ratboy*, which concerned a half-rodent freak of nature. The project had Eastwood's blessing but when she decided to rewrite the script he exploded with rage. "Clint warmed to my desire to direct," according to Locke, "because I think he enjoyed the idea that he was going to be my mentor." When she started to assert herself over the material, however, he went cold on it. Previously he thought Locke was going to have the same point of view as he would have: "I would be [his] little carbon copy."[48] But that was changed now; she'd infiltrated his power base.

Eastwood's biographer Patrick McGilligan wrote, "As long as the actress treated Clint as Daddy everything was hunky-dory but the minute she stepped out of his cocoon and sought to be perceived on equal terms—challenging him on his own turf—his attitude towards her changed and hardened."[49]

Locke wasn't the only actress talked down to in 1986. So was Sigourney Weaver when she was making *Aliens*. Weaver was one of the few action heroines around at this time but if she thought she was going to be placed on a par with the Sylvester Stallones and Arnold Schwarzeneggers of the world, she had another think coming. This was made clear to her the day she had an argument with the film's director, James Cameron, about a particular scene in which she didn't want to use a gun to deal with the extra-terrestrial. "What are you gonna do?" an exasperated Cameron asked her, "talk [him] to death?"[50] At times like this, Weaver pined, "I felt like a fugitive from a chick flick in his eyes."

In 1986 we also had the quasi-sensuous *9½ Weeks*, a would-be erotic fantasy that had all the suggestiveness of a dead haddock. Playing out like some kind of stylized shampoo commercial, it had Kim Basinger and Mickey Rourke exploring one another's nether regions with the aid of some culinary additives that director Adrian Lyne mistakenly assumed would ratchet up the eroticism. The trenchcoat brigade lapped it up and it became a hit, lining the pockets of both of its stars. "All I liked about it was the money," Basinger admitted, and who could blame her? What started as a light-hearted (if saccharine) romance became, in Lyne's hands, a kind of S&M precursor to *Fifty Shades of Gray*. To this end he tried to bring terror to Basinger's character, at one point entreating Rourke to slap her to get her "in the mood." In the original script Basinger walked away from Rourke but in Lyne's version she falls in love with her chains. The newly liberated woman wasn't chained to the kitchen sink any more; she was chained to the bedpost.

Lyne made *Fatal Attraction* the following year. This could have been a film women warmed to, dealing as it did with the pain of unrequited love, but under Lyne's sledge-hammer direction it more closely resembled a revenge tragedy presided over by a psycho-bitch from hell.

The film is a gory treatise on marital infidelity. This is suburban horror, all the more fearful for being so recognizable. Stephen King made a fortune from recounting such tales. Lyne is more prosaic in his delineations but his pitch towards melodrama is no less insistent. A man, Dan (Michael Douglas), sleeps with a woman and then tells her he's happily married. The story is probably 2000 years old. So why did it create so many reverberations? Probably because Lyne knew which cages to rattle, which prejudices to tap into.

His genius from a marketing point of view was in making the straying husband the victim of the piece instead of the woman he impregnates and then deserts. Because Glenn Close, his lover, with her burning eyes and her wild hair resembles a medieval witch dressed up in the clothes of a sophisticated career woman unlucky in love. Douglas eventually becomes a hero despite having done "the bad thing."

Lyne turned the story of films like *Room at the Top* on their head. His Joe Lampton cad is our new role model, the protector of stability in domestic households, aided and abetted by the loyal wife who cooks for him and raises his child. She doesn't cook rabbits. That delight is left to Close, who commits the cardinal sin of invading the family home at the end and thereby offending the frontier mentality, the stability at the core of Mr. America—even if he does waver beyond the marital bed betimes.

Richard Corliss aligned Close to the vamp status of actresses such as Theda Bara, pointing out that her "masculinized" aura is enshrined even in her name, Alex, while Lyne's grab-bag of slick thrills is "hack chic" and thus great date movie fodder. Quoting Lord Byron's dictum "Man's love is of man's life a thing apart/'Tis a woman's whole existence," Corliss believed Douglas could "shower off the sentiment as he showers off the sweat" while Close had to slit her wrists to show she cared.[51] Everything about her character screamed gothic. There was even something about the creaking elevator where she had her first sexual encounter with Douglas that put one in mind of a horror film, as if they were being transported to some Stygian dungeon or crypt.

The original script of *Fatal Attraction* (1987) was sympathetic to the character of Glenn Close, pictured here with Michael Douglas, but Adrian Lyne was directing the film and he decided it would make more money if she was turned into a monster instead. And so it came to pass.

James Deardon wrote the original story on which *Fatal Attraction* was based. In this version, Dan's wife, Beth, was a peripheral character. For the movie Lyne wanted her transformed into "an icon of good wifery" in order to blacken Alex more. In the new treatment there would be a chiaroscuro of Light and Dark, the

"Victorian hearth angel" pitted against the Monster from Hell—and prevailing like some distaff knight errant. Lyne also came up with the idea of having Alex dressed up in black leather and living in a barren loft in New York's meat market district, "ringed by oil drums that burned like witches' cauldrons." This might have been acceptable if he pitched the film as an escapist thriller but he went on to remark that he knew many single women like Alex in the publishing world, women who "lacked soul" and were aggressive in their work because they were "sort of overcompensating for not being men."[52]

Douglas rowed in behind Lyne when he said, "If you want to know, I'm really tired of feminists, sick of them. They've really dug themselves into their own grave."[53] Together they made a film which morphed from the story of a husband's infidelity to one of serial stalking, ending in rightful retribution. In the original script Alex committed suicide while listening to the music of Madame Butterfly but test audiences didn't respond enthusiastically enough. "It wasn't cathartic," Deardon stated. "They were all wound up to a pitch and then it all kind of went limp and there was no emotional payoff for them."[54] The new ending—which ignored the fact that Alex was pregnant with Dan's child when Beth (Anne Archer) shoots her—cost over $1 million to shoot but it was more than compensated for by ticket sales. The film was soon a talking point all over the world as Close became a kind of human (or rather inhuman) manifestation of AIDS: i.e., the ultimate punishment for illicit sex. But surely the point is that it's she who dies, not Douglas. Even so, most people today see the *Fatal* of the film's title as applying to him rather than her.

The final scene revved people's hate quotient up so high, by the end of it even women were screaming "Punch the bitch's lights out!" at the screen. "Everyone knows a girl like Alex," Lyne insisted. (If they did, then "Everyone" must live in Transylvania.) As if this wasn't bad enough, he went on to speak about his wife in the same mode: "She's the least ambitious person I've ever met. She's a terrific wife. She hasn't the slightest interest in doing [*sic*] a career. She kind of lives this with me and it's a terrific feeling. I come home and she's there."[55] These words were spoken in 1987 but we might as well have been back in the sixties with *The Donna Reed Show*.

Douglas seemed to carry his screen character home with him after the film wrapped, being cited for infidelity shortly afterwards by his wife Diandra. (She walked in on him unexpectedly at the Wiltshire Hotel in Beverly Hills and found him making love to another woman.) To save his marriage he promptly signed himself into a clinic claiming to be suffering from something he called "sex addiction." The vernacular term for this is "cheating" but "sex addiction" sounds more profound, particularly when one pays $19,500 a day to be treated for it, as Douglas did. One was left thinking that a whole generation of unfaithful husbands could have kept their wives sweet over the decades if they dreamed up such a condition. Perhaps Diandra could have countered that she was suffering from "money addiction" and sued the pants off him in the divorce courts.

Outrageous Fortunes

Dawn Steel became president of Columbia Pictures in 1987 and proved herself to be a tough contender in business, so much so that people started to joke that she lived up—or rather down—to her surname. Previous females in executive positions, including Sherry Lansing, were known as "geishas," i.e., compliant women who played by men's rules as if living in fear that they'd be kicked downstairs if they didn't. But Steel was a different breed. She made her own rules. "Men can like me or lump me," she asserted, "and if they lump me sometimes it's better because then I can tell them what to do with themselves." One producer gave her this dubious accolade: "If she was any more aggressive, they'd have to lock her up."[1]

Liberation now meant something different to women. It wasn't dropping out or going to San Francisco with flowers in your hair. More likely it was being elected chairman of the board. But the kind of films that were being made didn't reflect this. They looked as if it was mostly men who were plotting them. And of course they were.

In *Suspect* (1987) Cher played an unhappy attorney, complaining to a colleague in one scene, "I don't have a life. The last time I went to the movies was a year ago. The only time I listen to music is in my car. I don't date. I'd like to have a child but I don't even have a boyfriend so how can I? I don't think I can do it any more. I'm tired, I'm really tired." To put those words into the mouth of a male attorney—substituting "girlfriend" for "boyfriend"—would have been unthinkable.

Holly Hunter played a network producer in *Broadcast News*. The film would have us believe that it's impossible to combine this with a healthy social or marital life. Her work suffers because she can't find a man. Ditch the job, the film implies, and Mr. Right has a better chance of hoving into your path.

Diane Keaton appeared in *Baby Boom*. It was partly written by a woman, Nancy Meyers, so one might expect its sympathies to be feminist but when one strips away the surface details this becomes yet another hymn to motherhood. As the film begins, Keaton plays a woman who appears to be obsessed with her executive career, and also to be disarmingly bereft of anything approaching a maternal instinct. When she actually has a baby, and then gets sacked, she starts a business selling baby food to wealthy moms in the rural habitat to which she retreats after the city rejects her. Such food becomes so popular, one of the companies she used to deal with offers her a huge amount for the patent. The film starts to mix its drinks at this point but they stick in the audience's gullet. Will Keaton adopt a pose of "If you can't beat 'em, join 'em"? Or set herself up in opposition to them with her newfound franchise? Neither, as it happens. She continues to live her simple life with baby in tow and cozy country mothers beating a path to her door for their treasured apple sauce. The film ends with a fuzzy "country virtue, city vice" vibe that's a total cop-out to the foregoing.

Elaine May directed *Ishtar* (1987), a film that failed abysmally, thereby setting the cause of women directors back years, if not decades. A huge amount of money was poured into it but most of the budget went towards the salaries of its high-profile cast. Warren Beatty and Dustin Hoffman pocketed $5 million each, as opposed to May's $2 million. The responsibility of having to earn that kind of money back handcuffed her and prevented her from experimenting with any creative ideas she might have had.

It wasn't as if she didn't have talent. She already showed that on *A New Leaf* (1971). Jack Lemmon described her as a genius.[2] But the spectacular failure of *Ishtar*—coupled with another flop ten years before, *Mickey and Nicky*—basically put paid to May's career. Men were allowed to fail behind—and before—the camera more often than women, as we've seen already. Michael Cimino could have his *Heaven's Gate* and Kevin Costner his *Waterworld* but as far as female directors were concerned it was usually a case of "One strike and you're out."

The humiliation of women continued with the Whoopi Goldberg-Sam Elliott feature *Fatal Beauty*. A love scene between them was edited out when audiences balked at the ebony-ivory combination. Goldberg was disgusted, remarking that the scene would have been allowed to stay in if Elliott had "put some money on the bedside table" after coitus, black servility being suitably catered to.[3] Color also led to pigeonholing in the Cathy Tyson movie *Business as Usual*. Tyson played a victim of sexual harassment. She'd already been a prostitute in *Mona Lisa* (1986). "Woman equals bed scene equals nakedness equals beaten up equals raped or whatever," she said, "It's so exploitative within the framework of the business. You just get used to [it]."[4]

When women weren't being abused, they were being patronized, as was the case in *Three Men and a Baby* (1987). This purported to be a film about a group of "New Men" who were more than willing to take over the traditional female mothering role if put to it. But in the hands of director Leonard Nimoy it turned into a forgettable farce featuring a trio of "laddish" bachelors who took temporary time-outs from their chauvinistic endeavors to show us their cuddly side.

In some ways this was even more offensive than the traditional screen males who pooh-poohed (if that's not the wrong expression in the context) the notion of nappy-changing, or indeed anything else that smacked of "women's work." Nimoy tried to trick us into thinking he was making some kind of statement about shared duties whereas in reality all he was offering was an escapist *divertissement* that served to copperfasten conventional roles by proxy. When Tom Selleck, Steve Guttenberg and Ted Danson (the eponymous triad) "fill in" for the confused lady who dumps the baby on their doorstep, they're free to revert to their bachelor-like ways after she comes to her senses in the final reel and reclaims her bundle of joy.

Sally Field played an artist in the aptly titled *Surrender*. The manner in which her talent is subjugated to a 1950s-style desire for a husband is embarrassing to watch. In one scene we see a self-portrait of her in which she's drowning because there's no man in her life. Artistic creation plays a poor second to procreation on her priority list as she ditches her easel for Michael Caine, a divorced author who contemplates moving to Kuwait because women don't vote there. He gets to say lines like "We're all just meat to them." (That's women, not Kuwaitians.)

Jack Nicholson appeared with Cher and Susan Sarandon in *The Witches of Eastwick* (1987) and charmed each of them, despite playing the Devil. ("Typecasting," he joked.) Cher particularly adored him but she wasn't quite as entranced by her treatment at the hands of Warner Brothers, the studio behind the film: "The women were totally subjected and it was a bitch. First of all we were always referred to as 'the girls.' We had lousy facilities, lousy trailers. I had to come up with my own clothes and I [also] supplied Susan with three of her outfits." Cher finished her tirade with this salvo, "If I'd been fucked by my husband as much as I was by Warner Brothers, I'd still be married!"[5]

Bette Midler and Shelley Long starred in *Outrageous Fortune*, a film about two women dating the same man, a reversion of the more common plot concerning two men dating the same woman. It grossed $7 million and one imagined there might be a sequel but this didn't happen. The problem, according to Joe Roth, then chairman of 20th Century–Fox, was, "Much of what sells big in the movie business are outsized fantasy action pictures and men have a very difficult time seeing women in these roles. Male stars get paid more than female stars because men will go out to see men. Women will [also] go out to see men [but] men have a difficult time going out to see women. I think, frankly, it is sexism."[6]

Nicolas Kent saw this devolution of responsibility from the studios to the public as being part of a self-fulfilling prophecy. "Because producers and executives assume movies with a female lead will not make money, they don't try making them. And because writers know that it's difficult if not impossible to sell those kinds of stories to producers and executives, they don't bother to write them." Hollywood, he contended, used to make the same kinds of assumptions about black movies until people like Spike Lee and Robert Townsend started making them, and filling seats. And hadn't Bette Davis proved she could "carry" a movie without a male lead way back in the forties?[7]

There were exceptions, needless to say, but for every Sigourney Weaver or Uma Thurman as an action heroine there were five clones of Bruce Willis, Arnold Schwarzenegger, Harrison Ford, Sylvester Stallone, Dolph Lundgren, Jean-Claude van Damme, Vin Diesel and Mel Gibson. Former studio boss Ned Tanen summed the situation up: "Most females do not sell tickets at the box office. Tom Cruise will open a movie. Eddie Murphy will open a movie. [But] I can't think of one woman who will open a movie. It may get great reviews, it may be revered by the critics, but that doesn't mean the public wishes to see them in [it]."[8]

Gibson made *Lethal Weapon* in 1987. He was the "cop on the edge," partnered with a more balanced Danny Glover. It spawned a franchise and made Gibson even more rich and famous than he already was. There wasn't too much room for women in the film apart from the usual support roles. Therese Russell outlined the general casting operational procedures undergone in such situations: "Say they have Mel Gibson to do a film and they go through a list to find a female lead. If it's not Kim Basinger maybe it's Michelle Pfeiffer. If it's not Michelle Pfeiffer maybe it's somebody else. The women are interchangeable and it's cast on who thinks she's fanciable."[9] Few people would remember the women in this movie today. (Darlene Love, anyone? Traci Wolfe?)

Casting the smaller roles for women was even more primitive. Michael Keaton played a hustler going into drug rehab in *Clean and Sober* in 1988. A novice actress called Linnea Quigley auditioned for a role in it. She was quite excited at the prospect until she arrived at the studio and was told to take off her clothes and lie face down on a couch. After she did this, the producer and director looked her over, whispered "Thank you" to her and ushered her out. When the film was released, she went to it with her husband and saw that the part she'd auditioned for—unsuccessfully—was that of a dead naked lady. Her reaction? "I guess I don't do dead naked well."[10]

Working Girl (1988) purported to be a film celebrating women in executive capacities but one of them (Sigourney Weaver) was a bitch and the other (Melanie Griffith) a young woman who deposes Weaver by playing the kind of "little girl" part that might have been taken by somebody like Marilyn Monroe a few decades before. Griffith puts people before her job and becomes the heroine. As the "evil" executive, Weaver ends up with nothing. Griffith was rewarded with an Oscar nomination for her performance, having charmed her way into audiences' hearts by dint of her girl-next-door diffidence.

Her rivals for the award were Glenn Close (*Dangerous Liaisons*), Meryl Streep (*A Cry in the Dark*), Sigourney Weaver (*Gorillas in the Mist*) and Jodie Foster (*The Accused*). Somebody remarked that all four of them played victims. It was like a metaphor for the plight of women in movies since the beginning of the century. "Women first" might have been a good maxim in a lifeboat situation but on celluloid they usually came last. Maybe we could even say all five were victims if we include Griffith, she being a victim of how men think women should behave in the office. Foster didn't have a problem with this. She didn't see a disjunction between being a feminist and playing a victim.[11]

Foster won. *The Accused* tackled the thorny issue of how certain men seemed to believe that they were entitled to abuse, if not rape, a woman who dressed provocatively— or who had a promiscuous past. She was initially passed over for the part, not being deemed "rapeable" enough by the people in casting. This was meant as an insult. Foster then tarted herself up and got the part. She was now officially rapeable.

She was bossy on set.[12] This may have been a reaction to the boorish attitude of former producers who said things like, "Stand over there. Turn around. Well, your hips are all right. Yes, okay, maybe." Foster's attitude was, "Hold on. *You're* on trial here, not me. I'm looking *you* over, mister."[13] The culture had shifted.

Sherry Lansing produced the film. One hoped it wasn't going to sell out to male demands like her earlier *Fatal Attraction*. She argued that the earlier film was a sympathetic study of how a woman could lose her identity after being rejected in love (!) and employed the same euphemisms here: "If anyone thinks this movie is anti-feminist, I give up. Once you see [it], I doubt that you'll ever think of rape the same way again. Those images will stick in your mind and you'll be more sympathetic the next time you hear of someone being raped."[14] Her comments almost sound like those an unreconstructed man might make on the subject. What did she mean by "the same way"? Did she mean indifference? And what did "more" sympathetic mean? Did it suggest that people would only been "slightly" sympathetic to rape victims before they saw the movie? *The Accused* was mercifully free of the directorial blemishes of *Fatal Attraction* but Lansing often put her foot in her mouth when speaking of her movies.

Dawn Steel was more solid. Now president of Columbia, she was often referred to as "the most powerful woman Hollywood had ever seen," and also one of the most ruthless. Was it possible to be seen as one without the other where women were concerned? Men seemed to have a problem with the simple word "strong." "Steely" sounded better. And it was a good pun.

Steel made the same promises to women that Lansing had, but women had the right to be skeptical about her carrying through on them. Amy Madigan saw the situation like this: "Women's roles? Forget it. You're either the prostitute or this contemporary woman like the city D.A. who's divorced, has these two fabulous kids, can take care of them and also have a great sex life. That superwoman kind of thing."[15]

Shirley MacLaine despaired of women's pictures ever endearing themselves to audiences over men's ones. "The average habitual moviegoers are between eleven and seventeen years old," she contended. "They prefer action pictures. When action pictures, science fiction, crime dramas and stories of sexual perversity prevail, there isn't much room for women unless we play dominatrices or outer-planetary dark goddesses."[16]

Jodie Foster wasn't considered "rape-able" enough in *The Accused* (1988) when she first presented herself for the part so she had a makeover to attain that dubious honor.

In 1989 the Quigley poll of U.S. theater owners registered the fact that only one woman, Kathleen Turner, was on the top ten list of money-makers. She just scraped in at tenth place. This was in marked contrast to a similar poll conducted in 1981 when Jane Fonda, Goldie Hawn, Dolly Parton and Bo Derek were on the list. Clearly, something was going dreadfully wrong with women's pulling power. Maybe all the great female roles were things of the past. It was still believed by the major studios that women couldn't "carry" films any more, their status downgraded to the pre-feminist roles of wife, girlfriend, or token "best friend" of the main character. Films were being pitched mainly towards young male audiences who craved adventures or thrillers with stars like Bruce Willis, who was currently cleaning up with *Die Hard*.

Bonnie Bedelia played his wife in the film. She "envelopes" it, simpering on the sidelines as her man does all for love and glory. At one point Willis tells his policeman friend that Bedelia was "the best thing that ever happened to a bum like me," but the line is sandwiched in between scenes of derring-do in the same way as, say, an Errol Flynn embrace of Olivia de Havilland might have been sandwiched into a swashbuckler film from the 1930s. Bedelia's function was to look worried about her man and to turn up at the end and give him a hug. She bookends the movie like the dispensable adjunct of a hundred actioners, a woman who knows her place in the grand scheme of things, the nester to his hunter. She was glad of the work but remained bemused by the film's success, and the fact that it acted as the launch-pad for a raft of like-minded projects. "If someone came down from Mars and went into a multiplex," she reflected, "they'd come to the conclusion that the planet Earth was occupied by men who liked to shoot a lot."

They also liked to debunk women a lot. The Vietnamese director Trinh T. Minh-ha tackled the role women play in Vietnamese society in her 1989 feature *Surname Viet Given Name Nam*. At a New York screening a man in the audience jumped up from his seat and said, "There are so many important things to make a film about. Why did you make [one] about women?" The question shocked her. The cinema was still dominated by men, she concluded, quoting film theorist Laura Mulvey who held that even in such matters as closeups, men still made such domination manifest: "The look is always owned by men." They were either its object or its subject. If they were the ones pictured, this was simply to signify their desire for the woman.[17] It was disconcerting to be reminded that a speech given by Maureen O'Hara almost half a century before in Dorothy Arzner's *Dance, Girl, Dance* still seemed to haunt women. Despite all the strides made by Lansing and Steel and their peers, they were still seen as sex objects.

This worrying fact was highlighted in Atlanta in the summer of 1989 when Rob Lowe filmed himself having sex with two girls, one of whom was only sixteen, two years under the legal age for sex in Georgia. Her brother found the video and gave it to their mother, who turned it over to the police. Lowe was charged with using his celebrity status to seduce a minor but the charge was subsequently dropped and he got off with two years of community service, visiting schools and prisons to lecture on the dangers of drugs and delinquency. How was it that a sex offender was put in the position of being a guardian of virtue? One teacher rightly declared, "Having Rob Lowe lecturing our children on morals is like inviting Hitler to a Jewish wedding."[18]

The film world was equally shocked in July 1989 when the 21-year-old actress Rebecca Schaeffer was shot dead in the doorway of her Los Angeles apartment by obsessive fan Robert Bardo. Bardo decided to kill her either because he was angered at being cold shouldered by her security staff earlier or because Schaeffer went to bed with a man in the black comedy *Scenes from the Class Struggle in Beverly Hills*, thereby becoming just "another Hollywood whore."[19] He called on her unannounced one night shortly after seeing this film, having enlisted the services of a private detective who managed to get her address from the Department of Motor Vehicles for him. Taken aback by his persistent urge to get his foot inside her door, she tried to shut it on him, whereupon the crazed fan took out a gun and shot her dead. It was an absurd and senseless tragedy, a wake-up call to stars everywhere about the casual manner in which those who watch their movies could so easily obtain their addresses. No longer are such details available to members of the public from sources like the Department of Motor Vehicles but did Rebecca Schaeffer have to die to facilitate such a basic right to privacy?

There were two headline-grabbing divorces during the year. The most brutal was that of Burt Bacharach, who delivered his parting shot over the phone to Angie Dickinson with the words, "This will only take a minute."[20] And it did. After 24 years. Jane Fonda also split from her politician husband Tom Hayden, giving him an estimated $5 million to get out of the marriage. She'd contributed millions of dollars to his various campaigns throughout their marriage. She asked him to return at least some of this but his lawyers argued that it was classed a "gift." Fonda was amused at the terminology but didn't push to get it back.[21]

Clint Eastwood made *Sudden Impact,* his final film with Sondra Locke. By now their romance was winding down. Locke's career had suffered as a result of her involvement with him rather than being enhanced by it. By now she was beginning to think he featured her opposite him for no better reason than that she wasn't that well known. "He's seldom had a strong leading lady," the columnist Bob Rosenfield wrote. Eastwood was said to have resented the few times this wasn't the case, as for instance when he co-starred opposite actresses Shirley MacLaine and Meryl Streep. As Rosenfield phrased it, "The women in his movies are mostly window-dressing."[22]

To erase Locke from his life completely when their relationship reached meltdown, Eastwood took the radical step of having her ejected from his house. There were jokes about him changing the "locks" as well as the "Locke." But Sondra wasn't smiling. She was too shocked to find any amusement in the way he pulled the plug on their relationship after so many years. She launched a palimony suit against him, the first of its kind ever conducted by a woman who was married to somebody else at the time. The fact that her husband, Gordon Anderson, was gay made her action even more intriguing.

In the course of the case, Eastwood's cozy image as a bastion of frontier family values took a tumble. Locke told the court that in addition to the humiliation of her forcible removal from his home, he'd "persuaded" her to have two abortions during their time together. The legal proceedings dragged on through the end of 1989 and well into the following year. Then in August 1990 Locke was diagnosed with breast cancer. She had to have a double mastectomy as a result.

Eastwood accused her of using the cancer to gain sympathy for herself. "She plays the victim very well," he chastised. Unfortunately she had cancer and so she plays that card." Locke received over 300 letters of "outrage and sympathy" over his remark. Diane Blum, the executive director of the National Cancer Care Foundation, announced, "Breast cancer is a devastating disease and 45,000 American women die from it every year. These women do not think of themselves as victims. The last thing they need is to have their disease trivialized."[23]

Eastwood knew he'd gone too far. He saw public sympathy turning against him and offered Locke a directing contract with Warners if she agreed to drop all claims against him. Surprisingly, she settled for this. By now she had one directing job in the can (the impressive thriller *Impulse*, starring Theresa Russell) and contemplated more of the same. Unfortunately, things didn't work out like this, as we'll see.

Marlon Brando came out of retirement to make *A Dry White Season*, receiving an Oscar nomination for playing a civil rights lawyer campaigning against apartheid in South Africa. Its director Euzhan Palcy had to negotiate a double prejudice in Hollywood as a result of being both female and black. Brando empathized with her plight or he wouldn't have broken an eight-year hiatus from filmmaking to essay the role. For Palcy the fight to get the film up and running was like a corollary to the plot because there was a kind of apartheid in Hollywood too. She persuaded the studio to let her make it only after her promise to cast more white people in it than blacks. The backing was made possible by the fact that a major star (Brando) agreed to appear in it. Would a black woman director like Palcy have been allowed such power otherwise? Would she have been allowed such power if the film focused as much on black people as white ones?

For Brando the film represented a return to "the big time." But his time in the sun was short-lived. In May 1990, just as life was looking up for him, his son Christian shot Dag Drollet, the fiancé of his half-sister Cheyenne. Cheyenne blamed Brando *père* for "planting" the idea in Christian's head. She believed he had an almost hypnotic influence over the boy. Cheyenne believed Brando hated Drollet because he introduced his daughter to drugs. He was also suspected of having beaten her.

Brando helped Christian at the trial. He gave a courtroom speech that had a huge bearing on the charge being downgraded from murder to manslaughter. The Drollet family believed Brando's money allowed a murderer a "soft" sentence. Cheyenne went deeper into a shell after the trial and was in and out of psychiatric institutions for the next number of years. And then in 1995, just when people thought she was recovering from her traumas, she hanged herself. It was yet another grim example of what came to be known as "the Brando Curse." Much of her depression emanated from her relationship with her father. "He wants to control my perceptions," she said, "He's the devil himself. We might all live in a dark zone but his is worldwide."[24] She added, "He always broke the heart of all the women he went out with."[25]

The suicide of Jill Bennett was less widely reported than that of Cheyenne Brando but was no less heartrending. Bennett had been embroiled in a storm-tossed marriage with the playwright John Osborne, who was as cruel to her in death as he had been in life. In the second volume of his autobiography he wrote that her suicide was a "final fumbled gesture after a lifetime of gladrag borrowings, theft and plagiarism." It was also "one of the few original or spontaneous gestures in her loveless life."

Bennett left most of her estate to a dog's home, causing Osborne to snipe, "She had no love in her heart for people, and only a little more for dogs." At her funeral he said he regretted not being able to "look down upon her open coffin and drop a good large mess in her eye."[26] His attack on her was both unwarranted and untrue. A gifted actress, she took to drink as a result of frustrations with Osborne and her inability to conceive children. There was also a tragic love affair with a married man, Thomas Schoch, who left her to go back to his wife when his interest in her waned.

To add to the unnatural deaths that year there were some natural ones as well. Ava Gardner passed away quietly in London, having spent the last years of her life there to escape the glitz and glamour that were ultimately unfulfilling to her. After her beauty faded, the good parts dried up, so what reason was there to stay there? All she ever got from Hollywood, she droned, was "three lousy ex-husbands."[27] Greta Garbo died too. She'd left Hollywood at a much younger age than Gardner, but for roughly similar reasons. Her image as "the gloomiest Scandinavian since Hamlet" left one wondering why there wasn't some kind of support structure in place in Hollywood for those who were hunted and haunted by the public gaze and sought release from it. She said once, "I always have to climb over the garbage cans and hampers full of dirty linen and sneak up to my room on foot or in the service elevator."[28]

Whoopi Goldberg won an Oscar for playing a medium in Jerry Zucker's smash hit *Ghost*, scoring a double whammy in proving that being black and a woman meant one could still open a film. But maybe she was the exception to prove the rule, as Euzhan Palcy well knew. Hollywood manager Dolores Robinson saw the situation like this: "I used to say that if you're black and you're fat you can be a mother. If you're black and pretty you can be a prostitute. It was almost like that. Now the options have improved but not broadened. You've got twelve beautiful actresses trying to be Wesley Snipes' girlfriend, Eddie Murphy's girlfriend or Denzel Washington's girlfriend. Those are the [only] three roles."[29]

Awakenings was nominated for Best Picture in 1990 and Robert De Niro for Best Actor in the film but there was nothing for its director Penny Marshall. Was it because she was a woman? Similar concerns had been expressed back in 1986 when *Children of a Lesser God* was nominated for Best Picture but not Randa Haines for Best Director. It was ungracious, to say the least.

Another Marshall, Garry, directed *Pretty Woman*, one of the year's most profitable films. It made a star out of Julia Roberts but it glamorized prostitution out of all proportion, giving us to believe a woman could crawl out of this lifestyle and still have a happy-ever-after marriage with a knight in shining armor (or even shining Armani). Taking on the mantle of the new Shirley MacLaine, Roberts was a strange kind of "dirty angel" as she offered Richard Gere the kind of attention Linda Lovelace gave her clients in *Deep Throat*. But behind the sexual favors she was just your regular girl-next-door looking for love. All the work done by films like *Klute* in making call girls into three-dimensional characters was blotted out by this one's cute schmaltz. Were we really expected to believe Gere could carry Roberts off to his castle on his white steed without worrying at all about her history, or her ghetto origins?

The original script had Roberts dumped in a gutter at the end. This seemed a much more likely scenario than being whisked off to movie heaven by her Lancelot-like suitor, but the studio money men wanted a fairy tale finale and this they got. No doubt their instincts were correct because the film cleaned up at the box office.

Why did so many people go to see it? Probably because of its escapist slant rather than any feeling that such a scenario could unfold in real life. Michelle Pfeiffer commented, "What's interesting about a lot of today's women is that they believe the opposite of *Pretty Woman*. Prince Charming is not coming. He got hit by a truck and they're not looking any more."[30]

Pfeiffer reunited with Al Pacino that year for another Garry Marshall release, *Frankie and Johnny*. It was eight years since their original partnership in *Scarface*. Pfeiffer had grown more assertive in the interim and Pacino had lost his domineering qualities so their working relationship was a lot more amicable this time, even if the film wasn't quite as potent as Brian De Palma's scorcher. When Pfeiffer told him he'd become "much nicer" since *Scarface*, he was surprised as he hadn't remembered being distant on that set. "Maybe I was just a jerk and I didn't know it," he suggested. "On *Scarface* I didn't speak with Michelle much. I think it had something to do with her being early on in her career. She seemed much less involved."[31] The new Pfeiffer was more proactive, and well capable of keeping Pacino in line if he threatened to upstage her.

Pfeiffer co-starred with Sean Connery in another film she made at this time, Fred Schepisi's *The Russia House*. It was based on John le Carré's Cold War tale of post-*glasnost* espionage. Connery was twice her age but still the romantic lead, a fact that understandably irritated her. An exasperated Pfeiffer exclaimed, "When I'm sixty years old, are they going to let me do *Russia House*? I don't think so. You see the statistics and realize the longevity of a female career as opposed to a male [one] in this business is just so much shorter. I'm not worried about age but I'm very aware this is my window of time. I want to be allowed to age gracefully but they won't let you do that. So when I hear an actress say, 'You know what? I'm gonna have my face done and my tits raised and I'll get another ten years out of this business,' I say, 'More power to you—go do it.' I said my whole life I'd never have a facelift. But I understand the desire."[32] To quote Michelle Vogel, "For an actress in Hollywood terms, ten years is the difference between playing a goddess and a grandmother."

Age was also the underlying theme of Luis Mandoki's *White Palace*, in which Ivy League scholar James Spader gets swept off his feet by the older Susan Sarandon. The film gave us another twee ending and another superficial treatment of the age divide. Everything was sorted and wrapped in pink ribbons. Because Sarandon was older than Spader, she had to be sexier too to "make up" for this. What Meryl Streep called "The Hollywood Age Police" may not have imposed themselves on the film but why was it still such a big deal to have a woman older than her lover? If she was, why did that have to take over everything else that was happening in the film, or in their lives?

191

Sarandon was on firmer ground in *Thelma & Louise* (1991), Ridley Scott's ode to the frontier spirit as applied to a pair of women fed up with the men in their lives. They take to the road to wreak havoc and find a crazy, happy-sad love together. Was it a feminist film? Annette Kuhn saw it more as an adventurous romp with undertones of screwball comedy.[33] In another sense it seemed like sweet revenge for twenty years of male-oriented road movies. It was usually men who left women for an adventure but here the buccaneering ethos was appropriated by two crazy cowgirls. The iconography of every road movie, or even every C&W road song like "By the Time I Get to Phoenix," was sabotaged and re-aligned.

The fact that the film's release coincided with the trial of Clarence Thomas for his sexual harassment of Anita Hill caused some people see it as a footnote to that high-profile case. Many critics also thought it depicted men in a degrading light, featuring a number of "pathetic stereotypes of testosterone-crazed behavior." One reviewer even saw it as a fascist piece of work.

Its scriptwriter, Callie Khouri, begged to disagree with such viewpoints, claiming she'd written a screenplay not so much about feminists as outlaws. "We see plenty of movies of this genre with men," she argued, "I don't see why it shakes everyone up to see it with women." The fact that their aggressors were male wasn't meant to be seen in any anti-men light but neither was she going to contrive "some monstrous female" to be the villain. "Even if this were the most man-bashing movie ever made," she argued, "it wouldn't even begin to make up for the 99 percent of movies where the women are there to be caricatured as bimbos, or to be skinned and decapitated." She defended the dramatic ending where the two heroines drive off the edge of the cliff: "I just kept seeing this image of Thelma at the kitchen sink at the beginning and knowing she was never, never going to be there again."[34]

Thelma & Louise became a cult film, a long overdue distaff corollary to *Bonnie and Clyde.* The two women at its core had the kind of fun only men were previously permitted. By this time "women's pictures" had been rechristened "chick flicks" and though neither Susan Sarandon nor Geena Davis were sweet sixteen, they were allowed to act like that here, and also suggest a lesbian underpinning to their friendship. The freeze-frame at the end was straight out of *Butch Cassidy and the Sundance Kid,* as were some of the serio-comic exchanges between the pair, but this was still a welcome addition to the rite-of-passage bonding genre that had been the preserve of men up to now.

The Academy of Motion Picture Arts and Sciences designated 1991 "The Year of the Woman" so maybe it was appropriate that *Thelma & Louise* was one of its showpieces. It was nominated for Best Picture; also nominated were Sarandon and Davis for Best Actress, Khouri for Best Screenplay and Scott for Best Director.

Barbra Streisand wasn't quite as lucky with *The Prince of Tides,* a film she hoped would fare better at the Oscars than her previous directorial venture, *Yentl.* It was nominated for Best Picture but she wasn't cited for Best Director. To her this seemed like a contradiction in terms. Did the film direct itself? Once again the curse that afflicted *Children of a Lesser God* and *Awakenings,* two other films nominated for Best Picture without the (female) director being cited, made itself manifest. (Man-ifest?)

Jodie Foster could also have done with a Best Director nod for *Little Man Tate*, a charming tale in which she played a single mother raising an exceptionally gifted child on her own. Foster was a child star herself, and indeed was one of the few to have also had a successful adult career. She now added a third string to her bow by directing, and handled the job adeptly, her only worry being that some of her critics would say things like "She has fat thighs" as she went about her work.

For Foster, directing the movie was the beginning of her "reincarnation" as an individual entity in Hollywood, a woman who was slowly but surely finding her own voice behind the camera as well as in front of it. "I didn't want to be a vulnerable bimbo for some director to take advantage of," she explained.[35]

She didn't know how long she had left in her career after making the film: "This is not a business that is kind to women.... The female pioneers have to be ten times better than a man. Maybe some day there will be an old-girls network."[36]

She raised the budget for *Little Man Tate* on the strength of her earlier performance as Clarice in *The Silence of the Lambs*. Michelle Pfeiffer had been offered the Clarice role before her but turned it down, not appreciating the tone of the film, which she felt was in danger of glorifying its sick violence. "Anthony Hopkins' part was the most charming and smartest," she believed, "and he wins in the end."[37] That could never have happened with a female serial killer—or any kind of female killer.

Like Hopkins, Foster won an Oscar for her performance. Hers was harder won, being the less showy role. She remarked, "It's very rare to see a movie where the woman is in the role of a prince who goes out to slay the dragon and goes through turmoil to do it.... This is mythology that women are often not allowed to be a part of."[38] She wasn't here either, using her head (and heart) rather than her hands to get through to Hopkins.

By now Pfeiffer and Foster were two of the most vocal campaigners for women's rights in films, along with Barbra Streisand, Meryl Streep, Demi Moore and Julia Roberts. For a scene in *Sleeping with the Enemy* (1991) in which Roberts was called on to be soaked in water repeatedly while wearing only her underwear, she's rumored to have demanded that the entire film crew strip off with her.[39] If only Jean Seberg had been as assertive during *Saint Joan* she might have lived longer and had a more productive career.

Demi Moore commanded even more headlines when in December 1991, seven months pregnant, she agreed to pose naked on the cover of *Vanity Fair* magazine. This was viewed as a significant statement by women worldwide regarding the need to exhibit their bumps. "I was trying to tell people it's possible to have a career, be a mother and still be very sexy," she gushed. Not everyone looked like Demi Moore, however, or had her opportunities. Neither did *Vanity Fair* necessarily accede to her view. According to one author, the magazine was more interested in magazine sales than Moore's "having it all" boast.[40]

In some Bible belt towns, newsstands covered the magazine in brown paper to hide her protruding stomach. "They're afraid to imagine a pregnant woman as sexy," she railed. "Women can either be sexy or they can be a mother. I didn't want to have to choose so I challenged that." It was a noble ambition even if publicity was as much behind the move as women's rights.

Did *Vanity Fair* exploit her or vice versa? "I think we used each other," she allowed. The magazine was mentioned in 95 TV stories in the U.S., as well as featuring in 1500 newspaper articles, 64 radio shows and a dozen cartoons. Her fans applauded her actions while her enemies derided her for being a self-serving bitch. Neither reaction fazed her: "If you're a woman and you ask for what you want, you're treated differently than a man would be. It's a lot more interesting for journalists to write about me being a bitch than being a nice woman."[41]

The Stone Age

If *Thelma & Louise* seemed to open movies up to new parameters for women, in its aftermath we witnessed a step backwards. Other "chick flicks" of the time seemed less daring, more conservative, especially those with a lesbian subtext. Mary Stuart Masterson and Mary Louise Parker played lesbians in Jon Avnet's *Fried Green Tomatoes*, but we're never quite told that, even though this is 1991 rather than 1951. The reasons remained unclear. Did Avnet feel that the relationship between the pair of them would seem purer if it wasn't consummated? Was he afraid of losing his heterosexual audience if he featured Masterson and Parker in bed together? One can, of course, argue that they're just very close friends, but when we look at the film closely their relationship seems to go much further than that. They may not kiss or do anything more physical than hug one another but the expression in their eyes seems to tell a different story.

Leaving Normal (1992), a kind of *Thelma & Louise* lite, also left to the imagination any sexual undercurrent between its two female leads. Then there was *Single White Female* (1992). This started off intriguingly as a complex study of psychosis but sold out in its latter stages, opting for a slasher-type finale. None of these mainstream films depicted lesbianism head-on without overtones of mental illness.

The steamy Paul Verhoeven thriller *Basic Instinct,* starring Sharon Stone and Michael Douglas, also fell into this barrow. This was the film that made Stone's name as she essayed the role of a bisexual serial killer with some relish. Gay movements campaigned it for various reasons, causing Douglas to say, "Someone has to be the bad guy [*sic*], and it can't always be the Italians."

It was only five years since he'd disentangled himself from the panic-stricken embrace of Glenn Close in *Fatal Attraction*. Now he was in the throes of another disastrous liaison with another nutcase. Even by Hollywood's dismal standards, this was a new low.

Stone also had problems with the film, claiming Verhoeven tricked her into removing her underwear for the famous interrogation scene where she uncrosses her legs and caused (in one writer's view) even more consternation than Moses did when he parted the Red Sea in *The Ten Commandments*. Douglas Thompson wrote, "Somebody in Hollywood once pointed out that men put women on a pedestal and then look up

195

their skirts. With Sharon Stone, Hollywood looked up her skirt and then put her on a pedestal."[1]

Stone berated Verhoeven for showing the leg-crossing scene but when it proved the making of her, she "forgave" him. Verhoeven, for his part, castigated Stone as a difficult performer, a term that enraged her. "If I was a petite ethnic lawyer," she contended, "my behavior would be totally acceptable."[2]

Directors hadn't taken her seriously in the past because of her beauty: "I looked like an inflatable Barbie doll and nobody wanted me to play anything too edgy." Before *Basic Instinct* she'd been in forgettable adventure films, becoming frustrated by the fact that people couldn't see beyond her physical attributes to the character actress underneath: "I never thought that I looked on the outside like I was on the inside. On the inside I felt like a dark Semitic girl with curly hair. I never felt blond."[3]

Up to now Stone had been little more than eye candy. One day she was propositioned by a studio executive. When she told him what to do with himself, he was aghast. She was informed, in age-old manner, "You'll never work in this town again."[4] She laughed off the warning, feeling it was only a matter of time before she hit it big.

A *Playboy* spread shortly before production began on *Basic Instinct* gave men a preview of what to expect from Catherine Trammell, the tumescent character Stone played in the film. Why had she done it? For money, mainly—she'd just bought a house—but also to confront Hollywood's ageism against women full on. She was now in her thirties and was wondering if going *au naturelle* would lead to more film offers: "Leading ladies my age are typed and you need to be sexually appealing for parts you might be right for. It's a man's world. I'd taken my top off in three movies and nobody noticed. I felt I was re-owning my femininity."[5]

Many women were enraged by the character of Sharon Stone in *Basic Instinct* (1992) because of what was called her "lipstick lesbianism." Neither did her murderous nature help the image of women, nor the alliance of the two facts. But Michael Douglas, seen with her here, didn't complain any more than he did over the changes wrought in Glenn Close's character in *Fatal Attraction*.

As well as being beautiful and sexy, Stone was also clever. This led to problems. "In Hollywood," she said, "you can be tall, you can be blond, you can be pretty, but you can't be smart. You can't have too many opinions. Being blond is a great excuse when you're having a bad day: 'I'm blond. I can't help it.'" She told Joe Eszterhas, who wrote the screenplay for *Basic Instinct*, that her climb to the top was so rough, she "crawled the hill of broken glass and I sucked and I sucked until I sucked all the air out of my life."[6]

Stone made it clear from Day One of the film's shoot that she was part of the new generation of Hollywood actresses and wouldn't be treated as a second-class citizen by any director. She arrived on the set, as she put it, "packing heat." She waved a gun in a cinematographer's face and warned, "If I see one ounce of cellulite on the screen, you're a dead mother."[7]

GLAAD, the Gay and Lesbian Alliance, had many problems with the film, feeling legitimately that its gay characters (of whom Stone at least seemed to be one, however tentatively) reinforced negative stereotypes about lesbians. The idea of putting a disclaimer on the movie was considered but Douglas didn't think this was a good idea. If they went down that road, he believed, every film with a killer would have had to have had a disclaimer. Verhoeven said it was about evil in general rather than evil gay people. Everyone was quoting Scripture for their purpose.

Eszterhas refused to rewrite the script to pacify the politically correct. But its focus caused headaches. It presented a world where lesbian women hated straight men enough to want to kill them. For GLAAD representatives, this was tantamount to homophobia. But Stone disagreed: "My character is sociopathic and motivated by power. Gender choice is a secondary and irrelevant issue for her."[8]

She was more bothered by some intricate details in the sex scenes between herself and Douglas. Verhoeven wanted her to react to Douglas' lovemaking by thrusting her head back and simulating ecstasy after only a few seconds of canoodling, but she told him this wasn't the way women behaved in real life. If it was, she joked, Douglas thoroughly deserved his $14 million paycheck. Stone's mother had a different kind of problem with the movie. According to Stone, "She said the most shocking thing about it was that people were more concerned [about] whether or not I was a homosexual than whether or not I was a serial killer."[9]

Stone collaborated with Eszterhas for the second time on *Sliver*, a murder-voyeurism cocktail that followed hot on the heels of *Basic Instinct* but failed to ignite at the box office. William Baldwin was her co-star but he didn't get on with her. He thought she was playing a sexual game two ways, stripping for the cameras, then making intellectual pronouncements about exploitation. Stone had recently said of Hollywood, "If you have a vagina and a point of view in this town, that's a lethal combination."[10] Baldwin shot back, "We've seen too much of both from Sharon."

She argued that taking off her clothes in films wasn't so much her choice as a studio demand. Men didn't have to suffer the same indignities. Baldwin was shown naked from the back in the film but his contract forbade full frontal nudity. Robert Evans, who produced it, tried to rationalize this. "There isn't a leading man who will do full frontal nudity," he claimed, "and there isn't a leading lady who won't."[11]

This farcical comment overlooked the fact that women usually didn't have any choice in the matter. They'd always been the victims in life, said Stone, both inside and outside movies. "We're trained from an early age to submit to men and to bury our integrity beneath this veneer of femininity and stereotyped images of how we should behave."[12] She did her best to reverse this trend any way she could. She once dated a gay woman for an experiment, she revealed, whereas on dates with boring men she retreated to the rest room to read books.

On *Sliver*, because of the clout she'd built up from *Basic Instinct*, she was able to demand final cut on the sex scenes: "I had a rider in my contract that every frame of anything that's nude or partially nude or sexual in any way, I get to see and approve of or it doesn't go into the picture." Baldwin accused her of playing the system, of using sex any which way to become rich and jettisoning "real" feminists in the process. She saw things differently. If she played a man's game by her rules, it gave her a chance to change things from inside: "It was a nice feeling. No more cheap remarks [or] condescending remarks [from] casting agents and directors who think you're just a piece of meat who can be replaced by the next Hollywood blond thing waiting in line."[13]

Similar concerns about compromise were laid at the door of Demi Moore when she made *Indecent Proposal* (1994). In this movie Moore starred as a cash-strapped woman who agrees to go to bed with a high-rolling gambler (Robert Redford) for $1 million to alleviate the money problems of herself and her husband, Woody Harrelson. The film caused all sorts of controversies about everything from opportunism to glorified prostitution. Like *Fatal Attraction*, it was a Sherry Lansing-Adrian Lyne production, with the issues hyped up to increase the film's marketability.

Amy Holden Jones, the screenwriter, had made the very tasteful *Love Letters* some years before, and also directed Julia Roberts in one of her better earlier films, *Mystic Pizza*. But *Indecent Proposal* was more akin to Roberts' *Pretty Woman* in its orientation. The fact that Redford was gentlemanly, and rescuing Moore from a financial pickle, didn't make their transaction any more palatable than a 42nd Street deal. Neither did it make it any easier to take than, say, Richard Gere riding along on his white steed to "rescue" Roberts from hooker hell in *Pretty Woman*. From a certain point of view the civilized nature of these proceedings nearly made them more venal. They seemed to legitimize sex for sale, framing them in a more refined context than was usually the case.

Roger Ebert made a good point when he said audiences felt comfortable with the sex-for-money theme because it was the hunky Redford that Moore was bedding and not, say, the much more ordinary-looking Seymour Cassel who played his chauffeur in the movie. "Let's be blunt," wrote Ebert. "If Demi took the million and slept with Cassel, we'd think she was a whore."[14] The moral dilemma of the film was centered upon the object of the deal, not the rationale.

Moore tried to condone it by saying she argued with Lyne in a bid to make her character more than a sex object: "There was a scene where I wanted to keep my clothes on and I told him, 'They don't have to see my breasts in every shot, do they?'"[15] This was fine, but Moore went on to exhibit the selfsame breasts at various junctures in the future. (Dennis Pennis asked her once in jest, "Demi, if it wasn't gratuitous and it was tastefully done, would you consider keeping your clothes on for a movie?")

Michelle Pfeiffer denounced the sad state of the film industry as far as women were concerned at the 17th annual Women in Film luncheon. "So this is the year of the woman," she reflected. "Well yes, it's actually been a good [one]. Demi Moore was sold to Robert Redford for $1 million. Uma Thurman went to Mr. De Niro for $40,000, and just three years ago Richard Gere bought Julia Roberts for—what was it?—$3,000? I'd say that was real progress."[16] Thunderous applause greeted her referencing of the tawdry goings-on of *Indecent Proposal, Mad Dog and Glory* and *Pretty Woman* respectively. Her comments were especially brave considering Moore was in the audience, as was Sherry Lansing.

Pfeiffer was always more imaginative than Moore, even in her quote unquote "sex kitten" parts. This term acquired literal ramifications when she played Catwoman in *Batman Returns* in 1992. "It's a positive role model for women," she insisted. "I don't think [they're] gonna go out and start whipping people [as a result of it] but it's an empowering character." In a previous era her feline slithering might have been seen as little more than a sidebar frolic but here she more closely resembled a sensuous dominatrix.

Moore was in the news again in 1994 when she played a woman who sexually harasses her boss, Michael Douglas, in *Disclosure*. It was a novel idea, making the harasser beautiful, but someone other than Douglas should have been cast as her victim. He'd already been manhandled by Glenn Close and Sharon Stone, two other women on the edge, in recent high-profile offerings, and now a third beauty was added to the list of nutcases who were obsessed by him. It was quite a trio. What was the appeal of this man to bring out such intensity in demented ladies? Hardly his views on women. (Douglas was prone to making statements like, "The one thing that men and women have in common is that they both like the company of men."[17])

Some viewers had a problem believing Douglas would have been able to resist her charms in the film, perverse and all as they were portrayed. "Who's gonna turn you down?" some people asked her, and this she found objectionable. "What they were actually saying is that a man can't control himself if he's with a woman who may turn him on."[18]

That wasn't really the issue. Moore practically rapes Douglas in the scene in question. Her advances on him are much more erotic than, say, those of Glenn Close in *Fatal Attraction*. The idea of making a movie in which a woman sexually harasses a man was theoretically exciting but it didn't make any attempt to tackle the theme in an adult manner. Like so many of Moore's films, it promised much more than it delivered.

Later that year Faye Dunaway was sacked by Andrew Lloyd Webber from a musical version of *Sunset Boulevard* she planned to do on Broadway. Not a woman to be dismissed lightly, especially when the decision was based more on Webber's fickleness than her lack of talent (or, as he alleged, her inability to sing), she contested the decision and took him to court, suing him for breach of contract. The case rumbled on for almost a year, after which she received a generous out-of-court settlement, which sent out a warning to other producers who might consider dispensing with their stars willy-nilly.

Sally Field played Tom Hanks' mother in *Forrest Gump* even though she was only a few years older than him, in yet another example of Hollywood's rampant sexism-ageism tendency in this regard. Did mothers have to look as good as Field to be classified as legitimate screen material? Her casting reminded one of similar anomalies that seemed to be part and parcel of Hollywood's skewed age system through the decades. One remembered, for instance, that Angela Lansbury was only a few years older than Elvis Presley when she played his mother in *Blue Hawaii* in 1961. Four years later she was Laurence Harvey's mother in *The Manchurian Candidate* even though they were the same age. Glenn Close had been Mel Gibson's mother in *Hamlet* in 1991 even though she was only two years older than him. In the same year, Kate Nelligan played Nick Nolte's mother in *The Prince of Tides*, despite the fact that she was actually nine years *younger* than him (she would have had him at the age of minus nine). It went on again and again and nobody seemed to have an interest in stopping it, because "[m]others had to look beautiful no matter what age they were." Otherwise men wouldn't go to see them.

In 1994 O.J. Simpson was acquitted of murdering his wife Nicole. He was adjudged to be not guilty even though 99 percent of people asked for their view of the case believed he did it, based on the overwhelming forensic evidence. Simpson also had a history of beating his wife. Most people expected him to be found guilty as the trial began but things changed as it progressed. When the arresting officer, Mark Fuhrman, was found to be a racist—he'd used the "N" word often in the past—the trial seemed to turn into an indictment of him rather than Simpson. As prosecutor Marcia Clark remarked in her summing-up speech, people seemed to have forgotten the other "N" word of the trial: Nicole.

Simpson's acquittal sent out a scary message to abused women everywhere about the chances of them receiving justice if they went public. The leader of his defense team, Johnny Cochrane, had promised early on in the trial that if he had just one black person on the jury, that would be enough for him to win the case. In the event he got many more than that. Often in the past, black men had been convicted for offenses they didn't commit. The Simpson trial seemed like an overpayment of the debt of history. A savage double murder went unpunished due to legal loopholes and technical mumbo-jumbo. As a viewer of the proceedings put it after Simpson got off, "Money talks and bullshit walks."

Pierce Brosnan made his debut as James Bond in *GoldenEye* in 1995. Bond was still as chauvinist as ever, and surrounded by the familiar bevy of sexy women, but in this instance the script was politically correct enough to have Judi Dench rasp at him in one scene, "You are a sexist, misogynistic dinosaur, a relic of the Cold War." Maybe feminists emitted a cheer or two at this encounter but it was hardly worth getting excited about. It impacted little on the rest of the movie, or the general franchise. Somehow a reformed, woman-friendly 007 creation seemed nearly worse than the guns-and-girls character that had featured in the series over three decades. Dench's speech was too little, too late. We may not have loved the "dinosaur" but we'd grown to accept him. Could viewers have stomached Bond as a New Man, vacuuming the living room or dandling a baby on his knee? Maybe only if he was holding a Luger on the other one.

Paul Verhoeven diminished whatever slight screen credibility he had that year when he (mis)directed *Showgirls*, a salacious fairy story about a lap dancer abroad in the jungle of Las Vegas sleaze. It was scripted by Joe Eszterhas, who divided opinion on his previous collaboration with Verhoeven in *Basic Instinct,* but here he had few apologists, having sold out totally for the fast buck in a tale that had as little dignity as it had truth. It cost $40 million to make, which is a lot of money for a soft porn offering, especially when it had about as much eroticism as a Walt Disney movie. Its only saving grace was an unintentional humor which gave it a kind of cult appeal for those of us who thought we'd never see an exploitation movie quite as cringe-inducing as *Myra Breckinridge.*

Notwithstanding this, there were some positive signs for the future. Marcia Nasatir became vice-president of production at United Artists, a significant step forward in the journey towards sexual equality. "For a long time at UA," she recalled, "I was the only woman at the meetings. Many of the men had never taken meetings with a woman present before. They would use four-letter words, then suddenly turn to me and say, 'Oh, Marcia, excuse us.' I'd say something banal like, 'I've heard that word before.'" About three years later, another woman came to a meeting to take dictation and one of the men swore, afterwards apologizing to the secretary with the words "Rose, excuse us." For Nasatir this was a great moment: "They no longer saw me as a woman." She went on to become president of Twentieth Century–Fox and to oversee many big-budget releases like *The Big Chill, Hamburger Hill* and *Ironweed.* Speaking of women's role in society in general, she told a story about a friend of her mother's who'd become rich after her husband died, having gone into real estate as a result of the extra time on her hands. Nasatir concluded wryly, "In order to succeed as a woman, you have to kill your husband."[19]

The black lesbian director Michelle Parkerson made *Litany for Survival,* a documentary on the poet Audre Lorde. Another documentary, this one about breast cancer, was directed by another black lesbian, Barbara Hammer. Called *Eight in Eight*, it was made to heighten awareness of the disease. All too often in the past, directors saw breasts almost as a man's property rather than a woman's, and not just in stag movies either. Hammer wanted to reclaim it from exploitative overtones and also to use the film to encourage women to touch their own breasts frequently—something she found many women afraid to do—to check for tumors.

A third black director, Julie Dash, made *Daughters of the Dust*, one of the few Hollywood films with an all-black cast to get a mainstream release. Her aim in making it, she stressed, was to try to outgrow the "sexless Mammy role" blacks had filled since the days of Hattie McDaniel in *Gone with the Wind*, and the "mother-protector" one that was the heritage of everyone from Ethel Waters in *The Member of the Wedding* to Whoopi Goldberg in *Ghost*.

Elisabeth Shue was Oscar-nominated for playing a prostitute in *Leaving Las Vegas* in 1995. Also in '95, Mira Sorvino won for *Mighty Aphrodite* in the same "profession." Meryl Streep lamented Hollywood's continuing preoccupation with loose women. "If the Martians landed and did nothing but go to the movies this year," she reflected, "they'd come to the conclusion that the chief occupation of women on earth is hooking." One was reminded of Bonnie Bedelia's similar comment on Martians and movie violence a few years before.

Demi Moore received a salary of $12.5 million for *Striptease* (1996), a step in the right direction for women's rights but in the wrong one for her choice of material. The film reminded one of those "lusty fairy tales" Billy Wilder made so much better. It dealt with a woman who took to stripping to raise money for a court case to regain custody of her daughter from her shiftless ex-husband. This was a potentially interesting storyline but under Andrew Bergman's maudlin direction (and Moore's tacky performance) it became about as thought-provoking as a fortune cookie.

The film was really just another opportunity for Moore to show her charms in *déshabillé* mode. In interviews she talked it up as a serious study of a woman's fight for justice but it was really just another third-rate moneyspinner for the woman now called "Gimme More" instead of Demi Moore. She was the highest-paid actress of her time but what a pity it had to be for fluff like this. It degenerated into total farce after she became involved with the lascivious Burt Reynolds. Her screen daughter was played by her real-life one, Rumer, which seemed to make the whole thing even more tasteless.

Another 1996 offering, Milos Forman's *The People vs. Larry Flynt,* was more authentic

Demi Moore acquired the moniker "Gimme More" as a result of her perceived financial greed. She advanced the cause of women by posing nude when she was pregnant in 1991 but some of her subsequent movie choices, like *Disclosure* and *Striptease,* seem to have set such a movement backwards as a result of their dumbed-down sexual politics.

in its attempt to champion the cause of the pornography peddler of the title. On the other hand, as Alison Darren noted, it "fights shy of examining Flynt's relentless objectification of women," which isn't examined in the same way as his fight for constitutional equity and freedom of speech. *The First Wives Club* fared better. An ode to the abandoned and neglected wives of the world, it also featured a sideswipe at Hollywood's general attitude towards women: In one scene Goldie Hawn tells her plastic surgeon, "There are only three ages for women in Hollywood: babe, district attorney and *Driving Miss Daisy*."

In the fall of that year Clint Eastwood's former lover Sondra Locke took him to court again, having had all her movie ideas rejected by Warner Bros. In the years since their last legal tussle she'd offered the studio over thirty projects but so far none had come to fruition. She came to believe that Eastwood was the main culprit behind her multiple rejections, and that his "promise" that she'd get a directing deal at Warners, uttered six years previously, had been merely a sop to ward off her palimony claim. She also learned that the money Warner Bros. had supposedly been paying her over this time to develop film ideas (a whopping $1.5 million) had in fact come from Eastwood's own pocket. This meant her tenure at the studio was really just cosmetic. Eastwood had "arranged a work contract for me in which I would never work," was the way she put it.[20]

Eastwood eventually agreed to settle with her out of court. She saw this as a victory for "the little person everywhere" and a message that "people cannot get away with whatever they want to—just because they're powerful." The following year she wrote a book about the whole charade of their relationship. *The Good, the Bad and the Very Ugly* documented the manner in which he exerted such control over her career and personal life in the decade or so they spent together. Expecting him to be her Prince Charming, she was dismayed to find a "heavy iron door" instead, behind which he concealed all his secrets. If she attempted to peer behind that door, "he brought all his power and darkness down upon her."[21] "Think of Eastwood and Warner Bros. as a big powerful empire with high-tech weapons," she wrote. "Whatever you fire at them can't touch them. They'll deflect it like popcorn and only laugh at you."[22]

Another weird paternal relationship reached a head in 1997 when Woody Allen married his adopted daughter Soon-Yi Previn, thereby making Mia Farrow his mother-in-law as well as his ex-wife. Farrow had adopted Soon-Yi while married to Andre Previn. Soon-Yi's intimacy with Allen only came to light when Farrow discovered nude photographs of her in his apartment. She went on to accuse Allen of inappropriate behavior with their other children, resulting in drawn-out legal proceedings which saw him denied him unsupervised access to them.

Allen was 35 years older than Soon-Yi. Farrow remarked, "Woody is a great director. Just don't have children by him." (They had one together, Satchel). It was the end of a long saga of disenchantment for her, captured spikily in a "love gift" she'd given him some years before: a photograph of her and her nine children with cooking skewers piercing all of their hearts, and also her own. Written beside the photo were the words, "Once my heart was one and it was yours to keep. My child you used, and pierced my heart a hundred times and deep."[23]

Epilogue

Women continued to be abused by men and to scramble around for roles that reflected this or sought to ameliorate it. These arrived only in fits and starts. Maybe the most interesting one was Kim Basinger's "comeback cameo" in *L.A. Confidential*. For her this was a game-changing role, a step back into *noir*, a part Ava Gardner or Rita Hayworth might have played: "I'm taken aback by the readiness of people to equate sex symbol with vapid, dipsy, unintelligent—all those horrible names. Your looks will open doors there but [as for] the real doors of opportunity as an actress? Slam, slam, slam."[24]

The century ground to a halt without too much drama. *Boys Don't Cry* and *Girls Interrupted* offered strong roles for women, and Sam Mendes' *American Beauty* had some profound things to say about what Charles Bukowski called "the man-woman thing," but despite the strides that had been made for awareness of all the issues discussed in this book, one felt that women's voices would still have to be raised to be heard and that their path to the top of the Hollywood tree would be a "one step forward, two steps backward" one.

The "Me Tarzan, You Jane" era had ended but the "Frankly, my dear, I don't give a damn" one would continue, albeit in a more subtle guise. Women might have had more rights now, but they seemed to have less magic. They were sidelined in a different way to the old days, which made it all more eerie and subversive. The "tough broad" was gone, replaced often by the "cute chick." Girlpower became yawnful.

The war on salaries and sexism continues to be fought.

When parity is achieved, as with the big earners, it disguises the fact that there are still a lot of foot soldiers laboring in the trenches. When "issue films" get made, they grab headlines for a few weeks but then things revert to the way they always were, and may always be.

Ultimate sexual equality is probably an unrealizable goal because of our old friend the double standard. When Colin Farrell was listed in Wikipedia as a "Lothario," he said, "That's a polite word for a slut, isn't it? Imagine what they'd say if I was a woman."[25]

Epilogue

Maybe we should leave the last word to the inimitable Groucho Marx, who had a pet gripe about the fair sex: "I'm fed up of all this talk about prejudice against women in movies," he droned, "As far as I'm concerned it's a load of hooey. Every year, for the Oscars, for example, the Best Actress award is always won by a female."

As the man said, there's no answer to that.

Chapter Notes

Introduction

1. Clive Sutherland, ed., *Showbiz in Quotes* (London: Charles Letts, 1990), 60.
2. Gene Shalit, ed., *Great Hollywood Wit* (New York: St. Martin's Press, 2002), 165.
3. Sean French, *Jane Fonda* (London: Pavilion, 1997), 13.

Birth Pangs of a New Medium

1. *Photoplay*, January 1916, 109–11.
2. Ally Acker, *Reel Women: Pioneers of the Cinema, 1896 to the Present* (London: B.T. Batsford, 1991), 63.
3. Ibid., 4.
4. Joshua Zeitz, *Flapper: A Madcap Story of Sex, Style, Celebrity and the Women Who Made America* (New York: Three Rivers Press, 2006), 226–7.
5. Barry Norman, *Talking Pictures* (London: BBC, Hodder & Stoughton, 1987), 31.
6. Danny Peary, ed., *Close-Ups: Intimate Profiles of Movie Stars by their Directors, Screenwriters and Friends* (New York: Galahad Books, 1978), 124.
7. Ibid., 126.
8. Patrick McGilligan, *Fritz Lang: The Nature of the Beast* (London: Faber & Faber, 1997), 76–8.
9. Cari Beauchamp, *Without Lying Down: Frances Marion and the Powerful Women of Early Hollywood* (Berkeley: University of California Press, 1997), 221.
10. Selwyn Ford, *The Casting Couch: Making It in Hollywood* (London: Grafton Books, 1990), 46.
11. Ibid., 49.
12. Mick LaSalle, *Complicated Women: Sex and Power in Pre-Code Hollywood* (New York: St. Martin's Griffin, 2000), 21.
13. Sam Staggs, *Close-Up on Sunset Boulevard: Billy Wilder, Norma Desmond and the Dark Hollywood Dream* (New York: St. Martin's Griffin, 2002), 13.
14. Michael Munn, *Hollywood Rogues* (London: Robson, 1991), 28–30.
15. Ibid., 31–2.
16. Otto Friedrich, *City of Nets: A Portrait of Hollywood in the 1940s* (London: Headline, 1986), 186.
17. Marjorie Rosen, *Popcorn Venus: Women, Movies and the American Dream* (New York: Avon Books 1973), 85.
18. Laurie Jacobson, *Dishing Hollywood* (Nashville: Cumberland House, 2003), 124.
19. Don Macpherson and Louise Brody, *Leading Ladies* (London: Octopus, 1986), 23.
20. Rosen, *Popcorn Venus*, 100.

Entrances and Exits

1. Louise Brooks, *Lulu in Hollywood* (New York: Alfred A. Knopf, 1992), 92.
2. David Stenn, *Clara Bow: Running Wild* (New York: Doubleday, 1998), 126.
3. Sharon Smith, *Women Who Make Movies* (New York: Hopkinson & Blake, 1975), 20.
4. Charlotte Chandler, *She Always Knew How: A Personal Biography of Mae West* (London: Pocket Books, 2009), 101.
5. Booton Herndon, *Mary Pickford and Douglas Fairbanks: The Most Popular Couple the World Has Ever Known* (New York: W.W. Norton, 1997), 270.
6. Ibid., 183.
7. Andrea Sarvady, *Leading Ladies: The 50 Most Unforgettable Actresses of the Studio Era* (San Francisco: Chronicle Books, 2006), 63.
8. Peary, ed., *Close-Ups*, 143.
9. Donald Spoto, *Dietrich* (London: Corgi, 1993), 77.
10. Peary, ed., *Close-Ups*, 141.
11. Annette Tapert, *The Power of Glamour: The Women Who Defined the Magic of Stardom* (London: Aurum, 1999), 232.
12. Peary, ed., *Close-Ups*, 141.
13. Thomas Doherty, *Pre-Code Hollywood: Sex, Immorality and Insurrection in American Cinema 1930–1934* (New York: Columbia University Press, 1999), 126.
14. Norman, *Talking Pictures*, 80.

15. Charlotte Chandler, *The Girl Who Walked Home Alone: A Personal Biography of Bette Davis* (London: Simon & Schuster, 2006), 68.

16. Michelle Lovric, ed., *Wicked Women's Wit* (London: Prion, 2004), 142.

17. Ethan Mordden, *Movie Star: A Look at the Women who Made Hollywood* (New York: St. Martin's Press, 1983), 114.

18. David Bret, *Jean Harlow: Tarnished Angel* (London: JR Books, 2009), 105.

19. John Robert Colombo, ed., *Wit and Wisdom of the Movies* (London: Hamlyn, 1979), 110.

20. Chandler, *She Always Knew How*, 1–2.

21. Paul F. Boller, Jr., and Ronald L. Davis, *Hollywood Anecdotes* (London: Macmillan, 1987), 216.

22. Jessie Shiers, ed., *The Quotable Bitch: Women Who Tell It Like It Really Is* (Guilford, CT: Lyons Press, 2008), 154

23. Samantha Cook, *The Rough Guide to Chick Flicks* (London: Penguin, 2006), 147.

24. Howard Johns, *Hollywood Celebrity Playground* (Fort Lee, NJ: Barricade Books, 2006), 430–1.

25. Doherty, *Pre-Code Hollywood*, 127.

26. Ibid., 150.

27. Patrick McGilligan, *George Cukor: A Double Life* (London: Faber & Faber, 1991), 112.

Rigors of the Code

1. Michael Parkinson, *Parky's People* (London: Hodder & Stoughton, 2010), 48–9.

2. Paul McDonald, *The Star System: Hollywood's Production of Popular Identities* (London: Wallflower, 2005), 52.

3. Mordden, *Movie Star*, 183.

4. *Cahiers du Cinema*, 1966, 459–60.

5. Acker, *Reel Women*, 298.

6. Shiers, ed., *The Quotable Bitch*, 181.

7. Jacobson, *Dishing Hollywood*, 68.

8. Sarvady, *Leading Ladies*, 91.

9. William Arnold, *Shadowland* (New York: Berkley Books, 1982), 55–6.

10. Sarah Parvis, ed., *Good Girls Finish Last* (Kansas City: Andrews McMeel, 2004), 91.

11. Chandler, *The Girl Who Walked Home Alone*, 113.

12. McDonald, *The Star System*, 61.

13. C. Warner Sperling and C. Millner, with J. Warner, Jr., *Hollywood Be Thy Name: The Warner Bros. Story* (Rocklin, CA: Prima, 1994), 220.

14. Peary, ed., *Close-Ups*, 447.

15. Ibid., 448.

16. Beauchamp, *Without Lying Down*, 12.

17. Ibid., 142.

18. Francis Marion, *Off With Their Heads!* (New York: Macmillan, 1972), 28–9.

19. Beauchamp, *Without Lying Down*, 355.

20. Patrick Agan, *The Decline and Fall of the Love Goddesses* (Los Angeles: Pinnacle Books, 1979), 69.

21. Barbara Leaming, *If This Was Happiness: A Biography of Rita Hayworth* (New York: Ballantine, 1989), 56.

22. John Kobal, *Rita Hayworth: Portrait of a Love Goddess* (New York: Berkley Books, 1982), 136–7.

23. Leaming, *If This Was Happiness*, 48.

24. Paul Donnelley, *Judy Garland* (London: Haus, 2007), 42.

25. *McCall's*, January/February 1964.

26. James Robert Parish, *Hollywood Divas: The Good, The Bad and the Fabulous* (New York: McGraw-Hill, 2003), 92–3.

27. *Film Comment*, Winter 1965, 30.

28. Ibid., November 1973.

29. B. Ruby Rich, *Chick Flicks: Theories and Memories of the Feminist Film Movement* (Durham: Duke University Press, 1998), 46–7.

30. *L.A. Examiner*, November 14, 1939.

31. Bob Thomas, *Joan Crawford: A Biography* (London: Weidenfeld & Nicolson, 1978), 127–8.

32. Ford, *The Casting Couch*, 118–20.

33. Hugo Vickers, *Vivien Leigh* (London: Hamish Hamilton, 1988), 101.

34. Rosemarie Jarski, ed., *Hollywood Wit* (London: Prion, 2000), 101.

35. Sarvady, *Leading Ladies*, 93.

36. David Shipman, ed., *Movie Talk: Who Said What About Whom in the Movies* (London: Bloomsbury, 1988), 99.

37. McGilligan, *George Cukor*, 150.

38. Anne Edwards, *Vivien Leigh: A Biography* (New York: Simon & Schuster, 1977), 98–103.

39. *Sunday Independent*, January 12, 2014.

40. Donald Bogle, *Dorothy Dandridge* (New York: Amistad, 1997), 164.

Outside the Trenches

1. Stephen Randall, ed., *The Playboy Interviews: Larger Than Life* (Milwaukie, OR: M Press, 2006), 208.

2. Irving Wallace, Amy Wallace, David Wallechinsky and Sylvia Wallace, *The Secret Sex Lives of Famous People* (Chatham, Kent: Chancellor Press, 1993), 161.

3. Ronald L. Davis, *The Glamour Factory: Inside Hollywood's Big Studio System* (Dallas: Southern Methodist University Press, 1993, 74–5.

4. Maureen O'Hara, with John Nicoletti, *'Tis Herself: A Memoir* (London: Simon & Schuster, 2004), 33–4.

5. Ibid., 49–50.

6. Anna Lee, with Barbara Roisman Cooper, *Memoir of a Career on General Hospital and in Film* (Jefferson, NC: McFarland, 2007), 142

7. Davis, *The Glamour Factory*, 127.

8. Judith Mayne, *The Woman at the Keyhole: Feminism and Women's Cinema* (Bloomington: Indiana University Press, 1990), 101.

9. O'Hara with Nicoletti, *'Tis Herself*, 84–5.

10. Ibid., 75.

11. Leonard Moseley, *Zanuck: The Rise and Fall of Hollywood's Last Tycoon* (London: Panther, 1985), 131.

12. Ibid., 207–8.

13. Ibid., 116.

14. Ford, *The Casting Couch*, 128–9.

15. Kirk Crivello, *Fallen Angels: The Lives and Untimely Deaths of 14 Hollywood Beauties* (London: Futura, 1998), 94.

16. David Bret, *Doris Day: Reluctant Star* (London: JR Books, 2008), 19.

17. Donnelley, *Judy Garland*, 46–7.

18. Michael Freedland, *Judy Garland: The Other Side of the Rainbow* (London: JR Books, 2010), 57.

19. David Niven, *Bring on the Empty Horses* (New York: Putnam, 1975), 460–1.

20. Doug McClelland, *Susan Hayward: The Divine Bitch* (New York: Pinnacle Books, 1973), 38–9.

21. Ibid., 114.

22. Sarvady, *Leading Ladies*, 111.

23. J. Haskins and K. Benson, *Lena: A Personal and Professional Biography of Lena Horne* (New York: Stein & Day, 1984), 115.

24. Davis, *The Glamour Factory*, 314.

25. Sarvady, *Leading Ladies*, 75.

26. Ava Gardner, *Ava: My Story* (London: Transworld, 1990), 56–8.

27. Jill Bauer, *From I Do to I'll Sue: An Irreverent Compendium for Survivors of Divorce* (London: Robson, 1994), 122–3.

28. Ibid., 88.

29. Friedrich, *City of Nets*, 152

30. Agan, *The Decline and Fall of the Love Goddesses*, 70.

31. Jarski, ed., *Hollywood Wit*, 250.

32. George Carpozi, *That's Hollywood, Volume 2* (New York: Manor Books, 1978), 172.

33. Jeremy Pascall and Clyde Jeavons, *A Pictorial History of Sex in the Movies* (London: Hamlyn, 1975), 93.

34. Macpherson, *Leading Ladies*, 154.

35. Norman, *Talking Pictures*, 35.

36. Donnelley, *Judy Garland*, 19.

37. Davis, *The Glamour Factory*, 126.

38. Chandler, *The Girl Who Walked Home Alone*, 111.

39. *Hollywood Reporter*, December 1944.

40. *New York Times Magazine*, July 21, 1957.

41. *L.A. Times*, February 23, 1944.

42. Sutherland, ed., *Showbiz in Quotes*, 21.

43. McClelland, *The Divine Bitch*, 72–3.

44. Agan, *The Decline and Fall of the Love Goddesses*, 189.

45. Beverly Linet, *Susan Hayward: Portrait of a Survivor* (New York: Atheneum, 1980), 93.

46. Nigel Cawthorne, *The Sex Lives of the Hollywood Goddesses* (London: Prion, 1997), 176.

47. Shipman, ed., *Movie Talk*, 213–4.

48. Ibid.

49. David Thomson, *Rosebud: The Story of Orson Welles* (London: Abacus, 1997), 390.

50. Peter Conrad, *Orson Welles: The Stories of His Life* (New York: Faber & Faber, 2003), 232.

51. Leaming, *If This Was Happiness*, 109.

52. Peter Ford, *Glenn Ford: A Life* (Madison: University of Wisconsin Press, 2011), 62.

53. Jarski, ed., *Hollywood Wit*, 270.

54. Gardner, *Ava*, 91.

55. Ibid., 54.

56. Frances Farmer, *Will There Really Be a Morning?* (London: Fontana, 1983), 217.

57. Ibid.

Postwar Transitions

1. Tom Hickman, *The Sexual Century* (London: Carlton, 1999), 87.

2. Boze Hadleigh, *Bette Davis Speaks* (New York: Barricade Books, 1996), 144.

3. Sian Facer, ed., *Rita Hayworth in Her Own Words* (London: Hamlyn, 1992), 28.

4. Ibid., 31.

5. Conrad, *Orson Welles*, 232–3.

6. Parish, *Hollywood Divas*, 132.

7. Thomson, *Rosebud*, 277.

8. Facer, ed., *Rita Hayworth in Her Own Words*, 35.

9. Doug McClelland, *Hollywood Talks Turkey: The Screen's Greatest Flops* (Boston: Faber & Faber, 1989), 159.

10. Friedrich, *City of Nets*, 265.

11. Ibid., 265–6.

12. Shipman, ed., *Movie Talk*, 214.

13. *Take One*, Vol. 4, No. 1, 1972.

14. *L.A. Times*, December 28, 1965.

15. Lizzie Francke, *Script Girls: Women Screenwriters in Hollywood* (London: BFI, 1994), 82.

16. Acker, *Reel Women*, 197.

17. Ibid., Vol. 3, No.3, 1972.

18. Francke, *Script Girls*, 78.

19. Davis, *The Glamour Factory*, 148.

20. Ibid., 111.

21. Sheilah Graham, *My Hollywood: A Celebration and a Lament* (London: Michael Joseph, 1984), 85.

22. Norman, *Talking Pictures*, 58–9.

23. Ibid., 40.

24. Ibid., 64.

Scandals and Torments

1. Ford, *Glenn Ford*, 118.

2. Gary Carey, *All the Stars in Heaven: The Story of Louis B. Mayer and MGM* (London: Robson, 1981), 260.

3. Johns, *Hollywood Celebrity Playground*, 120–1.

4. Davis, *The Glamour Factory*, 115.

5. Acker, *Reel Women*, 199.

6. Colombo, *Wit and Wisdom of the Moviemakers*, 67.

7. Crivello, *Fallen Angels*, 101–2.

8. Jacobson, *Dishing Hollywood*, 220.
9. *Ireland's Big Issues*, 14 August-September 4, 2013.
10. Graham, *My Hollywood*, 121.
11. Parkinson, *Parky's People*, 293.
12. James Robert Parish, *The Hollywood Book of Scandals* (New York: McGraw-Hill, 2004), 117.
13. Charlotte Chandler, *A Personal Biography of Ingrid Bergman* (New York: Applause Theater and Cinema Books, 2007), 161.
14. Ibid., 170–1.
15. Friedrich, *City of Nets*, 406.
16. Chandler, *A Personal Biography of Ingrid Bergman*, 174.
17. Ibid., 171.
18. Anne Lee, *Memoir*, 205
19. Freedland, *Judy Garland*, 115.
20. *Sunday Independent*, September 29, 2013.
21. Francke, *Script Girls*, 65.
22. *Action*, May-June 1967.
23. Patrick McGilligan, *Film Crazy: Interviews with Hollywood Legends* (New York: St. Martin's Press, 2000), 221.
24. Ibid., 223.
25. Ibid., 225.

The Eisenhower Years

1. Macpherson, *Leading Ladies*, 162.
2. Staggs, *Close-Upon Sunset Boulevard*, 179–82.
3. Hadleigh, *Bette Davis Speaks*, 60.
4. Sam Staggs, *All About All About Eve* (New York: St. Martin's Griffin, 2000), 31–2.
5. Margaret Moser, Michael Bertin and Bill Crawford, *Movie Stars Do the Dumbest Things* (Los Angeles: Renaissance Books, 1999), 58–9.
6. Rex Reed, *Conversations in the Raw* (New York: New American Library, 1969), 17.
7. Stephen Farber and Marc Green, *Hollywood Dynasties* (New York: Delilah Books, 1984), 144.
8. Ibid., 146.
9. Freedland, *Judy Garland*, 123
10. Eddie Muller, *Dark City Dames: The Wicked Women of Film Noir* (New York: Regan Books, 1987), 112.
11. Norman, *Talking Pictures*, 58.
12. Charles Higham, *Howard Hughes: The Secret Life* (London: Virgin, 2004), 186.
13. Ibid., 187.
14. Johns, *Hollywood Celebrity Playground*, 219.
15. Higham, *Howard Hughes*, 172–3.
16. Davis, *The Glamour Factory*, 125.
17. Shipman, ed., *Movie Talk*, 97.
18. Jarski, ed., *Hollywood Wit*, 251.
19. Elia Kazan, *A Life* (New York: Anchor Books, 1989), 435.
20. O'Hara with Nicoletti, *'Tis Herself*, 184.
21. Randall, ed., *The Playboy Interviews*, 121.
22. Agan, *The Decline and Fall of the Love Goddesses*, 181.

23. Johns, *Hollywood Celebrity Playground*, 130.
24. Veronica Lake, with Donald Bain, *Veronica* (London: W.H. Allen, 1969), 160.
25. Doug McClelland, ed., *StarSpeak: Hollywood on Everything* (Boston: Faber & Faber, 1987), 265.
26. Jane Ellen Wayne, *Grace Kelly's Men* (New York: St. Martin's Press, 1991), 88.
27. Parish, *Hollywood Divas*, 155.
28. Bauer, *From I Do to I'll Sue*, 19.
29. Christine Gledhill, ed., *Stardom: Industry of Desire* (London: Routledge, 1991), 43.
30. Moser, Bertin and Crawford, *Movie Stars Do the Dumbest Things*, 188.
31. Graham, *My Hollywood*, 113.
32. Ford, *The Casting Couch*, 152.
33. Agan, *The Decline and Fall of the Love Goddesses*, 84–5.
34. Bob Thomas, *King Cohn: The Life and Times of Hollywood Mogul Harry Cohn* (Beverly Hills: New Millennium Press, 1967), 329–30.
35. Wayne, *Grace Kelly's Men*, 109–10.
36. Gardner, *Ava*, 191.
37. Robert Laguardia and Gene Arceri, *Red: The Tempestuous Life of Susan Hayward* (London: Robson, 1986), 86–8.
38. Ibid., 105.
39. Anita Loos, *A Girl Like I* (New York: Viking, 1966), 167.
40. Ibid., 187.
41. *New York Times*, October 11, 1988.

The Lipstick Sex

1. Simone de Beauvoir, *The Second Sex* (London: Jonathan Cape, 1953), 510.
2. Jennifer Scanlon, *Bad Girls Go Everywhere: The Life of Helen Gurley Brown* (New York: Oxford University Press, 2009), xii.
3. Macpherson, *Leading Ladies*, 157.
4. Wayne, *Grace Kelly's Men*, 140.
5. Donnelley, *Judy Garland*, 95.
6. McGilligan, *George Cukor*, 227–8.
7. Gerold Frank, *Judy* (New York: Da Capo, 1999), 394.
8. Sutherland, *Showbiz in Quotes*, 94.
9. Dorothy Dandridge and Earl Conrad, *Everything and Nothing: The Dorothy Dandridge Tragedy* (New York: Abelard & Schuman, 1970), 178.
10. Karyn Kay and Gerald Peary, eds., *Women and the Cinema* (New York: E.P. Dutton, 1977), 176.
11. *TV Guide*, October 8, 1966.
12. O'Hara with Nicoletti, *'Tis Herself*, 261.
13. Ibid., 188.
14. Ibid., 192.
15. Henry E. Scott, *Shocking True Story: The Rise and Fall of Confidential, America's Most Scandalous Scandal Magazine* (New York: Pantheon, 2010), 95–9.
16. Phyllis Gates, *My Husband, Rock Hudson* (London: Headline, 1987), 87.

17. Ibid., 104.
18. Ibid., 152.
19. Ibid., 138–9.
20. *Photoplay*, August 1955.
21. Ibid.
22. Dyhouse, *Glamour*, 114.
23. Norman, *Talking Pictures*, 98.
24. Johns, *Hollywood Celebrity Playground*, 30.
25. *Daily Mail*, June 12, 1980.
26. Thomas, *King Cohn*, 322–3.
27. Ibid., 324.
28. Willi Frischauer, *Behind the Scenes of Otto Preminger* (New York: William Morrow, 1973), 142.
29. Mike Steen, *Hollywood Speaks: An Oral History* (New York: G.P. Putnam, 1974), 85.
30. Ibid., 86.
31. Kashner and Macnair, *The Bad and the Beautiful*, 207–8.
32. Peary, ed., *Close-Ups*, 181–3.
33. Ibid., 172.
34. Sarvady, *Leading Ladies*, 147.
35. Graham, *My Hollywood*, 114–5.
36. Guus Luijters, ed., *Marilyn Monroe in Her Own Words* (London: Omnibus Press, 1990), 60.
37. Moser, Bertin and Crawford, *Movie Stars Do the Dumbest Things*, 188.
38. Michelle Vogel, *Gene Tierney: A Biography* (Jefferson, NC: McFarland, 2011), 158–61.
39. Gene Tierney, with Mickey Herskowitz, *Self Portrait* (New York: Wyden Books, 1979), 192.
40. Vogel, *Gene Tierney*, 166.

Changing of the Guard

1. Vickers, *Vivien Leigh*, 240.
2. Boze Hadleigh, *Hollywood Babble On: Stars Gossip about Other Stars* (London: Birch Lane Press, 1994), 182.
3. McClelland, *Hollywood Talks Turkey*, 63.
4. Wallace, Wallace, Wallechinsky and Wallace, *The Secret Sex Lives of Famous People*, 228.
5. Michael Feeney Callan, *Pink Goddess: The Jayne Mansfield Story* (London: W.H. Allen, 1986), 107.
6. Martha Sexton, *Jayne Mansfield and the American Fifties* (Boston: Houghton Mifflin, 1975), 199.
7. Christopher Downing, *Burton Stories: Anecdotes, Sayings and Impressions of Richard Burton* (London: Futura, 1990), 49.
8. Davis, *The Glamour Factory*, 119.
9. Parkinson, *Parky's People*, 287–8.
10. Johns, *Hollywood Celebrity Playground*, 220.
11. Jarski, ed., *Hollywood Wit*, 169.
12. Kobal, *Portrait of a Love Goddess*, 261.
13. Ibid., 271.
14. Facer, *Rita Hayworth in Her Own Words*, 48.
15. Ibid.
16. David Richards, *Played Out: The Jean Seberg Story* (New York: Random House, 1981), 59.
17. *The Times*, November 22, 1962.

18. Frischauer, *Behind the Scenes of Otto Preminger*, 152.
19. *Show*, August 1963.
20. McClelland, *Hollywood Talks Turkey*, 108.
21. Frischauer, *Behind the Scenes of Otto Preminger*, 161.
22. Agan, *The Decline and Fall of the Love Goddesses*, 207.
23. *Radio Times*, June 24, 1971.
24. *Film Yearbook*, 1984.
25. Joan Smith, *Misogynies* (London: Vintage, 1996), 118.
26. Maurice Zolotow, *Billy Wilder in Hollywood* (New York: Limelight Editions, 1996), 264–6.
27. Agan, *The Decline and Fall of the Love Goddesses*, 238.

The Swinging Sixties

1. Hadleigh, *Hollywood Babble On*, 112.
2. Shalit, ed., *Great Hollywood Wit*, 117.
3. Jarski, ed., *Hollywood Wit*, 151.
4. McClelland, ed., *StarSpeak*, 327
5. Lawrence Grobel, *The Hustons* (London: Bloomsbury, 1990), 495.
6. Jarski, ed., *Hollywood Wit*, 166.
7. Peary, ed., *Close-Ups*, 322.
8. Colin Jarman, ed., *The Guinness Dictionary of Poisonous Quotes* (London: Guinness, 1991), 138.
9. Joey Berlin, ed., *Toxic Fame: Celebrities Speak on Stardom* (Detroit: Visible Ink, 1996), 214.
10. Zolotow, *Billy Wilder in Hollywood*, 108.
11. Shalit, ed., *Great Hollywood Wit*, 143.
12. Roy Pickard, *Shirley MacLaine* (Kent, UK: Spellmount Books, 1985), 85.
13. Jarski, ed., *Hollywood Wit*, 99.
14. Boze Hadleigh, *The Lavender Screen: The Gay and Lesbian Films—Their Stars, Makers, Characters and Critics* (Secaucus, NJ: Carol, 1993), 36.
15. Alison Darren, *Lesbian Film Guide* (London: Cassel, 2000), 45.
16. Parkinson, *Parky's People*, 294–6.
17. Shiers, ed., *The Quotable Bitch*, 169.
18. *New York Times*, September 18, 1977.
19. *Village View*, July 6, 1989.
20. Boze Hadleigh, ed., *Holy Matrimony* (Kansas City: Andrews McMeel, 2003), 79.
21. Wayne, *Grace Kelly's Men*, 295.
22. Ibid., 296.
23. Ruuth, *Cruel City*, 82.
24. Crivello, *Fallen Angels*, 36.
25. Alexander Walker, *Vivien: The Life of Vivien Leigh* (London: Orion, 1987), 355–6.
26. Edwards, *Vivien Leigh*, 244–5.
27. Peary, ed., *Closeups*, 314.
28. Walker, *Vivien*, 395.
29. Tony Hall, ed., *They Died Too Young: The Brief Lives and Tragic Deaths of the Mega-Star Legends of our Time* (London: Parragon, 1997), 69.

30. Arthur Miller, *Timebends: A Life* (London: Methuen, 1988), 528.
31. Hall, ed., *They Died Too Young*, 69.
32. George Jacobs and William Stadiem, *The Last Word on Frank Sinatra* (London: Pan, 2004), 169.
33. Miller, *Timebends*, 531.
34. Ibid., 529.
35. Ibid., 532.
36. Peary, Ed., *Close-Ups*, 319.
37. *Marilyn Monroe, My Story* (New York: Stein & Day, 1986), 237–8.
38. Norman Mailer, *Marilyn: A Biography* (New York: Putnam, 1987), 15.
39. Smith, *Misogynies*, 122–4.
40. Luijters, ed., *Marilyn Monroe in Her Own Words*, 55.

Life After Marilyn

1. Basinger, *The Star Machine*, 320.
2. Sutherland, ed., *Showbiz in Quotes*, 90.
3. *New York Times*, March 10, 1968.
4. Randall, ed., *The Playboy Interviews*, 136.
5. *Variety*, September 24, 1962.
6. Graham Tarrant, ed., *Actors on Actors* (London: Aurum, 1995), 62.
7. Darren, *Lesbian Film Guide*, 216–7.
8. Macpherson, *Leading Ladies*, 194.
9. Hadleigh, *Hollywood Babble On*, 110.
10. Peter Manso, *Brando: The Biography* (New York: Hyperion, 1994), 218.
11. Ibid., 688.
12. Pickard, *Shirley MacLaine*, 86.
13. Minty Clinch, *Burt Lancaster* (New York: Stein & Day, 1984), 120.
14. Gardner, *Ava*, 269.
15. Shalit, *Great Hollywood Wit*, 161.
16. French, *Jane Fonda*, 13.
17. Shalit, *Great Hollywood Wit*, 47.
18. Patrick McGilligan, *Alfred Hitchcock: A Life in Darkness and Light* (Chicester, West Sussex: John Wiley & Sons, 2003), 628.
19. John Russell Taylor, *Hitch: The Life and Work of Alfred Hitchcock* (London: Faber & Faber. 1978), 247
20. Davis, *The Glamour Factory*, 74.
21. Donald Spoto, *Spellbound by Beauty: Alfred Hitchcock and His Leading Ladies* (London: Arrow, 2009), 173–4.
22. Ibid., 272.
23. Taylor, *The Life and Work of Alfred Hitchcock*, 251.
24. McGilligan, *A Life in Darkness and Light*, 643.
25. Gardner, *Ava*, 268.
26. Ibid., 256.
27. Ibid., 258–9.
28. Ibid., 259–60.
29. C. McGivern, *The Romy Schneider Story* (Berkshire: Reel Publishing, 2006), 50–1.
30. Ibid., 58–9.

31. Ibid., 41.
32. Ibid., 53.
33. Manso, *Brando*, 487.
34. Ibid., 566–7.
35. G. Haddad-Garcia, *The Films of Jane Fonda* (Secaucus, NJ: Citadel Press, 1981), 110.
36. *The Sun*, November 4, 1964.
37. *Sunday Express*, March 22, 1964.
38. *American Film*, November 1981.
39. *Sunday Times*, October 17, 1976.
40. French, *Jane Fonda*, 54–5.
41. Farber and Green, *Hollywood Dynasties*, 147.
42. Gail and Jim Piazza, *The Academy Awards: The Complete Unofficial List* (New York: Black Dog & Leventhal, 2008), 162.
43. *Sunday Times*, May 2, 1971.
44. Ruuth, *Cruel City*, 81.

The Sexual Revolution

1. Francke, *Script Girls*, 92.
2. Michael Viner and Terrie Maxine Frankel, *Tales from the Casting Couch* (Beverly Hills: Dove Books, 1995), 74.
3. Shipman, ed., *Movie Talk*, 213.
4. Ruth Barton, *Hedy Lamarr: The Most Beautiful Woman in Film* (Lexington: University Press of Kentucky, 2012), 208.
5. Douglas Thompson, *Hollywood People* (London: Pan Books, 1995), 233.
6. Lee Server, *Ava Gardner* (London: Bloomsbury), 448.
7. Graham, *My Hollywood*, 125.
8. Dwayne Epstein, *Lee Marvin: Point Blank* (Tucson: Schaffner Press, 2013), 177.
9. Thompson, *Hollywood People*, 128.
10. Rex Harrison, *A Damned Serious Business: My Life in Comedy* (London: Bantam, 1990), 199.
11. Boze Hadleigh, *Leading Ladies* (London: Robson, 1992), 128.
12. Russo, *The Celluloid Closet*, 164.
13. Acker, *Reel Women*, 225.
14. Ibid.
15. French, *Jane Fonda*, 69–71.
16. Kashner and Macnair, *The Bad and the Beautiful*, 202.
17. Hadleigh, *The Lavender Screen*, 56.
18. Graham, *My Hollywood*, p .125.
19. Johns, *Hollywood Celebrity Playground*, 222.
20. Pickard, *Shirley MacLaine*, 86.
21. Manso, *Brando*, 642–3.
22. Sheridan Morley and Ruth Leon, *Judy Garland: Beyond the Rainbow* (London: Pavilion, 1999), 141.

Leaving the Doll's House

1. Collier, *The Fondas*, 179.
2. *The Sun*, August 11, 1972.

3. Ibid.
4. *Sunday Mirror*, September 24, 1972.
5. Farmer, *Will There Really Be a Morning?*, 113
6. Arnold, *Shadowland*, 186–7.
7. Crivello, *Fallen Angels*, 83–4.
8. Ibid., 84.
9. Jacobson, *Dishing Hollywood*, 44.
10. *National Inquirer*, September 1, 1968.
11. Wheaton, *Forever Young*, 178.
12. Jarski, ed., *Hollywood Wit*, 273.
13. Parkinson, *Parky's People*, 322.
14. French, *Jane Fonda*, 91.
15. Ibid., 95.
16. *Newsweek*, September 25, 1985.
17. Acker, *Reel Women*, 213.
18. *Variety*, December 8, 1971.
19. *Women and Film*, Vol. 2, No.7, 1974.
20. Cook, *The Rough Guide to Chick Flicks*, 54.
21. Marshall Fine, *Bloody Sam: The Life and Films of Sam Peckinpah* (New York: Hyperion), 2005, 201.
22. John Baxter, *Stanley Kubrick: A Biography* (London: HarperCollins, 1997), 248–9.
23. *Film Yearbook*, 1986.
24. Rosen, *Popcorn Venus*, 253.
25. *New Musical Express*, June 15, 1974.
26. Tim Adler, *Hollywood and the Mob* (London: Bloomsbury, 2007), 176–7.
27. Linda Lovelace, with Mike McGrady, *Out of Bondage* (New York: Berkley Books, 1987), 9.
28. Tarrant, ed., *Actors on Actors*, 46.
29. Bacon, *Hollywood Is a Four Letter Town*, 217
30. Marc Eliot, *Steve McQueen: A Biography* (London: Aurum, 2011), 258.
31. Christopher Sandford, *Steve McQueen: The Biography* (London: HarperCollins, 2002), 159.
32. Ibid., 244.
33. Ibid., 210.
34. McClelland, ed., *StarSpeak*, 328.
35. Crivello, *Fallen Angels*, 214–5.
36. Patricia Bosworth, *Jane Fonda: The Private Life of a Public Woman* (London: Robson, 2011), 384.
37. Agan, *The Decline and Fall of the Love Goddesses*, 44–6.
38. Colombo, *Wit and Wisdom of the Moviemakers*, 66.
39. *New York Times*, July 29, 1973.
40. *Women and Film*, Vol. 2, No. 7, Summer 1975.
41. *New York Daily News*, April 13, 1977.
42. Raquel Welch, *Beyond the Cleavage* (New York: Weinstein Books, 2010), 255–6.
43. Ruuth, *Cruel City*, 44.
44. Christopher Sandford, *Polanski* (London: Arrow, 2009), 249–50.
45. Oliver Reed, *Reed All About Me: The Autobiography of Oliver Reed* (London: W.H. Allen, 1979), 172.
46. Bauer, *From I Do to I'll Sue*, 113.
47. *Playboy*, November 1965.
48. *Film Yearbook*, 1988.
49. McGilligan, *Film Crazy*, 229.
50. Acker, *Reel Women*, 205.
51. Charlotte Brunsdon, ed., *Films for Women* (London: BFI, 1987), 17–19.
52. Peter Biskind, *Easy Riders, Raging Bulls: How the Sex-Drugs-and-Rock-'n-Roll Generation Saved Hollywood* (London: Bloomsbury, 1998), 253.
53. Ibid., 253–4.
54. Julian Upton, *Fallen Stars: Tragic Lives and Lost Careers* (Manchester: Critical Vision, 2004), 107.
55. Ibid., 109.
56. Johns, *Hollywood Celebrity Playground*, 262–3.

The Beginnings of Cynicism

1. *New York Times*, August 20, 1976.
2. J.T. Jeffries, *Jessica Lange* (New York: St. Martin's Press, 1986), 3.
3. Ibid., 7.
4. Jarman, ed., *The Guinness Dictionary of Poisonous Quotes*, 137.
5. Jeffries, *Jessica Lange*, 106.
6. John Marriott and Robin Cross, *The World's Greatest Hollywood Scandals* (London: Chancellor Press, 1997), 131.
7. Graham, *My Hollywood*, 224.
8. Peary, ed., *Close-Ups*, 203–4.
9. *People*, May 5, 1980.
10. Thompson, *Hollywood People*, 240.
11. Sandford, *Polanski*, 290.
12. Mordden, *Movie Star*, 92.
13. Thomas, *Joan Crawford*, 257–8.
14. Wallace, Wallace, Wallechinsky and Wallace, *The Secret Sex Lives of Famous People*, 109.
15. *Savvy*, October 1988.
16. Donald Zec, *Marvin: The Story of Lee Marvin* (London: New English Library, 1979), 191.
17. Epstein, *Lee Marvin*, 225.
18. Zec, *Marvin*, 228
19. Ford, *The Casting Couch*, 178.
20. Wheaton, *Forever Young*, 237.
21. Crivello, *Fallen Angels*, 175.
22. French, *Jane Fonda*, 15.
23. *American Film*, March 1979.

Fatal Attractions

1. Acker, *Reel Women*, 281–2.
2. Nick Holt, ed., *The Wit and Wisdom of Movies* (Oxford: House of Raven Books, 2005), 68.
3. Nicolas Kent, *Naked Hollywood: Money, Power and the Movies* (London: BBC, 1991), 92.
4. Welch, *Beyond the Cleavage*, 38–40.
5. Thompson, *Hollywood People*, 223.
6. Biskind, *Easy Riders, Raging Bulls*, 416.
7. Ford, *The Casting Couch*, 216.
8. Upton, *Fallen Stars*, 23.
9. Alexander Walker, ed., *No Bells on Sunday: The Rachel Roberts Journals* (New York: Harper & Row, 1984), 238.

10. Jacobson, *Dishing Hollywood*, 183.
11. McGivern, *The Romy Schneider Story*, 100.
12. Ibid., 112.
13. Ruuth, *Cruel City*, 69.
14. Jeffries, *Jessica Lange*, 34–5.
15. Ibid., 28.
16. Ibid., 30.
17. Hadleigh, ed., *Hollywood Bitch*, 230.
18. Brunsdon, ed., *Films for Women*, 152.
19. Darren, *Lesbian Film Guide*, 166.
20. Biskind, *Easy Riders, Raging Bulls*, 396.
21. Russo, *The Celluloid Closet*, 294.
22. Hadleigh, ed., *Hollywood Bitch*, 230.
23. Shipman, ed. *Movie Talk*, 144.
24. Hadleigh, ed., *Hollywood Bitch*, 223.
25. Boze Hadleigh, *Celebrity Feuds: The Cattiest Rows, Spats and Tiffs Ever Recorded* (London: Robson, 2000), 36.
26. Boze Hadleigh, ed., *Celebrity Diss and Tell* (Kansas City: Andrews McMeel, 2005), 143.
27. Russo, *The Celluloid Closet*, 275.
28. Ibid., 293.
29. Hadleigh, *The Lavender Screen*, 95.
30. Francke, *Script Girls*, 107.
31. Hadleigh, ed., *Celebrity Diss and Tell*, 264.
32. *Film Yearbook*, 1988.
33. *Los Angeles Herald-Examiner*, November 10, 1983.
34. Douglas Thompson, *Pfeiffer: Beyond the Age of Innocence* (London: Warner Books, 1993), 65–6.
35. Ibid., 66.
36. John Harkness, *The Academy Awards Handbook* (New York: Pinnacle Books, 1994), 256.
37. Anthony Holden, *The Oscars: The Secret History of Hollywood's Academy Awards* (London: Warner Books, 1993), 344–5.
38. James Spada with Christopher Nickens, *Streisand: The Woman and the Legend* (New York: Pocket Books, 1983), 365.
39. Shalit, ed., *Great Hollywood Wit*, 135.
40. Russo, *The Celluloid Closet*, 280.
41. Smith, *Misogynies*, 36–7.
42. Acker, *Reel Women*, 214–5.
43. French, *Jane Fonda*, 162.
44. Thompson, *Hollywood People*, 214.
45. Acker, *Reel Women*, 41.
46. Annette Kuhn, *Women's Pictures: Feminism and Cinema* (London: Verso, 1982), 238.
47. Judith M. Redding and Victoria A. Brownworth, *Film Fatales: Independent Women Directors* (Seattle: Seal Press, 1997), 225.
48. Patrick McGilligan, *Clint: The Life and Legend* (London: HarperCollins, 1999), 386.
49. Ibid., 388.
50. K. Madsen Roth, ed., *Hollywood Wits* (New York: Avon Books, 1995), 164.
51. *Time*, November 16, 1987.
52. Susan Faludi, *Backlash: The Undeclared War Against Women* (London: Vintage, 2002), 149–50.
53. Smith, *Misogynies*, 31–2.
54. Faludi, *Backlash*, 151.
55. Ibid., 150.

Outrageous Fortunes

1. *New Yorker*, May 29, 1989.
2. *Life*, July 28. 1967.
3. Gledhill, ed., *Stardom*, 53.
4. *City Limits*, No. 310, 1987.
5. Thompson, *Pfeiffer*, 108–9.
6. Kent, *Naked Hollywood*, 93.
7. Ibid., 94–5.
8. Ibid., 93.
9. Thompson, *Hollywood People*, 236.
10. Viner and Frankel, *Tales from the Casting Couch*, 239–40.
11. Philippa Kennedy, *Jodie Foster: A Biography* (London: Pan, 1995), 193.
12. Kennedy, *Jodie Foster*, 224–5.
13. Ibid., 79.
14. *San Francisco Examiner*, October 14, 1988.
15. *Washington Post*, May 17, 1985.
16. Shirley MacLaine, *My Lucky Stars: A Hollywood Memoir* (London: Bantam, 1996), 235.
17. Redding and Brownworth, *Film Fatales*, 96–7.
18. Michael Munn, *Hollywood Rogues: The Off-Screen Antics of Tinseltown's Hellraisers* (London: Robson, 1991), 157–8.
19. Robert L. Snow, *Stopping a Stalker: A Cop's Guide Making the System Work for You* (New York: Da Capo, 1998), 73–4.
20. Bauer, *From I Do to I'll Sue*, 235.
21. French, *Jane Fonda*, 166.
22. Hadleigh, *Celebrity Feuds*, 24.
23. Sondra Locke, *The Good, the Bad and the Very Ugly: A Hollywood Journey* (New York: William Morrow, 1997), 370.
24. Manso, *Brando*, 1012.
25. Ibid., 1016.
26. Upton, *Fallen Stars*, 118.
27. Carpozi, Jr., *That's Hollywood*, Vol. 2, 82.
28. Hadleigh, ed., *Celebrity Diss and Tell*, 224.
29. Thompson, *Hollywood People*, 27–8.
30. Thompson, *Pfeiffer*, 218.
31. Ibid., 221.
32. Ibid., 198–9.
33. Kuhn, *Women's Pictures*, 230.
34. Francke, *Script Girls*, 129–31.
35. Thompson, *Hollywood People*, 42.
36. Kennedy, *Jodie Foster*, 270.
37. Thompson, *Pfeiffer*, 214.
38. Kennedy, *Jodie Foster*, 246.
39. Cook, *The Rough Guide to Chick Flicks*, 186.
40. Faludi, *Backlash*, 132.
41. Nigel Goodall, *Demi Moore: The Most Powerful Woman in Hollywood* (Edinburgh: Mainstream 2000), 90–1.

The Stone Age

1. Douglas Thompson, *Sharon Stone: Basic Ambition* (London: Little, Brown, 1994), 3.
2. Parish, *Hollywood Divas*, 247.
3. Ibid., 248.
4. Thompson, *Sharon Stone*, 40.
5. Ibid., 107.
6. Joe Eszterhas, *The Devil's Guide to Hollywood: The Screenwriter as God* (London: Duckworth, 2006), 41.
7. Ibid., 306.
8. Thompson, *Sharon Stone*, 122.
9. Ibid., 169.
10. Shiers, ed., *The Quotable Bitch*, 170.
11. Thompson, *Sharon Stone*, 166.
12. Ibid., 164.
13. Ibid., 169.
14. Peter Keough, ed., *Flesh and Blood: The National Society of Film Critics on Sex, Violence and Censorship* (San Francisco: Mercury House, 1995), 69.
15. Goodall, *Demi Moore*, 114–5.
16. Thompson, *Pfeiffer*, 268.
17. *Playboy*, November 1980.
18. Goodall, *Demi Moore,* 121.
19. Acker, *Reel Women,* 151–2.
20. Locke, *The Good, the Bad and the Very Ugly*, 4.
21. Hadleigh, *Celebrity Feuds*, 25.
22. Locke, *The Good, the Bad and the Very Ugly*, 370.
23. Parish, *The Hollywood Book of Scandals*, 226.
24. Ciaran Carty, *Intimacy with Strangers: A Life of Brief Encounters* (Dublin: Lilliput Press, 2013), 57.
25. *Irish Times*, December 21, 2013.

Bibliography

Acker, Ally, *Reel Women: Pioneers of the Cinema, 1896 to the Present*. London: B.T. Batsford, 1991.

Adler, Tim. *Hollywood and the Mob*. London: Bloomsbury, 2007.

Agan, Patrick. *The Decline and Fall of the Love Goddesses*. Los Angeles: Pinnacle Books, 1979.

Allen, Virginia. *The Femme Fatale: Erotic Icon*. Troy, NY: Whistler Publishing, 1983.

Anger, Kenneth. *Hollywood Babylon*. London: Arrow Books, 1986.

Arnold, William. *Shadowland*. New York: Berkley Books, 1982.

Austin, John. *Hollywood's Babylon Women*. New York: SPI Books, 1994.

Bacon, James. *Hollywood is a Four Letter Town*. New York: Avon Books, 1976.

Bainbridge, John. *Garbo*. New York: Holt, Rinehart and Winston, 1971.

Ballinger, Alexander, and Danny Graydon. *The Rough Guide to Film Noir*. London: Penguin, 2007.

Basinger, Jeanine. *A Woman's View: How Hollywood Spoke to Women, 1930–1960*. New York: Alfred A. Knopf, 1993.

Bauer, Jill. *From I Do to I'll Sue: An Irreverent Compendium for Survivors of Divorce*. London: Robson, 1994.

Baxter, John. *Stanley Kubrick: A Biography*. London: HarperCollins, 1997.

Beauchamp, Cari. *Without Lying Down: Frances Marion and the Powerful Women of Early Hollywood*. Berkeley: University of California Press, 1997.

Berlin, Joey, ed. *Toxic Fame: Celebrities Speak on Stardom*. Detroit: Visible Ink, 1996.

Birchill, Julie. *Girls on Film*. New York: Pantheon, 1986.

Biskind, Peter. *Easy Riders, Raging Bulls: How the Sex-Drugs-and-Rock-'n'-Roll Generation Saved Hollywood*. London: Bloomsbury, 1998

Bloom, Claire. *Leaving a Doll's House: A Memoir*. London: Virago, 2012.

Bogdanovich, Peter. *The Killing of the Unicorn*. London: Futura, 1984.

Bogle, Donald. *Dorothy Dandridge*. New York: Amistad, 1997.

Bret, David. *Doris Day: Reluctant Star*. London: JR Books, 2008.

_____. *Jean Harlow: Tarnished Angel*. London: JR Books, 2009.

Brownlow, Kevin. *The Parade's Gone By*. New York: Alfred A. Knopf, 1979.

Brunsdon, Charlotte, ed. *Films For Women*. London: BFI, 1987.

Callan, Michael Feeney. *Pink Goddess: The Jayne Mansfield Story* London: W.H. Allen, 1986.

Carey, Gary. *All the Stars in Heaven: The Story of Louis B. Mayer and MGM*. London: Robson, 1981.

Carpozi, George, Jr. *That's Hollywood Volume 2*. New York: Manor Books, 1978.

Carty, Ciaran. *Intimacy with Strangers: A Life of Brief Encounters*. Dublin: Lilliput Press, 2013.

Cashin, Fergus. *Mae West: A Biography*. London: W.H. Allen, 1982.

Cawthorne, Nigel. *Sex Lives of the Hollywood Goddesses*. London: Prion, 1997.

Chafe, William H. *The Paradox of Change: American Women in the 20th Century*. New York: Oxford University Press, 1991.

Chandler, Charlotte. *It's Only a Movie: A Personal Biography of Alfred Hitchcock*. London: Simon & Schuster, 2005.

_____. *A Personal Biography of Ingrid Bergman*. New York: Applause Theatre and Cinema Books, 2007.

_____. *A Personal Biography of Mae West*. London: Pocket Books, 2009.

_____. *The Star Machine*. New York: Vintage, 2009.

Clinch, Minty. *Burt Lancaster*. New York: Stein & Day, 1984.

Coffee, Lenore. *Recollections of a Hollywood Screenwriter*. London: Cassell, 1973.

Cole, Janis, and Holly Dale. *Calling the Shots: Profiles of Women Filmmakers*. Kingston, Ontario: Quarry Press, 1993.

Collier, Peter. *The Fondas: A Hollywood Dynasty*. London: HarperCollins, 1991.

Conrad, Peter. *Orson Welles: The Stories of His Life*. New York: Faber & Faber, 2003.

Cook, Samantha. *The Rough Guide to Chick Flicks*. London: Penguin, 2006.

Crivello, Kirk. *Fallen Angels: The Lives and Untimely Deaths of 14 Hollywood Beauties*. London: Futura, 1998.

Dandridge, Dorothy, and Earl Conrad. *Everything and Nothing: The Dorothy Dandridge Tragedy*. New York: Perennial, 2000.

Darren, Alison. *Lesbian Film Guide*. London: Cassel. 2000.

Davis, Ronald L. *The Glamour Factory: Inside Hollywood's Big Studio System*. Dallas: Southern Methodist University Press. 1993.

De Beauvoir, Simone. *Brigitte Bardot and the Lolita Syndrome*. New York: Arno Press, 1960.

De Lauretis, Teresa. *Alice Doesn't: Feminism, Semiotics and Cinema*. New York: Macmillan, 1985.

Djikstra, Bram. *Idols of Perversity: Fantasies of Feminine Evil in Fin-de-Siecle Culture*. New York: Oxford University Press, 1986.

Doane, Mary Ann. *The Desire to Desire: The Woman's Film of the 1940s*. New York: Grossman, 1969.

Doherty, Thomas. *Pre-Code Hollywood: Sex, Immorality and Insurrection in American Cinema, 1930–1934*. New York: Columbia University Press, 1999.

Donati, William. *Ida Lupino: A Biography*. Lexington: University Press of Kentucky, 1996.

Donnelley, Paul. *Judy Garland*. London: Haus, 2007.

Dooley, Roger. *From Scarface to Scarlet: American Films in the 1930s*. New York: Harcourt Brace, 1979.

Downing, Christopher, ed. *Burton Stories: Anecdotes, Sayings and Impressions of Richard Burton*. London: Futura, 1990.

Dressler, Marie. *My Own Story*. Boston: Little, Brown, 1934.

Dyhouse, Carol. *Glamour: Women, History, Feminism*. London: Zed Books, 2010.

Edwards, Anne. *Vivien Leigh: A Biography* New York: Simon & Schuster, 1977.

Eliot, Marc. *Steve McQueen: A Biography*. London: Aurum, 2011.

Erens, Patricia. *Sexual Stratagems: The World of Women in Film*. New York: Horizon Press, 1979.

Eszterhas, Joe. *The Devil's Guide to Hollywood*. London: Duckworth, 2006.

Eyman, Scott. *Mary Pickford: America's Sweetheart*. New York: Donald L. Fine, 1990.

Faludi, Susan. *Backlash: The Undeclared War against Women*. London: Vintage, 2002.

Farber, Stephen, and Marc Green. *Hollywood Dynasties*. New York: Delilah Books, 1984.

Farmer, Frances. *Will There Really Be a Morning?* London: Fontana, 1983.

Fine, Marshall. *Bloody Sam: The Life and Films of Sam Peckinpah*. New York: Hyperion, 2005.

Ford, Peter. *Glenn Ford: A Life*. Madison: University of Wisconsin Press, 2011.

Ford, Selwyn. *The Casting Couch: Making It in Hollywood*. London: Grafton Books, 1994.

Francke, Lizzie. *Script Girls: Women Screenwriters in Hollywood*. London: BFI, 1994.

Frank, Gerold. *Judy*. New York: Da Capo, 1999.

Freedland, Michael. *Judy Garland: The Other Side of the Rainbow*. London: JR Books, 2010.

French, Brandon. *On the Verge of Revolt: Women in American Films of the 1950s*. New York: Ungar, 1978.

French, Sean. *Jane Fonda: A Biography*. London: Pavilion, 1997.

Friedrich, Otto. *City of Nets: A Portrait of Hollywood in the 1940s*. London: Headline, 1986.

Frischauer, Willi. *Behind the Scenes of Otto Preminger*. New York: William Morrow, 1974.

Gamman, Lorraine, and Margaret Marshment, eds. *The Female Gaze*. Seattle: Real Comet Press, 1989.

Gardner, Ava. *Ava: My Story*. London: Transworld, 1990.

Gates, Phyllis, and Bob Thomas. *My Husband, Rock Hudson*. London: Headline, 1987.

Gish, Lillian, with Ann Pinchot. *The Movies, Mr Griffith and Me*. Englewood Cliffs, NJ: Prentice-Hall, 1969.

Gledhill, Christine, ed. *Stardom: Industry of Desire*. London: Routledge, 1991.

Golden, Eve. *Platinum Girl: The Life and Legends of Jean Harlow*. New York: Abbeville Press, 1991.

Goodall, Nigel. *Demi Moore: The Most Powerful Woman in Hollywood*. Edinburgh: Mainstream, 2000.

Graham, Sheilah. *My Hollywood: A Celebration and a Lament*. London: Michael Joseph, 1984.

Grant, Neil, ed. *Rita Hayworth in Her Own Words*. London: Hamlyn, 1992.

Grey, Ian. *Sex, Stupidity and Greed: Inside the American Movie Industry*. New York: Juno Books, 1997.

Grobel, Lawrence. *The Hustons*. London: Bloomsbury, 1990.

Hadleigh, Boze. *Bette Davis Speaks*. New York: Barricade Books, 1996.

_____. *Celebrity Feuds: The Cattiest Rows, Spats, and Tiffs Ever Recorded*. London: Robson, 2000.

_____. *The Lavender Screen: The Gay and Lesbian Films—Their Stars, Makers, Characters and Critics*. Secaucus, NJ: Carol, 1993.

Hall, Tony, ed. *They Died Too Young: The Brief Lives and Tragic Deaths of the Mega-Star Legends of our Time*. Bristol: Parragon, 1996.

Harrison, Rex. *A Damned Serious Business: My Life in Comedy*. London: Bantam, 1990.

Haskell, Molly. *From Reverence to Rape: The Treatment of Women in the Movies*. Chicago: University of Chicago Press, 1987.

Haskins, J., and K. Benson. *Lena: A Personal and Professional Biography of Lena Horne*. New York: Stein & Day, 1984.

Herndon, Booton. *Mary Pickford and Douglas Fairbanks: The Most Popular Couple the World Has Ever Known*. New York: W.W. Norton, 1977.

Hickman, Tom. *The Sexual Century*. London: Carlton, 1999.

Higham, Charles. *Brando: The Unauthorized Biography*. London: Grafton Books, 1987.

_____. *Howard Hughes: The Secret Life*. London: Virgin, 2004.

Holt, Nick, ed. *The Wit and Wisdom of Movies*. Oxford: House of Raven, 2005.

Hotchner, A.E. *Doris Day: Her Own Story*. London: W.H. Allen, 1976.

_____. *Sophia: Living and Loving*. London: Corgi, 1980.

Jacobson, Laurie. *Dishing Hollywood: The Real Scoop on Tinseltown's Most Notorious Scandals*. Nashville: Cumberland House, 2003.

Johns, Howard. *Hollywood Celebrity Playground*. Fort Lee, NJ: Barricade Books, 2006.

Kael, Pauline. *Deeper Into Movies*. Boston: Little, Brown, 1969.

Kaplan, E. Ann. *Women and Film: Both Sides of the Camera*. New York: Methuen, 1983.

Kashner, Sam, and Jennifer Macnair. *The Bad and the Beautiful: A Chronicle of Hollywood in the Fifties*. London: Little, Brown, 2002.

Kay, Karyn, and Gerald Peary, eds. *Women and the Cinema*. New York: Dutton, 1977.

Kennedy, Philippa. *Jodie Foster*. London: Macmillan, 1995.

Kent, Nicolas. *Naked Hollywood: Money, Power and the Movies*. London: BBC, 1991.

Keough, Peter, ed. *Flesh and Blood: The National Society of Film Critics on Sex, Violence and Censorship*. San Francisco: Mercury House 1995.

Kobal, John. *Rita Hayworth: Portrait of a Love Goddess*. New York: Berkley Books, 1982.

Kuhn, Annette. *Women's Pictures: Feminism and Cinema*. London: Verso, 1982.

Laguardia, Robert, and Gene Arceri. *Red: The Tempestuous Life of Susan Hayward*. London: Robson, 1986.

Lake, Veronica, with Donald Bain. *Veronica*. London: W.H. Allen, 1969.

LaSalle, Mick. *Complicated Women: Sex and Power in Pre-Code Hollywood*. New York: St. Martin's Griffin, 2003.

Leaming, Barbara. *If This Was Happiness: A Biography of Rita Hayworth*. New York: Ballantine, 1989.

Lee, Anna, with Barbara Roisman Cooper. *Anna Lee: Memoir of a Career on General Hospital and in Film*. Jefferson, NC: McFarland, 2007.

Locke, Sondra. *The Good, the Bad and the Very Ugly: A Hollywood Journey*. New York: William Morrow, 1997.

Lovelace, Linda, with Mike McGrady. *Out of Bondage*. New York: Berkley Books, 1987.

Luijters, Guus. *Marilyn Monroe in Her Own Words*. London: Omnibus Press, 1990.

MacLaine, Shirley. *Don't Fall Off the Mountain*. New York: W.W. Norton, 1970.

Macpherson, Don, and Louise Brody. *Leading Ladies*. London: Octopus, 1986.

Madsen, Axel. *The Sewing Circle: Hollywood's Greatest Secret—Women Who Loved Other Women*. London: Birch Lane Press, 1995.

Manion, Dominique, and James Ursini. *Femme Fatale: Cinema's Most Unforgettable Lethal Ladies*. New York: Limelight Editions, 2009.

Mann, May. *Jayne Mansfield: A Biography*. St. Alban's, Herts: Mayflower, 1975.

Manso, Peter. *Brando: The Biography*. New York: Hyperion, 1994.

Marriott, John, and Robin Cross. *The World's Greatest Hollywood Scandals*. London: Chancellor Press, 1997.

Marx, Samuel, and Joyce Vanderveen. *Deadly Illusions: Jean Harlow and the Murder of Paul Bern*. New York: Random House, 1990.

McClelland, Doug. *Hollywood Talks Turkey: The Screen's Greatest Flops*. Boston and London: Faber & Faber, 1989.

_____. *Susan Hayward: The Divine Bitch*. New York: Pinnacle Books, 1973.

_____, ed. *Hollywood on Hollywood: Tinseltown Talks*. Winchester, MA: Faber & Faber, 1985.

McDonald, Paul. *The Star System: Hollywood's Production of Popular Identities*. London: Wallflower, 2005.

McGilligan, Patrick. *Alfred Hitchcock: A Life in Darkness and Light*. West Sussex: John Wiley & Sons, 2003.

_____. *Clint: The Life and the Legend*. London: HarperCollins, 1999.

McGivern, C. *The Romy Schneider Story*. Berkshire, England: Reel Publishing, 2006.

Moedelski, Tania. *The Women Who Knew Too Much: Hitchcock and Feminist Theory*. New York: Methuen, 1988.

Moore, Lucy. *Anything Goes: A Biography of the Roaring Twenties*. London: Atlantic Books, 2008.

Mordden, Ethan. *Movie Star: A Look at the Women Who Made Hollywood*. New York: St. Martin's Press, 1983.

Moser, Margaret, and Michael Bertin, and Bill Crawford. *Movie Stars Do the Dumbest Things*. Los Angeles: Renaissance Books, 1999.

Mosley, Leonard. *Zanuck: The Rise and Fall of Hollywood's Last Tycoon*. London: Granada, 1985.

Muller, Eddie. *Dark City Dames: The Wicked Women of Film Noir*. New York: Regan Books, 1987.

Munn, Michael. *Hollywood Rogues: The Off-Screen Antics of Tinseltown's Hellraisers*. London: Robson, 1991.

Naughton, John. *Movies: A Crash Course*. London: Simon & Schuster, 1998.

Negri, Pola. *Memoirs of a Star*. Garden City: Doubleday, 1970.

Newquist, Roy. *Conversations with Joan Crawford*. Secaucus, NJ: Citadel Press, 1980.

Niven, David. *Bring on the Empty Horses*. New York: Putnam, 1975.

Norman, Barry. *Talking Pictures*. London: Hodder & Stoughton, 1987.

O'Hara, Maureen, with John Nicoletti. *'Tis Herself: A Memoir*. London: Simon & Schuster, 2004.

Paris, Barry. *Garbo: A Biography*. New York: Alfred A. Knopf, 1995.

Parish, James Robert. *The Hollywood Book of Scandals*. New York: McGraw-Hill, 2004.

_____. *Hollywood Divas: The Good, The Bad and The Fabulous*. New York: McGraw-Hill, 2003.

Parkinson, Michael. *Parky's People: The Lives, the Laughs, the Legend*. London: Hodder & Stoughton, 2010.

Pascall, Jeremy, and Clyde Jeavons. *A Pictorial History of Sex in the Movies*. London: Hamlyn, 1975.

Peary, Danny, ed. *Closeups: Intimate Profiles of Movie Stars by Their Costars, Directors, Screenwriters and Friends*. New York: Galahad Books, 1978.

Penley, Constance, ed. *Feminism and Film Theory*. New York: Routledge, 1988.

Pickard, Roy. *Shirley MacLaine*. Kent: Spellmount, 1985.

Randall, Stephen, ed. *The Playboy Interviews: Larger Than Life*. Milwaukie, OR: M Press, 2006.

Redding, Judith M., and Victoria A. Brownworth. *Film Fatales: Independent Women Directors*. Seattle: Seal Press, 1997.

Reed, Oliver. *Reed All About Me: The Autobiography of Oliver Reed*. London: W.H. Allen, 1979.

Rich, B. Ruby. *Chick Flicks: Theories and Memories of the Feminist Film Movement*. Durham: Duke University Press, 1998.

Richards, David. *Played Out: The Jean Seberg Story*. New York: Random House, 1981.

Rosen, Marjorie. *Popcorn Venus: Women, Movies and the American Dream*. New York: Avon Books, 1973.

Russo, Vito. *The Celluloid Closet: Homosexuality in the Movies*. New York: Harper & Row, 1985.

Ruuth, Marianne. *Cruel City: The Dark Side of Hollywood's Rich and Famous*. Malibu, CA: Roundtable, 1991.

Sandford, Christopher. *McQueen: The Biography*. London: HarperCollins, 2002.

_____. *Polanski*. London: Arrow Books, 2009

Sarvady, Andrew. *Leading Ladies: The 50 Most Unforgettable Actresses of the Studio Era*. San Francisco: Chronicle Books, 2006.

Scott, Henry E. *Shocking True Story: The Rise and Fall of Confidential, America's Most Scandalous Scandal Magazine*. New York: Pantheon, 2010.

Sexton, Martha. *Jayne Mansfield and the American Fifties*. Boston: Houghton Mifflin, 1975.

Shalit, Gene, ed. *Great Hollywood Wit*. New York: St. Martin's Press, 2002.

Shiers, Jessie, ed. *The Quotable Bitch: Women Who Tell It Like It Really Is*. Guilford, CT: Lyons Press 2008.

Shipman, David. *Movie Talk: Who Said What About Whom in the Movies*. London: Bloomsbury, 1988.

Shulman, Irving. *Harlow: An Intimate Biography*. New York: Dell, 1964.

Smith, Joan. *Misogynies*. London: Vintage, 1996.

Sochen, June. *Herstory: A Woman's View of American History*. New York: Alfred A. Knopf, 1974.

_____. *Mae West: She Who Laughs, Lasts*. Arlington Heights, IL: Harlan Davidson, 1992.

Spada, James, with Christopher Nickens. *Streisand: The Woman and the Legend*. New York: Pocket Books, 1983.

Sperling, C. Warner, and C. Millner, with J. Warner, Jr. *Hollywood Be Thy Name*. Rocklin, CA: Prima, 1994.

Staggs, Sam. *All About All About Eve*. New York: St. Martin's Griffin, 2000.

_____. *Close-Up on Sunset Boulevard: Billy Wilder, Norma Desmond and the Dark Hollywood Dream*. New York: St. Martin's Griffin, 2002.

Starr, Tamara, ed. *In Her Master's Voice: 5000 Years of Putdowns and Pin Ups*. London: Penguin, 1991.

Steen, Mike. *Hollywood Speaks: An Oral History*. New York: G.P. Putnam, 1974.

Sutherland, Clive, ed. *Showbiz in Quotes*. London: Charles Letts, 1990.

Swanson, Gloria. *Swanson on Swanson*. New York: Random House, 1980.

Tarrant, Graham, ed. *Actors on Actors*. London: Aurum, 1995.

Tasker, Yvonne. *Working Girls: Gender and Sexuality in Popular Cinema,* London: Routledge, 1998.

Taylor, John Russell. *Hitch: The Authorized Biography of Alfred Hitchcock*. London: Abacus, 1981.

Thomas, Bob. *Joan Crawford: A Biography*. London: Weidenfeld & Nicolson, 1978.

_____. *King Cohn: The Life and Times of Hollywood Mogul Harry Cohn*. Beverly Hills: New Millennium Press, 1967.

Thompson, Douglas. *Hollywood People*. London: Pan Books, 1995.

_____. *Pfeiffer: Beyond the Age of Innocence*. London: Warner Books, 1995.

_____. *Sharon Stone: Basic Ambition*. London: Little, Brown, 1994.

Thomson, David. *The Story of Orson Welles*. London: Abacus, 1997.

Tierney, Gene, with Mickey Herskowitz. *Self-Portrait*. New York: Wyden Books, 1979.

Underwood, Peter. *Death in Hollywood: The Lives, Loves and Deaths of Hollywood's Brightest Stars*. London: Piatkus, 1992.

Upton, Julian. *Fallen Stars: Tragic Lives and Lost Careers*. Manchester: Critical Vision, 2004.

Vermilye, Jerry. *Ida Lupino*. New York: Pyramid, 1977.

Vickers, Hugo. *Vivien Leigh*. London: Hamish Hamilton, 1988.

Vieira, Mark A. *Sin in Soft Focus: Pre-Code Hollywood*. New York: Harry N. Abrams, 1999.

Viner, Michael, and Terrie Maxine Frankel, eds. *Tales from the Casting Couch*. Beverly Hills: Dove Books, 1995.

Vogel, Michelle. *Gene Tierney: A Biography*. Jefferson, NC: McFarland, 2011.

Walker, Alexander. *Vivien: The Life of Vivien Leigh*. London: Orion, 1987.

_____, ed. *No Bells on Sunday: The Rachel Roberts Diaries*. New York: Harper & Row, 1984.

Walsh, Andrea S. *Women's Film and Female Experience, 1940–1950*. New York: Praeger, 1984.

Wayne, Jane Ellen. *Grace Kelly's Men*. New York: St. Martin's Press, 1991.

Welch, Raquel. *Beyond the Cleavage*. New York: Weinstein Books, 2010.

Wheaton, Rona. *Forever Young: Untimely Deaths in the Screen World*. London: Warner Books, 1994.

Zec, Donald. *Marvin: The Story of Lee Marvin*. London: New English Library, 1979.

Zeitz, Joshua. *Flapper: A Madcap Story of Sex, Style, Celebrity and the Women Who Made Modern America*. New York: Three Rivers Press, 2006.

Zierold, Norman. *The Moguls*. New York: Avon Books, 1972.

Zolotow, Maurice. *Billy Wilder in Hollywood*. New York: Limelight Editions, 1996.

Index

Numbers in **bold italics** indicate pages with photographs.

227

Index